£29.50

BOOK LOAN

Please return or renew it no later
than the last date shown below

DISPLAY	3 0 MAY 2003	
ε 1 JUN 1990		
3 1 MAY 1991		
CANCELLED		
19 CANCELLED		
CANCELLED		
2 0 DEC 2002		

STRATEGIC PLANNING IN NATIONALISED INDUSTRIES

The nationalised industries account for a vital section of British industry, and the strategies they adopt are of considerable importance to our industrial future. This book discusses the problem of strategic planning in these industries, with contributions from academics, managers and civil servants with a wide variety of experience in this field.

At a time when 'privatisation' has put the future of the nationalised industries into the melting pot, the book analyses the differences between strategic planning in the public and private sectors, and the extent to which the strategic issues in these industries are independent of the form of ownership. The potential conflict between increasing the competitive pressures in these industries on the one hand, and making them profitable candidates for privatisation on the other, is discussed with particular reference to the future of British Telecom.

There are contributions on the framework of government control, alternative methods of monitoring performance, planning and forecasting under conditions of uncertainty, the use of computer models, reviews of strategic decision-making in the energy and transport industries, and a postscript on the future of the public corporations.

This review of the practice and problems of strategic planning in this field will be of interest to all those concerned with the future of the public sector together with students of management and economics.

John Grieve Smith, the editor, has had many years' experience of planning in the public sector both in the nationalised industries and Whitehall, including ten years as Planning Director at the British Steel Corporation.

STRATEGIC PLANNING IN NATIONALISED INDUSTRIES

Edited by
John Grieve Smith

M

First published 1984 by
THE MACMILLAN PRESS LTD
London and Basingstoke
Companies and representatives
throughout the world

Typeset by
Wessex Typesetters Ltd
Frome, Somerset

Printed in Hong Kong

British Library Cataloguing in Publication Data
Strategic planning in nationalised industries.
1. Government business enterprises—
Great Britain
I. Grieve Smith, John
338.0941   HD4145
ISBN 0–333–36551–8

Contents

Preface

This book is based on the papers prepared for a conference held at Robinson College, Cambridge, from 14 to 16 September 1983. The conference was financed by the Panel on the Economics of Industry and Public Enterprise of the Social Science Research Council (as it was then called). I was Chairman of this Panel, but the conference was largely organised by John Grieve Smith, one of the members of the Panel. He has provided the introduction and postscript to this volume, in addition to one of the chapters.

The conference, and the consequent book, were intended to stimulate constructive discussion on strategic planning in the state-owned sector of British industry, an area which has received comparatively little attention in the general run of literature on business strategy. Those attending the conference included senior managers concerned with strategic planning, civil servants and academics. This mixture of backgrounds was a stimulating one which led to a high level of informed discussion, and helped the (mainly academic) authors in preparing the final versions of their contributions.

In choosing strategic planning as the subject for the conference, we wished to investigate how far nationalised industries were similar to large private firms in the planning and investment problems they faced, and thus how far similar techniques of planning could be employed independently of their position in the public or private sector. We knew also that considerable difficulties arise in the relationships between the government and these industries, and we wanted to evaluate the influence of these relationships on the quality of the strategic planning of the industries, and on the nature of their investment policies.

These issues, and others relating to the problem of managing such huge enterprises, loomed large in the conference. Our discussions of these subjects were greatly enriched by the fact that so many practitioners from nationalised industries were present. However, the conference took place at a time when the future of the nationalised industries was dominated by the prospect of the 'privatisation' of certain sectors. The paper by Beesley and Gist bears most closely on this subject, but the subject naturally came up in virtually all our discussions. It became clear that the problem of privatisation was, in practice, closely bound up with the problem of whether strong private monopolies were likely to take the place of previously nationalised concerns. This raised the question of the need for regulatory agencies to oversee the activities of the newly privatised firms (as, for example, with the Office of Telecommunications). Little thought appears to have been given to the problems of regulating industries in this way in this country, and US experience on the subject, which is of course considerable, has scarcely been examined. In addition, another problem which has hardly been explored is that of the role of the government in enterprises where there is a large private stake but where the government retains a large stake also. It would seem inappropriate for the government to continue to act as it did when the industries were wholly nationalised, but so far the question of how it might best act has been little discussed.

Finally, it became clear that the question of public or private ownership was not necessarily synonymous with the difference between monopoly and competition. The government will undoubtedly find it easier to sell off nationalised concerns, in whole or part, if these concerns retain a strong monopoly position. From the point of view of the public interest, however, it might be desirable to attempt to introduce an element of competition into newly privatised industries, even though this may make the problem of disposal more difficult.

These and other issues, which are only now beginning to be seriously discussed, were raised at the conference. The problems of strategic planning, ownership and organisation in these industries inevitably interact, and we hope that the papers in this book will make a useful contribution to the lively debate which is now taking place.

Z. A. SILBERSTON

Notes on the Contributors

M. E. Beesley is a founding Professor of Economics at the London Business School. Lecturer in Commerce at Birmingham University, then Reader in Economics at LSE, he became the Department of Transport's Chief Economist for a spell in the 1960s. His main teaching interest is the contribution of economics to developing organisations' strategy. He started the Small Business Unit at the LBS, which encourages students to take a practical, as well as academic interest in forming and running small concerns. At the other end of the scale, he has advised on company problems of monopoly and restrictive trade practices and on the relationships between nationalised industries and their Ministries. He directs the Institute of Public Sector Management. His widely known work in transport economics has taken him to such countries as Australia, USA, India, Pakistan, Hong Kong, South Korea, Sabah and many in Europe. His independent economic study *Liberalisation of the Use of British Telecommunications Network* was published in 1981 by HMSO.

Ann P. Brown is Lecturer in Operational Research at the City University Business School. She joined the British Steel Corporation in 1967 as a member of the Central Operational Research Group, and worked on a planning model to establish the siting and use of deep-water ports in the United Kingdom. In 1971 she joined the City University Business School where she has divided her time between teaching, consultancy and research. Her teaching has spanned the whole range of quantitative modelling techniques at both MBA and Undergraduate Level. Her various consultancy projects have included a project in forecasting for London transport and a costing exercise for SITPRO. She has supervised MBA student projects with such companies as: Marconi-Radar, Chemical Bank International, STC, Post Office and Drake & Scull. Her research topics include the study of global modelling techniques.

I. C. R. Byatt has been Deputy Chief Economic Adviser at HM Treasury since 1978. Before that, he was in charge of the Public Expenditure Economic Unit and as such was heavily involved in the preparation of the 1978 White Paper on nationalised industries – in particular the development of the concept of the required rate of return. He has had wide experience in various government departments working on public expenditure matters. He has also taught at Durham University and the London School of Economics. He has published a book on the electrical industry in Britain and contributed articles on electricity pricing to learned journals.

G. F. Dudley is a Research Fellow in the Department of Politics, University of Strathclyde. His principal research interests are: public policy (especially the implementation process, dynamics of policy change and policy succession); steel policy; transport policy; regulation and de-regulation. He is currently working with Professor Richardson on a project, sponsored by the European University Institute in Florence, on British steel policy. He has published articles on steel policy, transport policy, and pressure groups.

P. Gist is a consultant in the economics of transport and telecommunications. He worked with Professor Michael Beesley on his report *Liberalisation of the Use of British Telecommunications Network*, published by HMSO in 1981, and is currently researching the role of market forces as a regulatory device in the telecommunications industry in the UK and USA.

John Grieve Smith had many years' experience of planning in the public sector before moving to Cambridge, where he is now Senior Bursar of Robinson College, and lectures on business strategy. He joined the planning branch of the newly formed UK Atomic Energy Authority in 1957 after working as an economist in the Cabinet Office and Treasury for eight years. In 1961 he moved to the Iron and Steel Board to become head of its economic department. After three years in the Department of Economic Affairs as Assistant Director of the Planning Division, he returned to the steel industry, and until 1981 was Director of Planning at the British Steel Corporation. He then spent a year as Industrial Management Teaching Fellow at the City University Business School.

A. J. Harrison is currently a co-editor of *Public Money*, the public sector policy journal. Before leaving the Government Economic Service to establish *Public Money*, he was a senior economic adviser in the Department of the Environment. He has published a number of books and articles on the application of economics to public policy problems.

John Heath is Professor of Economics at the London Business School, and Director of the full-time Master's Programme. Currently he is a Board Member of the British Airports Authority and adviser on Corporate Strategy to the British Railways Marketing Board. Formerly he was Director of the Economic Services Division of the Board of Trade. He has been a Lecturer in Economics at the University of Manchester and has worked for Spicers Ltd.

Andrew Likierman is Senior Lecturer and Director of the part-time Master's Programme at the London Business School. He also holds a number of outside appointments, including Advisor to the House of Commons Treasury and Civil Service Select Committee and member of the Audit Committee of Freightliners Ltd, a British Rail subsidiary. He has worked in the Cabinet Office as a member of the Central Policy Review Staff (the government's Think Tank) and has served on several government enquiries. He was a lecturer at Leeds University and a Visiting Fellow of the Oxford Management Centre. He is the author or co-author of three books and numerous articles, mainly in the field of financial control, covering both public and private sectors and specialising in nationalised industries.

Richard Pryke is Senior Lecturer in Economics at the University of Liverpool and well known as a specialist on British public enterprise. He was heavily involved in the Labour Party's work on steel prior to its renationalisation and was a member of the working party which paved the way for the National Enterprise Board. After research on nationalised industries at Cambridge, he wrote *Public Enterprise in Practice*, which appeared in 1971. This surveyed the first twenty years of nationalisation and concluded that, after a disappointing first decade, the nationalised industries made rapid strides to improve their efficiency. However, ten years later in another study, *The Nationalised Industries*, he found that, with some exceptions, the industries had performed badly since 1968. He is also the author (with John Dodgson) of a book on British Rail.

Ray Rees is Professor of Economics at University College, Cardiff. After leaving the LSE he spent a year as a junior economist at the Electricity Council; then in 1965 he joined the new economics department at Queen Mary College, University of London, and moved to Cardiff in 1978. His non-academic experience includes: the four years 1968–72 as an Economic Advisor on nationalised industries at HM Treasury; Economics Assessor to the Armitage Enquiry on heavy lorries and the environment; and Expert Witness for the Secretary of State for Trade in the case of TWA Air Canada and Others v. the BAA and Secretary of State for Trade. He has published a book, *Public Enterprise Economics*, and numerous papers in academic journals and books.

J. J. Richardson is Professor of Politics at the University of Strathclyde. His current interests include: British politics – especially the policy-making and implementing process and the role of interest groups; policy analysis and comparative public policy; Scandinavian politics – especially developments in the Swedish policy style; government and industry; aspects of local government. He has been a local councillor, OECD consultant, occasional lecturer at Civil Service College, and Visiting Professor at the universities of Bergen, Stockholm, Umea and State University of New York. His books include *Policy Styles in Western Europe* (ed.); *Governing under Pressure: The Policy Process in a Post Parliamentary Democracy* (with A. G. Jordan); *Pressure Groups in Britain* (ed. with R. Kimber); *Campaigning for the Environment* (ed. with R. Kimber); *The Policy-Making Process*.

Bernard Taylor is Director of Planning and Development at the Administrative Staff College, Henley-on-Thames, and has been closely associated with the development of Corporate Planning in Britain. Professor Taylor is editor of *Long Range Planning* journal and founding editor of the *Journal of General Management*. He has produced ten books dealing with various aspects of business strategy and planning, and has lectured widely in Britain, North America and on the Continent of Europe. Recently he completed an assignment for the United Nations with the National Council for

Applied Economic Research in New Delhi. He has held responsible positions in marketing with Procter & Gamble and in education and training with Rank Xerox and the Institute of Marketing. He founded the Post-Experience Programme at the University of Bradford Management Centre.

K. J. Wigley is a Senior Economic Adviser in the Department of Energy. He heads a Branch responsible for the preparation of energy projections and the provision of economic and statistical advice on electricity, coal, energy conservation and fuel substitution matters. He has worked on energy modelling while on the research staff of the Department of Applied Economics at Cambridge University, and was the author of *The Demand for Fuel, 1948–1975* published by Chapman & Hall in 1968 in the series *A Programme for Growth*. He was Lecturer in Economics in the Department of Engineering at Cambridge and a Fellow and Director of Studies in Economics at Corpus Christi College, Cambridge. In 1975 he joined the Civil Service as Director of Studies in Economics and Financial Management at the Civil Service College and worked in the Department of Health and Social Security before joining the Department of Energy in 1980.

List of the Conference Participants

Mr Terence BOLEY	The Electricity Council
Miss Ann BROWN	City University Business School
Mr Ian BYATT	H.M. Treasury
Mr James DRISCOLL	Nationalised Industries' Chairmen's Group
Mr Peter GIST	London Business School
Mr Rufus GODSON	British Gas Corporation
Mr John GRIEVE SMITH	Robinson College, Cambridge
Mr Anthony HARRISON	*Public Money*
Professor Peter HART	University of Reading
Mr David HEALD	University of Glasgow
Professor John HEATH	London Business School
Mr Anthony KNIGHT	British Telecom
Mr Andrew LIKIERMAN	London Business School
Mr Peter MILNER	Central Electricity Generating Board
Mr Michael PARKER	National Coal Board
Dr John PRIDEAUX	British Railways Board
Dr Richard PRYKE	University of Liverpool
Professor Ray REES	University College, Cardiff
Professor Jeremy RICHARDSON	University of Strathclyde
Professor Aubrey SILBERSTON	Imperial College of Science and Technology
Mr Walter SIMPSON	National Girobank
Mr Robert SPEIRS	Britoil
Mr David STEEL	University of Exeter
Dr Martin STOPFORD	British Shipbuilders
Mr Roger TABOR	The Post Office

Professor Bernard TAYLOR

Dr Stephen WATSON
Mr Roger WHITE
Mr Kenneth WIGLEY

The Management College
Henley
University of Cambridge
National Water Council
Department of Energy

NOTE

The participants all attended in their personal capacity and not as representatives of their respective organisations.

Introduction and Summary

PART I STRATEGIC PLANNING

The problems of business strategy facing those public corporations which are customarily referred to as the 'nationalised industries', are to a large extent similar in nature to those facing large enterprises in the private sector. We therefore start with a review of **the state of the art** of strategic planning (Taylor, Chapter 1).

Over the past decade the practice of strategic planning has matured and developed in response to pressures from inside and outside the business. What started out as a unique system of corporate planning based on a simple model of problem-solving and decision-making, has evolved into a broad range of philosophies and techniques, each of which can provide management with a sensible approach to tackling its strategic problems.

A small or medium-size firm may adopt only one of these approaches – typically a system controlling the allocation of resources, or a framework for generating strategies for new ventures. However, in the large corporation, such as General Electric USA, or Shell International, most or all of these approaches will be present. The philosophies and the techniques are for the most part compatible and complementary.

Five main styles or modes of planning have emerged in recent years:

(1) *Central Control System*, the view of planning as a system for acquiring and allocating resources. Conventional budgeting is being supplemented by a 'funds allocation' procedure based on a systematic evaluation of each business, its general environment, its competitive situation, and its strategy for the future. Also, instead of operating as a simple financial holding company, the top management of multi-industry, multi-national businesses are setting out to manage their investments as a 'portfolio of businesses'.

1

(2) *A Framework for Innovation*, the idea that planning should provide a framework for the generation of new products and new processes and the entry into new markets and new businesses. It is being recognised that the process of corporate development – improving the competitive performance of existing businesses generating new products, penetrating new markets, expanding internationally and creating or acquiring new businesses – is a prime task of top management and needs to be fostered and managed with separate budgets, plans, project teams, task forces, etc.

(3) *Futures Research*, the concept of planning as exploring and creating the future. Futurists believe that the future cannot be forecast. Therefore decision-makers should consciously assess the uncertainties, then develop and work towards a vision of the future. In businesses which have to cope with a great deal of uncertainty – for example, in new and growing technologies, in countries which are politically unstable, or in fluctuating international markets – managers have been forced to 'plan' in terms of alternative futures using simulations, scenarios and contingency plans rather than traditional forecasting.

(4) *Political Planning*, the perspective which sees planning as a process of resolving conflicts between interest groups and organisations inside and outside the business. The managements of most large business corporations now find themselves in a continual dialogue with governments, international agencies, trade unions, social pressure groups and the media. To handle this socio-political area, some large American companies now have public affairs' departments and external consultants who monitor social trends, forecast emerging socio-political issues and formulate action programmes to safeguard the interests of the business and to help to contribute to the solution of social problems, such as unemployment and the decline of city centres.

(5) *Strategic Management*, the notion that planning should be concerned not just with formulating strategies but with developing the commitment, the skills and the talents required to implement the strategies. Executives who have tried to implement these kinds of changes have found that it is often not enough to set demanding targets, and ask for new strategies. It is a major problem to recruit and train managers who have the

capacity to 'think strategically'. Often the organisation structure has to be changed to give more initiative to the separate
businesses, or to co-ordinate strategies internationally in
worldwide product divisions. The way managers are appraised
and rewarded also needs to be adjusted to demonstrate that the
development of new strategies and new businesses is just as
important as the achievement of this year's targets.

The particular problems of **strategic planning in the nationalised
industries**, as compared with other large corporations, arise partly
from the nature and circumstances of the industries themselves and
partly from their relationship with the government (Grieve Smith,
Chapter 2). From the point of view of methods and techniques the
problems of planning in a nationalised industry are similar to those
of any large integrated enterprise operating predominantly in one
industry (by 'integrated' we mean here that the operation of the
various divisions in the company is interdependent, as in an oil
company or airline, as opposed to the subsidiaries in a highly
diversified conglomerate). Thus the central control concept is a
major strand in their approach to planning. In addition there is an
inevitable concern with quantitative forecasting, as key decisions in
many cases depend on assessments of future demand in relation to
current capacity – for example, in electricity generating. Increasingly in recent years the problems of forecasting against a changing
macro-economic background have underlined the need to pay more
attention to the methods of dealing with uncertainty.

In considering techniques for managing strategic innovation, one
fact that has to be borne in mind is that the statutory corporations
have far less room to manoeuvre than their counterparts in the
private sector. The corporations were set up to produce coal or steel
or provide air travel, and they are not free to drop the production of
these goods and switch to something else if the prospects for their
original products are poor. Thus in considering product/market
strategy they are mainly limited to products within their statutory
field and to the UK as their primary market. (The major exception
to this in the public sector was the National Enterprise Board which
was free to operate in virtually any field.)

Those working in nationalised industries are no newcomers to the
art of political management. One of the less-desirable consequences
of this is that their planning is frequently geared as much to the

dictates of government/industry relations as to the internal management needs of the corporations themselves. This creates special problems which do not appear to have a parallel in similar enterprises in the private sector. Serious difficulties arise where the corporations' plans become an instrument for extracting money from the government, or even merely for convincing the government that top management have the situation satisfactorily under control. Plans prepared as a basis for policy discussions with the government frequently tend to be less realistic than those prepared primarily for internal use. Political pressures (in the broadest sense) also tend to limit the extent to which the planning process is a wide-ranging look at the strategic alternatives open to the enterprise.

The nationalised industries are not, however, unique in having to operate amid a welter of outside pressures and influences in addition to those of the market. As Taylor points out, top management of the large American corporation now increasingly sees a key part of its job as dealing with outside bodies, as well as customers, and it is unrealistic for management in such key industries to believe that a return to the private sector would remove all these complications.

The importance of strategic planning lies in the fact that the decisive factor in the long-term development of the public corporations (as with their private sector counterparts) is the nature of their strategy and whether it is appropriate to the problems and opportunities they face. Effective strategic planning must aim to ensure that such strategies are based on the best possible analysis and forecasts, and that sufficient agreement is reached among the parties involved to provide the necessary degree of stability. The fact that different interests have different objectives and that the future is fraught with uncertainty makes it difficult to establish stable strategies for many of these industries, but the more difficult the task, the greater the need.

PART II CONTROL AND STRUCTURE

The nationalised industries are so diverse that any **framework of government control** has either to be very general or carefully tailored to the needs of each (Byatt, Chapter 3). Over the years successive governments have relied mainly on a framework of general financial control. This started with the statutory obligation to break even, together with the provision for government approval of investment programmes, and was tightened in the mid-1950s by removing their ability to borrow medium- or long-term on their own account. The further instruments of setting financial targets and more recent annual external financing limits have reinforced the government's control. In addition, successive White Papers on the Nationalised Industries have laid down a number of policy guidelines of a general financial or economic nature.

This apparatus of control may be regarded as directed to three main types of objective. The first is ensuring that nationalised industries conform to macro-economic policy objectives; in particular that they do not pre-empt too much of the nation's savings and investment. The focus has shifted from control of total investment programmes to control of external borrowing, and from a concern with price restraint to a concern with the PSBR. The focus may shift again in the future as macro-economic policy develops; but while the nationalised industry sector is large, this macro-economic concern will persist.

The second objective is to ensure that nationalised industries contribute to the efficient allocation of resources, in particular that their pricing policies are properly related to their costs and that they earn an adequate return on investment. Economic pricing has been defined as marginal cost pricing, subject to the need to cover accounting costs, and White Papers have argued that the structure of prices should reflect the structure of (marginal) costs. They have been against cross-subsidisation and in favour of explicit rather than implicit subsidies.

Investment was covered in rather different ways in successive White Papers. The 1961 White Paper concentrated on the effect of prices on the demand for investment and the need for more self-financing. The 1967 White Paper concentrated on project appraisal and the achievement of comparability with the private sector. The 1978 White Paper returned to the influence of the 'opportunity cost of capital' on the determination of total investment and focused on monitoring *ex post* achievement rather than *ex ante* appraisal.

The third objective is to ensure that the industries are run as efficiently as possible. Financial targets, however necessary, do not guarantee success in this area. The White Papers have therefore advocated monitoring by means of performance and service measures. External investigations of nationalised industry efficiency began with references to the National Board for Prices and Incomes and the Price Commission, and are now in the hands of the Monopolies and Mergers Commission.

Corporate planning has received increasing emphasis in recent years as a process for improving resource allocation and raising the efficiency of nationalised industry operations, and also as a means of developing a more constructive relationship between the industries and government. The 1976 report of the National Economic Development Office argued the need for the government and the industries to agree on a business strategy and recommended the establishment of 'Policy Councils' to carry this out. The 1978 White Paper preferred to increase the emphasis given to discussions of each industry's corporate plan within existing institutional arrangements. The 1979 Conservative government took this process further. It began a process of agreeing objectives with the industries, and instituted collective Ministerial consideration both of forward-looking Corporate Plans and of backward-looking Performance Reviews.

Likierman (Chapter 4) examines critically the case frequently made by those working in the industries that the **impact of financial constraints** makes strategic planning in the nationalised industries much more difficult than in the private sector. Four major complaints can be identified:

(1) meeting financial performance criteria may be incompatible with other objectives which are central to a strategic plan;
(2) the timescale under which financial targets and cash constraints are set makes strategic planning almost impossible;
(3) changes of government and changes of policy by government provide an unfavourable climate for strategic planning;
(4) in some cases governments do not even provide financial targets for the industries.

In practice, however, the system is more flexible than its critics allow, in that short-term financial targets and constraints tend to be adjusted in accordance with the realities of the situation. Hence the relationship between financial constraints and strategic planning may not in fact be so very different from the private sector that a completely new set of rules has to be applied.

Likierman goes on to discuss the issues arising in the case of 'hybrid' industries – those which the government has 'privatised' by selling a bare majority of the shares to the private sector, while retaining a significant percentage itself. These industries appear to be in a quite different and somewhat peculiar position from those industries remaining wholly publicly owned, in that the government has reserved some key powers for itself, while not indicating when and how it might use them. It is not clear how the government would react if the industry should wish to act more like a private sector organisation by, for example, diversifying its activities, or raising additional cash from its shareholders.

It is possible that the government will wish to sell off or run down shareholdings as soon as possible, so that the ambiguities will be only short-term. Otherwise it cannot be long before some of the key questions need answering. The need to protect the rights of other shareholders in a company governed by normal Stock Exchange regulations will significantly influence whether the government wishes or is able to exercise the same kind of pressure as is applied to the wholly owned industries.

With these complex relationships yet to be resolved, strategic planning in these hybrid industries could in practice be considerably more difficult than in their private counterparts.

Dudley and Richardson in Chapter 5 on the **political framework** give a political scientist's view of the complex relationships between the management of the nationalised industries, the government, trade unions and various pressure groups. The principal sources of government power *vis-à-vis* the industries are well known: its ability to appoint (and occasionally sack) chairmen and board members; its position as sole source of finance; and its direct control of investment (and in many instances, prices). But the industries themselves also have considerable political power. This arises from three main factors: their position as major industrial organisations; their advantage as a repository of expertise which Whitehall cannot hope to match; and the leverage arising from their statutory position under the nationalisation acts.

Acting in combination through the Nationalised Industries' Chairmen's Group, the corporations constitute a powerful and effective lobby. An example is the treatment of the nationalised industries in the Private Member's Bill put forward by Norman St John-Stevas MP which would, as originally drafted, have made the industries subject to investigation by the Controller and Auditor General. This provision was subject to intense lobbying and eventually replaced by a compromise proposal under which the Select Committee on Public Accounts would be involved with government-sponsored Monopolies and Mergers Commission inquiries. In addition, commercial auditors would conduct value-for-money inquiries on behalf of Whitehall sponsoring departments, the results of which would be made available to the Public Accounts Committee and the relevant Select Committees.

Other interests such as trade unions, consumer councils and environmental pressure groups have found it difficult to break into the heart of the Whitehall policy-making process. Indeed the unions have generally shown little desire to participate in decision-making, as opposed to reacting to board proposals as they emerge. Consumer Councils have tended to exercise very little power; but environmental groups have recently found a powerful instrument for publicity and delay by participating vigorously and at length in public planning inquiries. Parliament itself is in a somewhat paradoxical position: it is the body to whom the industries owe their formal status and authority; yet it is effectively debarred from any significant influence on both the strategic development and day-to-day operations of the industries.

Both Byatt, and Dudley and Richardson, see the reality of the relationship between the government and the nationalised industries as far more complex than the original Morrisonian doctrine of the 'arm's length relationship' would suggest. Byatt believes there are severe limits on how far it is possible to go in systematising the relationship between the industries and government. The 'arm's length' relationship is a pipe-dream. The 'holding company' analogy provides some insights but has limitations. The 'banker/client' model is again only part of the story. Perhaps the political context of the relationship inevitably involves both fuzziness and conflict. In Dudley and Richardson's view the fundamental issue to be resolved remains the 'balance of expertise', particularly between the industry and the government, and they see the current search for more effective external and independent review procedures as the most fruitful attempt to solve this problem.

Harrison (Chapter 6) considers the theory and practice of

monitoring performance but (contrary to Dudley and Richardson's view) is sceptical as to whether further monitoring by outside bodies will solve the problem. He casts doubt on the thesis that the key is to clarify the industries' objectives. These will always be subject to conflicting pressures and interpretations. Harrison's preferred solution is to develop the process of 'self-monitoring' by the industries themselves. This would involve, for a start, the publication of accounts showing the results for particular activities in detail. But in addition to the publication of more regular accounting and physical statistics, there should be three significant innovations:

(1) major submissions to the Board or Ministries should be published;
(2) information on key policy options should be made public;
(3) the key assumptions made in forward planning should be published, not simply the forecasts themselves.

(It is noteworthy that the Sizewell inquiry has led to publication of information of this kind in the case of nuclear power stations.)

Harrison believes that such a process, by exposing people to 'peer review', would harness management's professional talents to creative rather than defensive tasks. It would put Parliament and the wider public (particularly the opinion-formers) in a position to be more-effective critics of the industries.

Beesley and Gist's approach is more fundamental (Chapter 7). In an examination of the **role of market forces** they consider the scope for improving the industries' performance by subjecting them to increased competition. This could be achieved either with or without 'privatisation', and they focus primarily on the question of how competition might play a useful role while the industries remained in public ownership. The two main ways in which this might be achieved are:

(1) by relaxing restrictions on the entry of new firms to markets where nationalised industries at present have a statutory monopoly; or
(2) by splitting the public corporations into separate autonomous parts while leaving them in state ownership.

The potential benefits from increased competition could be a greater incentive to innovate both in methods of production and in products themselves; increased competition should also keep prices down and hence expand markets.

Following Beesley and Littlechild's article in *Lloyds Bank Review*,[1] the public corporations may be classified in terms of two characteristics: (i) whether they have good or bad market prospects; and (ii) whether if market forces were given full rein they would tend to end up in single or multiple ownership.

Beesley and Gist suggest that splitting up the present monolithic organisations should be considered in industries with good market prospects but with monopolistic tendencies: for example, establishing separate local telecommunications and gas distribution networks, making each airport independent, and breaking up British Rail. Each such board would be locally appointed or elected, with separate accounts, and would borrow under government guarantee subject to central rules.

Relaxation of entry restrictions would be particularly relevant in industries with good demand prospects and without 'natural' monopolistic tendencies: for example, electricity generation, telecommunications (excluding local networks), gas production, coal, airways. Pricing rules should be devised to avoid unfair competition between established interests and newcomers. These would be based on non-discrimination and the forbidding of predatory pricing.

The most important attempt so far to introduce competition to a nationalised industry with monopolistic tendencies has been in telecommunications. When the government initially embarked on a programme of easing entry to telecommunications markets they apparently did so with no clear idea that privatisation of British Telecom would follow. The intervening period saw attempts to combine more freedom to enter with the continuance of traditional controls over a nationalised industry. After privatisation, however, the Director General of Telecommunications and his office will be responsible for overseeing competition in the industry and setting the ground rules.

Beesley and Gist are concerned that the proposals in the 1983 Telecommunications Bill (before Parliament at the time of writing) do not go far enough to stimulate increased competition. Competition *has* been increased, but only selectively. They argue in detail that the rules of the game as envisaged in the draft licence are too restrictive and not sufficiently explicit. In particular they criticise provisions in the bill enjoining the Secretary of State and Director General of Telecommunications to ensure that a universal service is provided.

The recent history of British Telecom suggests that privatising a statutory monopoly, in conjunction with lifting restrictions on entry to the industry, may do nothing to increase competition unless the appropriate liberalisation measures are also adopted. The needs of privatisation *per se* and the requirements of a policy designed to increase the role for market forces may well be opposed, in that share values will be higher for a privatised monopoly than a company subject to competition. Beesley and Gist conclude that the priorities associated with a progamme of privatisation seem to have substantially reduced the pace of liberalisation.

PART III   METHODS AND TECHNIQUES

Rees (Chapter 8) discusses the relation between **prices and planning** in three major nationalised industries: electricity, coal and gas. Taking a view on future price movements is an essential step in any strategic evaluation. This applies both to selling prices and the buying-in prices for the various inputs: for example, fuel, materials, and labour. Rees discusses the problems raised by such forecasts and also considers pricing policy in these industries.

In the case of electricity, the fairly sophisticated marginal cost 'message' transmitted by the bulk supply tariffs which the CEGB charges to the area boards is not brought home to domestic consumers at the point of consumption. Recent developments in metering technology may, however, enable domestic consumers' charges to be geared more closely to marginal costs at different times of the day and year.

The NCB bases its planning on forecasts of world prices for coal on a number of different scenarios. But it appears to be planning to meet the entire UK demand out of domestic production, even though this would seem to imply a substantial margin of capacity at which unit costs exceed the world price. This has the further implication that, in so far as it is shielded from import competition, the NCB could charge more than the world price. Rees concludes that the NCB should base its prices on world levels and its long-term aim should be to close pits whose costs are above the prices obtained.

Economic efficiency in gas pricing requires that the price of gas sold in the industrial market be equal to the world price of industrial fuel oil, in terms of thermal content. Capacity of gas production should be at the level at which the long-run marginal cost of gas (i.e. the cost of new supplies from the North Sea) is about equal to the world fuel oil price. Rees believes this is broadly what seems to be happening.

Wigley (Chapter 9) discusses the **role of forecasting**, and its relationship with strategic planning and decision-taking. He compares the preparation of traditional forecasts, albeit with a range of possible outcomes, with the preparation of scenarios in the sense of a number of possible 'futures' with consistent assumptions about social, political, economic and technological developments, and concludes that each approach has something to learn from the other. The contrast between wholly 'rational' decision-making and that based solely on judgement is artificial. Analytical work is unlikely to reduce significantly the essential uncertainty attaching to the future and may even widen our perception of it. Analysis can, however, provide a quantitative basis for discussion of the effects of uncertainty on the key factors involved.

Ideally a strategic plan should: identify objectives for the organisation concerned; set out alternative assumptions about the future; analyse the effects on the organisation (and where appropriate on the assumptions themselves) of alternative strategies on each assumption; and arrive at the key considerations in deciding a 'preferred' strategy.

For a commercial organisation this means making alternative forecasts for: (a) external factors such as the general level of economic activity, prices of inputs, actions of competitors, etc.; and (b) product prices and sales, production costs, and investment requirements. For each set of assumptions the plan would ideally need to prepare the revenue, capital and flow-of-funds accounts for each of a number of years ahead.

The results of such an analysis should provide a basis for considering alternative strategies. For example, in deciding on investment in productive capacity there may be a choice between the flexibility of a mix of smaller and varied types of plant and the returns to scale of larger plant of similar types with series ordering. It might also consider such major issues as the future scale of the organisation relative to its competitors, possible diversification, etc. In practice, time and resources are scarce and the number of alternative assumptions and strategic options examined is strictly limited.

Rees makes the related point that it is not just the number and relevance of the alternatives examined that are important, but also the use to which such analysis is put in the decision-making process. A distinction needs to be made between the use of scenarios to help arrive at a judgement and their use to examine the robustness of a judgement already arrived at. Rees suggests that managements tend to arrive at what they regard as a current decision, based partly on subjective judgement, and quite probably on the 'internal objectives' of the industry. The analysis of sensitivities, or the more sophisticated consideration of scenarios, then tends to be viewed primarily as a means of testing the 'robustness' of the preferred decision to changes in the assumptions. It plays a role in the process of advocacy and debate, at the end of which the decision will be validated and resources committed (or not, as the case may be). Wide scope for the subjective judgement of industry management must always exist: the idea of an objective set of 'decision rules' or techniques for choices under risk, which could be imposed upon managers, is a chimera. History has shown the structure of incentives and control in the nationalised industries to be such that very wasteful investment expenditures can be made. The problem is to reconcile the necessary degree of managerial judgement which must exist in the face of uncertainty, with the avoidance of costly mistakes. Scenario planning is a small but useful step toward the solution of this problem.

The inevitably quantitative nature of many of the planning issues in these industries makes them strong candidates for the use of computer models. In Chapter 10, Brown discusses the use and development of **planning models** in six major industries, mainly for long-term capacity planning.

The six industries fall into two groups. The first comprises three energy industries: the National Coal Board, British Gas and the Central Electricity Generating Board. The second is made up of three 'network' based services: British Airways, British Rail and British Telecom.

In the analysis of strategic issues (such as the possible implementation of a new technology), evaluation of the options involves definition of the tactical (or year-by-year) path to the long-term goal. For enterprises with complex supply systems (and hence with many options for development, modernisation and closure) this type of analysis can be assisted by the use of models representing the economics of the business at operational level. One of the major difficulties of designing such models, however, is to balance the amount of detail necessary to ensure reasonable confidence in the results, against the need to ensure sufficient simplicity for the strategic issues to remain recognisable.

The most fundamental problem of all is, of course, the quality of the data (principally forecasts) fed into the model: although this is equally difficult whether such evaluations are done with the aid of models or 'by hand'. As discussed above, strategic evaluations depend on a wide range of forecasts, including sales volume and selling prices, input prices, operating standards, capital costs, etc. While the results of the calculations emanating from computer models are no better, or worse, than the quality of the forecasts they embody, their 'number-crunching' abilities do make it feasible to consider much more thoroughly the implications of varying the key forecasts or assumptions. In this sense they can make a valuable contribution to the problem of decision-making in the face of uncertainty.

The current explosion in the use of mini- and micro-computers is likely to produce a generation of managers increasingly disposed towards the use of computer models. Brown suggests that computer developments will contribute to the increasing accessibility and ease of use of models. In particular, software developments will encourage the possibility of building a greater variety of models to meet varying purposes. The increasing ease and ability with which 'what if?' questions can be answered should lead to a greater managerial willingness to evaluate alternatives.

PART IV TRANSPORT AND ENERGY

In Chapter 11, on **planning in transport**, Heath discusses the way in which British Rail's corporate planning process has developed from being seen primarily as part of their continuing negotiations with government, to becoming an instrument of internal management. Earlier Corporate Plans were largely intended to secure government support for policies which BR wished to pursue, but with the 1983–8 Corporate Plan, this has changed in two respects. The Plan is now more internally orientated; and it is seen as a guide to action based on decisions already taken, rather than as a means of arriving at strategic decisions. The process of strategy formation, with its inevitably heavy content of negotiations with the government, is now separated from corporate planning which has become essentially a tool of internal management.

This change in the role of corporate planning has been associated with the setting-up in 1982 of five 'profit-accountable' business units: InterCity; London and the South East; Provincial Passenger Services; Freight; and Parcels. Corporate planning has been largely, but not wholly, decentralised to these new business units, with the central corporate planning function remaining responsible for integrating the plans of the separate units. A new Strategy Committee, at Board level, agrees the basic policy assumptions and ground rules for the individual business plans. It is also responsible for developing higher-level strategic planning.

The rail business can be divided into two parts: the 'commercial' business units (InterCity, Freight and Parcels) and the 'social' railway (the Provincial Services and the London and South East commuter services). The government sets financial objectives for the commercial units; but in the case of the 'social' railway, the government is effectively purchasing rail services on behalf of the community through the Public Service Obligation.

Any system of organisation for a complex network raises problems of one kind or another. Whereas previously the balance of functional interests was a key problem, now it is the reconciliation of conflicting interests of the units, particularly where the commercial make an impact on the social. Nevertheless, Heath sees the new system as a major advance on the old; though there is still much to be done.

Heath's second example is strategic planning in the British Airports Authority, where privatisation has become the immediate strategic preoccupation. The major issue is whether the airports will continue to be managed as a single concern, or split up into independent companies. The BAA raises an interesting point about the government's ability to specify strategic objectives. An attempt to persuade the BAA to adopt a set of objectives proposed by the government was thwarted by the fact that the BAA had potentially conflicting statutory duties laid down by Parliament.

BAA's corporate plans differ from those of British Rail in that they make assumptions about future government decisions on airport strategy for example, on Stansted versus a fifth terminal at Heathrow) on the grounds that they would otherwise have no effective basis for long-term planning. Although its favourable financial results would tend to reduce government intervention, the sensitivity of future airport development and the fact that such developments are subject to major public inquiries, mean that its affairs are inevitably closely related to government – and it seems unlikely that privatisation would alter that.

In a review of **strategy for coal and electricity** (Chapter 12), Pryke is highly critical of the records both of successive governments and of the corporations. In the case of coal, he suggests that the Board has been over-optimistic both about the level of demand and the returns from its capital expenditure projects. Moreover, it has been prepared to go on producing coal at a loss and has devoted a substantial proportion of its investment to pits that have been persistently unprofitable.

Pryke criticises the CEGB for not having invested in Pressurised Water Reactors, instead of oil- and coal-fired plant and Advanced Gas Cooled Reactors. He therefore welcomes the CEGB's decision to construct a PWR at Sizewell, and its desire to follow this up with further stations of the same type. It should be recognised, however, that the Board's case rests on the assumption that there is likely to be a large and continuing rise in the cost of coal, and it is quite possible that the world price will increase more slowly than is being assumed and that the exchange rate will deteriorate less. On the other hand, the Board bases its case on the price that it will be charged by the NCB, although what is relevant in terms of economic welfare is the cost of producing the coal that the station will displace. Pryke contends that the government ought to have recognised that the NCB practises cross-subsidisation and instructed the CEGB to base its estimates on the prospective marginal cost of British coal. This will remain high even if, over the period between 1982 and 2000, the NCB closes down exhausted pits that mostly have high costs and which produce 36 million tonnes. After the turn of the century the marginal cost of British coal may decline, as more new mines come into operation and the remaining high-cost pits are closed, but the appropriate response would then be to limit the construction of nuclear capacity in order that Sizewell B and successor stations remain on base load, and provide large fuel savings, throughout their lives.

Pryke concludes that unless the government is prepared to play a more constructive strategic role we should devise an alternative system in which public ownership and monopoly are, wherever possible, replaced by private ownership and competition.

POSTSCRIPT

In a postscript on the **future of the nationalised industries**, Grieve Smith suggests that there is a genuine need to reconsider their organisation and structure, but the question at issue is not simply where to draw the frontier between the public and private sector – if indeed there can or should be a clear-cut frontier. It may, for example, be more important in practice to consider whether the bulk of our seaports (or airports) should be in one organisation or separate competing enterprises, than whether they are publicly or privately owned.

There is a need to examine carefully a number of different elements in the discussion about the future of the public corporations, apart from the extent to which they should be financed by public or private capital. In the case of public utilities, the two key issues are: the extent to which public or private utilities are given monopoly rights or otherwise protected against competition; and the method and rules by which the government or some public body will control or regulate public utilities in public or private ownership (for example rival telephone networks). The privatisation of British Telecom has highlighted these issues.

There are, however, as great or greater problems to be faced in those industries that are already subject to intense international competition, and are of such a size and nature that governments are almost inevitably involved one way or another in their strategic development: for example, aerospace, airways, shipbuilding and steel. These problems arise from the constraints on wholly or partly state-owned enterprises operating in competitive markets, in particular the attitude towards diversification and joint ventures, and the method and extent to which the government will use its power in relation to hybrid organisations in which it is a substantial shareholder. Under the present statutory and administrative framework the nationalised industries are for the most part locked into providing specified groups of products on a purely national basis. It does not necessarily require the introduction of private capital to ease these restrictions, and give them more room to manoeuvre.

There are two alternative approaches to government relations with the 'hybrid' (part-public/part-private) enterprise. One is to use the Company Act company but to clarify and formalise the conventions under which the government will use its powers as the major shareholder. The other is to legislate afresh for a new form of corporation with part-public, part-private capital and with the government's powers specified (and limited) by statute. The former approach is more flexible, but in a sense too much so: because the government can always alter the rules in the middle of the game, and the management and private shareholders only know where they are for as long, or as short, a time as current policy prevails.

Recent obsession with the Public Sector Borrowing Requirement and 'privatisation' has led the government to concentrate almost exclusively on establishing private shareholdings in as many of these organisations as possible, without adequate consideration of the industrial implications. Indeed the preparation of some organisations for privatisation seems to have become an end in itself, dominating both their financial arrangements and their immediate planning. Since the industries in question (aerospace, off-shore oil and gas, telecoms, airways, airports, steel) all represent crucial elements in the British economy and are ones in which the governments of most of our fellow EEC partners are involved in one way or another, it is important to consider any potential changes in terms of their effects on the long-term strategy and operating policy of these industries. Strategy and structure must be considered together with a view to seeking a political and organisational structure capable of: (a) providing the infrastructure needed by industry and the public; (b) maintaining or creating industrial organisations which have sufficient resources and market power to develop new products and technologies, and are free if necessary to ally themselves with other enterprises, British or foreign; and (c) facilitating industrial change by minimising the creation of vested interests in existing products and technology.

NOTES AND REFERENCES

1. Beesley and Littlechild, 'Privatisation; Principles, Problems and Priorities', *Lloyds Bank Review*, No. 149 (July 1983).

Part I
Strategic Planning

1 The State of the Art

BERNARD TAYLOR

Strategic Planning has a central role in the management of the modern corporation. It also provides a practical approach to changing the way an enterprise is managed. For planning to succeed, however, it needs to be seen not just as a set of techniques, but as part of a coherent programme of change.

In this chapter I would like to describe five approaches to Strategic or Corporate Planning. Each represents an important school of thought in management thinking and practice. Each view has a large body of supporters, both academics and practitioners. And each offers a coherent philosophy and a range of practical systems and techniques for implementing them.

In determining their approach to planning, the chief executive and his planning staff need to examine the different methodologies that are available to discover which system best meets their needs. They should then adapt the approach to suit their own organisation. For corporate planning systems do not come ready-made. They have to be tailor-made to fit each enterprise. The decision is important, because typically it takes two or three years to introduce a particular planning approach, and if it is to be effective it requires wholehearted commitment both from the Board and from operating management.

In any large organisation, of course, it is likely that several different planning approaches will be present at any one time. And in one part of the business, planning is likely to move through various phases – with the management adopting different planning philosophies at different stages in the development of the firm. Corporate planning, like other managerial activities, is a process which grows and evolves – and sometimes has major setbacks and needs to be re-launched. It is rare to find an enterprise where all the available planning approaches are being employed equally effectively.

23

TABLE 1.1. *Strategic planning: five practical approaches*

	Central control system	*Strategic management*	*Political planning*	*Framework for innovation*	*Futures research*
The Focus	Allocation and control of resources	Managing organisational change	Mobilising power and influence	Developing new business	Exploring the future
Important Ideas	A rational decision-making and control process	A community with common values and culture	Interest groups and organisations competing for resources	A vehicle for commercialising innovation	A management with a real awareness of future uncertainty
The Elements	1. Specific objectives 2. A balanced portfolio of investments 3. Action programmes and budgets 4. Monitoring and control	1. Organisation development 2. Staff development 3. Organisation structure 4. Management systems	1. Monitoring and forecasting social and political trends 2. Assessing the impact on the firm 3. Organising and implementing action programmes	1. Commitment to innovation 2. Funds for new development 3. Strategies for corporate development 4. Organising project teams and action programmes	1. Developing alternative futures 2. Assessing social and economic impact 3. Defining key decisions
The Techniques	1. SWOT analysis* 2. Business portfolio analysis 3. Gap analysis 4. Extrapolative forecasting 5. Extended budgeting	Group work on: 1. Stakeholder analysis 2. SWOT analysis* 3. Portfolio analysis etc.	1. Public affairs 2. Civic affairs 3. Employee communication 4. Social issue analysis 5. Country risk analysis 6. Media relations	Programmes for: 1. Divestment 2. Diversification 3. Acquisition 4. New product development 5. Market penetration and development	1. Scenarios 2. Delphi studies 3. Cross impact analysis 4. Trend analysis 5. Computer simulation 6. Contingency planning

*An analysis of strengths, weaknesses, opportunities and threats.

Table 1.1 sets out the five main approaches to planning in broad outline under four headings: (i) *The Focus* – the main objective or purpose; (ii) *Important Ideas* – the characteristic view or philosophy of planning; (iii) *The Elements* – the key steps or stages in the process; (iv) *The Techniques* – some of the techniques that are widely used. As with any classification system, the categories are not watertight, but they do represent quite distinct traditions in current thinking and practice.[1]

PLANNING AS A CENTRAL CONTROL SYSTEM

From the beginning, one of the main drives behind the development of corporate planning has been the desire of top management to have a better control over the allocation of capital and other key resources.

The Philosophy

The philosophy of 'planning and control' is fundamental to management. Early thinkers on management like Henri Fayol described the management process in terms of 'planning, command, coordination and control'. An analogy is often made with an army or another hierarchical organisation, where decisions are taken at the top, instructions are passed down through the enterprise, and the leaders get back information that enables them to measure actual results against the plan.

The business enterprise is also frequently compared with a machine which can be regulated by an engineering control system. Automatic control systems, such as the domestic thermostat, contain certain basic elements: a Sensor; a Standard of Performance; a Collator, which compares actual performance with the standard; and an Actor, which takes action to make up any deficiency in performance or to change the standard.

Writers and practitioners on planning have seen corporate planning as a comprehensive control system which could be used to regulate the operations of a whole firm – a logical extension of departmental control systems such as stock control, sales control and production control. They were also attracted by the idea of the business as a total system with an integrated information and control system.

It is perhaps natural that accountants should have seen corporate planning as an adjunct to the budgetary control system. There is, however, an important distinction to be drawn between strategic planning and management control – though they are obviously related. Strategic planning includes, for example, choosing company objectives, planning the organisational structure, setting policies for personnel, finance, marketing and research, choosing new product lines, acquiring a new division, and deciding on non-routine capital expenditures. Management control is concerned with formulating budgets, determining staff levels, formulating personnel, marketing and research programmes, deciding on routine capital expenditures, measuring, appraising and improving management performance, etc.[2]

The Processes

The rise of corporate planning in the 1960s coincided with a period of diversification and international expansion in large companies. In many cases these same firms were divided into product divisions which were designated as profit centres or cost centres. Divisional general managers were appointed and each was instructed to manage his division as if it were an independent business. Unfortunately, some of these executives took the instruction too literally and top management saw their subordinates riding off in all directions. Corporate planning was seized upon as a technique which might enable the main board to re-establish some control over the situation. Traditional budgeting systems proved woefully inadequate to the task of controlling a multi-divisional business – particularly when the divisional managers usually formed a majority in the main board and sat in judgement on their own capital projects.[3] The solution commonly adopted was:

(1) to re-structure the board so as to reduce the power of the divisional managers by bringing in heads of functional departments, non-executive directors, and others who could form a board representing the whole corporation rather than specific local interests;

(2) to require each division (later each Strategic Business Unit) to produce a Strategy and Action Plan against which its performance could be monitored.

This enabled top management and the management of each principal business to have a debate about future prospects in terms of the total market, the company's products and services, and the cash which might be generated immediately and in the long term.

Corporate planning for a divisionalised company can be divided into four stages:

(1) *Corporate Guidelines and Forecasts* Headquarters issues a statement which might include: financial and market objectives; corporate policies on personnel etc.; assumptions and forecasts about the business environment; an indication of the funds available and priorities for investment.
(2) *Divisional Strategy* Corporate and divisional executives discuss key strategic issues, a tentative allocation of resources, and new corporate projects.
(3) *Divisional Action Programmes* Divisional and departmental executives discuss alternative programmes, new divisional projects, and resources required.
(4) *Divisional Budgets* Departmental staff and divisional staff discuss detailed five-year and annual budgets.

The division's performance is then monitored against this strategy, the action programmes, and budgets.

The corporate staff groups (finance, personnel, manufacturing, etc.) and the planners themselves, are involved in the corporate planning process through:

(1) preparing the planning guidelines for divisions;
(2) reviewing divisional strategies and plans;
(3) advising the board or an executive committee in approving the plans;
(4) monitoring divisional performance against the plans.

Of course, the best staff groups operate in a supportive way, working by influence rather than through confrontation.

The Problems

The close association between planning and financial control has led to all kinds of problems. In particular there has been a tendency:

(1) to confuse strategic planning with extended budgeting;
(2) to produce three-year or five-year plans simply by extrapolating or pushing forward the present operations;
(3) to prepare company plans by merely consolidating the operational plans of divisions and subsidiaries;
(4) to stress the numbers rather than the quality of the thinking.

This still goes on. It is common to find corporate plans which consist of comprehensive and detailed operational plans and budgets – without any discussion of objectives, organisation structure or alternative strategies.

Another problem with the Five Year Plan and Budget is that it can easily degenerate into a sterile but time-consuming routine. Corporate planning has provided many examples of this: highly structured planning systems which required many man-hours to build and maintain – and resulted in plans which were 'wrong to three points of decimals'.

Nevertheless, the resource allocation process is at the core of most planning systems, and the Operational Plan and budget is the basic planning document. Other 'qualitative' and 'informal' approaches to planning have been developed to compensate for its inflexibility and its narrow scope.

PLANNING AS A FRAMEWORK FOR INNOVATION

One powerful reason, then, for the growth of business planning was the need to establish a central steering mechanism for the direction and co-ordination of large, diverse, multi-national operations. An equally strong and opposite motivation was the desire to promote initiative at the local level – in particular to prevent centralisation and bureaucracy from stifling creativity and innovation.

Over time, the need for continuous change and innovation has become accepted by many leading businessmen and writers on business as an article of faith. To quote Peter Drucker, the businessman's philosopher: 'In a world buffeted by change, faced daily with new threats to its safety, the only way to conserve is by innovating. The only stability possible is stability in motion.'[4] The implications of this philosophy were spelled out for businessmen, politicians and public officials by John Gardner, the former US Secretary of Health Education and Welfare, in his best-selling book *Self-Renewal*. He wrote:

> A society whose maturing consists simply of acquiring more firmly established ways of doing things is headed for the graveyard – even if it learns to do these things with greater and greater skill. In the ever-renewing society what matures is a system or framework within which continuous innovation, renewal and rebirth can occur.[5]

For a competitive business this process of self-renewal is fundamental to survival. In the short term a management can make profits by mortgaging the future – and many managements are tempted to do this in the present crisis. But in a rapidly changing situation, unless there is continual reinvestment in staff training, market development, new products, and up-to-date equipment, management are likely to find themselves overtaken by their competitors. As the Boston Consulting Group consultants concluded in their enquiry into the failure of the British motorcycle industry:

> The result of the British industry's historic focus on short-term profitability has been low profits and now losses in the long term. The long-term result of the Japanese industry's historic focus on market share and volume, often at the expense of short-term profitability, has been the precise opposite: high and secure profitability.[6]

This process of entrepreneurship has long been acknowledged as a central function of the businessman. It involves:

- identifying a market opportunity
- developing a product to match it
- raising the necessary finance and matching the risk to the opportunity

- mobilising the staff and the other resources necessary to provide the required service
- producing and distributing the product at a profit.

To quote Donald Schon:

> The firm defines itself as a vehicle for carrying out a special kind of process. It defines itself through its engagement in entrepreneurship, the launching of new ventures, or in commercializing what comes out of development. The principal figure in the firm becomes the manager of the corporate entrepreneurial process; and the question is this: what are the potentials in development for new commercial ventures?[7]

In a one-man business the owner can be his own entrepreneur, but in a large corporation the process has to be formalised and systematised. To quote Peter Drucker again:

> Every one of the great business builders we know of – from the Medici to the founders of the Bank of England down to Thomas Watson in our days – had a definite idea, a clear 'theory of business' which informed his actions and decisions. Indeed a clear simple and penetrating 'theory of the business' rather than 'intuition' characterizes the truly successful entrepreneur, the man who not only amasses a large fortune but builds an organization that can endure and grow long after he is gone.
>
> But the individual entrepreneur does not need to analyse his concepts and to explain his 'theory of business' to others, let alone spell out the details. He is a one person thinker, analyst and executor. Business enterprise, however, requires that entrepreneurship be systematized, spelled out as a discipline and organized as work.[8]

In many corporations, strategic planning is regarded as a form of 'organised entrepreneurship'. Patrick Haggerty, the former Chairman of Texas Instruments, described their planning system as a 'framework for innovation'. He said:

> Self Renewal at Texas Instruments begins with deliberate, planned innovation in each of the basic areas of industrial life –

creating, making and marketing. With our long range planning system we attempt to manage this innovation so as to provide a continuing stimulus to the company's growth.

The Management of Corporate Development

Most management systems are concerned with operational problems. Operational plans start with the present situation and push it forward – in terms of sales quotas, production targets, stock levels, budgets, etc. The horizon is typically one year, occasionally two years – or perhaps three to five years for a specific product or facility. Other management systems – performance appraisal, salaries and incentives, promotions and career development – also help to focus managers' ideas on the short term. A major problem for the large corporation is how to persuade staff to spend some of their time thinking and planning for new products, new markets, new production and administrative processes, and maybe entirely new kinds of businesses – joint ventures, mergers and acquisitions, new social and political initiatives.

How, for a start, can top management produce a strategy and a programme for the development of the business? Typically, this involves the formation of *ad hoc* groups which report directly to top management: project teams, venture groups, a diversification task force, a group to deal with acquisitions or international expansion, etc. In the present recession we have also seen task forces formed to look at closures, divestments, rationalisation and organisational restructuring.

The challenge is to develop a 'vision of success' for the total enterprise and its parts and then to produce action plans, budgets and timetables to realise the vision. The techniques which are in common use provide broad frameworks for discussion and analysis. For example:

(1) *Gap Analysis* describes the planning task by identifying the gap between the company's objectives and its likely achievement in terms of profits, sales, cash flow, etc. Management is invited to:
   (a) set an objective – in quantitative terms – for example, rate of return on investment or market share;
   (b) forecast the 'momentum' line for the present business assuming no major changes;

(c) plan to fill the gap with projects for increased efficiency, expansion and diversification.

(2) *SWOT Analysis* provides a series of check-lists for auditing the company's Strengths and Weaknesses, and the Opportunities and Threats in the business environment. The business is assessed against leading competitors in world markets in terms of its technology, market position, financial base, production efficiency, management and organisation. The opportunities and threats are considered in the light of trends in the environment – economic, socio-political, technological, and competitive. Then the two analyses are compared to see what are the market opportunities which match the firm's resources, what new resources are required, etc.

(3) *Business Portfolio Analysis* The process of funds allocation (i.e. allocation of both fixed and working capital) is frequently discussed on the basis of a matrix showing the pattern of businesses in the company's 'portfolio'. Many large companies have their own Matrix or Screen, typically displaying on one scale the prospects for the industry and on the other the strength of the company's market position. The criteria for the industry's attractiveness might include: growth potential, expected changes in markets and in technology, the strength of competition from existing competitors and possible newcomers, and government and environmental constraints. The analysis of one's own company strengths requires a comparison with leading competitors in terms of market share, production capability, relative costs, technical expertise, patent position, marketing, distribution and service, and government support.

(4) *PIMS (Profit Impact of Market Strategy)* The PIMS data base which was set up originally by General Electric, USA, is derived from around a thousand 'businesses' in the USA and Western Europe over a period of up to ten years. The programme collects 300 items of information about each business and attempts to discover which factors have most effect on profitability (return on investment): for example, market share, product quality, marketing expenditure, capital investment v. sales, etc. The data base is used primarily by holding companies in assessing the performance of divisions and subsidiaries and in making decisions about investment and divestment.

STRATEGIC MANAGEMENT

In practice, the majority of managers find the task of strategic planning difficult and they require a good deal of help. This is partly a matter of temperament. Operating managers tend to be chosen for their ability to get things done, and it has been well said that 'A man of action, forced into a state of thought, is unhappy until he can get out of it.'

It is largely the size and complexity of the task – to try to plan for the long-term development of the total enterprise in all its dimensions. It is also the problem of planning with little solid information in a situation of great uncertainty where all the elements interact. Inevitably, the manager has to rely on his judgement and imagination much more than he does in operational management.

Faced with these practical difficulties in generating new strategies, leading companies such as General Electric in the USA and Philips in Europe have started to think not just in terms of strategic planning but in terms of strategic management, i.e. changing the whole management system. This increasingly popular approach takes the view that policy-making is a learning process and strategic planning is the specific activity through which the members of an organisation learn to adapt to radical changes in the external environment.

The Philosophy

Consider the changes which are taking place and their impact on human institutions – fluctuations in supply and demand, the advent of new technologies, the appearance of social and political movements, the rise and fall of governments. All these trends are rendering established institutions and traditional ways of thinking and acting obsolete. In a rapidly changing world, organisations must adapt or go under. To quote Donald Schon: 'Our society and all of its institutions are in continuing processes of transformation . . . we must learn to understand, guide, influence and manage these transformations . . . We must invent and develop institutions which are "learning systems" – systems capable of bringing about their own transformation.'[9] This is the theory of natural selection again:

the view that organisations must adapt or be replaced by others which are better-suited to their environment.

How, then, can we build institutions which learn to adapt to their environment? Is it possible to develop management's ability to cope with change? Can we help organisations or teams of people to set objectives, to be more aware of the changes taking place around them, and to develop their own plans for the future – and can management learn to do this on a continuing basis?

Those who support the view of planning as part of a process of social change usually reject the theory that planning is a logical search for solutions, a cognitive decision-making process which establishes the area of search and certain performance criteria, collects and analyses data, assesses alternatives and makes an optimal choice. We are, after all, dealing not with inert objects but with people who have their own ideas, beliefs and motivations.[10]

In place of this model of planning as rational and sequential, behavioural scientists frequently present it as a trial-and-error process. Managers and administrators are encouraged to adopt an experimental approach; not looking for comprehensive solutions or great leaps forward but attempting to engineer incremental changes, with the top managers and their advisers not moving too far ahead of the group.[11]

The Approach

This 'behavioural' view of planning is more human, less comprehensive, more easily related to the organisations which we all know and work in. Planning is seen as a *process* through which individuals and teams can learn to cope with an unpredictable and rapidly changing environment. The fact that a forecast or a plan turns out to be wrong is therefore not an indication that the management is incompetent or that planning is not feasible, but rather as confirmation that we are living in an uncertain world and we need to reassess our situation continually. However, we should learn by experience and our involvement in forecasting, strategy-making, planning, programming and budgeting should help us to get a better 'feel' for the trends in the environment and should improve the organisation's capacity to respond to them.

Planning is seen as one element in a wider programme of organisational change. This may involve many other measures:

(1) *Moves affecting individual managers:* retiring or re-training existing managers, recruiting new managers, promoting and developing staff for new roles.
(2) *Changes in organisation structure:* these might include, for example:
  (a) dividing the company into semi-autonomous units such as product divisions;
  (b) establishing new groupings to co-ordinate policy by geographical regions, by product groups or by Strategic Business Units (i.e. parts of the organisation which have a common business strategy); or
  (c) reorganising the Board and revising the capital investment procedures to strengthen the role of the Board as a policy-making body.
(3) *Changes in management systems:*
  (a) changing the procedures for staff appraisal, promotion and payment, to encourage management to give a higher priority to new company-wide programmes: for example, social responsibility, new business development or staff development;
  (b) the introduction of improved information systems for finance, manpower and production;
  (c) the development of planning and control systems to focus management attention on cash flow, productivity, planning for manpower, etc.;
  (d) the provision of new procedures for environmental assessment to give managers a better understanding of the external trends which are likely to affect their business.

In adopting the organisational learning mode of planning, the planner takes on the role of a 'change agent'. His task is not merely to produce a product, 'the plan', but rather to intervene in 'the process', i.e. to work with management at various levels to help them to define their problems and to produce new programmes directed at changing the orientation of the organisation to fit new circumstances. Sometimes, the firm is engaged in a slow evolution. Occasionally there is a major crisis. Often the problem is to help a management team to adjust to some kind of radical change or discontinuity:

(1) the integration and rationalisation of several companies into a larger, divisionalised operation, following a programme of diversification or a series of mergers;
(2) the closure or sale of a number of businesses, and the slimming down of central staff functions following a reduction in demand or expropriation by government;
(3) developing the capacity to design, sell and manage total systems or turn-key projects – as opposed to selling individual products – to developing countries or to the communist world;
(4) the introduction of a sea-change in technology such as containerisation in shipping or the use of micro-processors and fibre optics in telecommunications.

One of the problems with the 'organisational learning' approach is that these radical changes occur infrequently in the life of an individual firm. It is therefore difficult for a manager to gain experience of closures and divestments, or mergers and acquisitions, within one company, except in a large multi-divisional business. In cases of radical change, therefore, it is often necessary for top management to bring in consultants or to recruit managers from outside the company who have acquired the relevant experience in other businesses.

However, the strategic planner who adopts a social learning approach does not act merely as a change agent intervening as and when required to carry out an attitude study, diagnose an organisational problem, to improve working relationships between individuals and departments. He is concerned to develop the competence of management teams in various parts of the organisation to take a 'strategic' view of their businesses, to identify the key issues for decisions and to take the action which they regard as necessary for the survival and growth of the enterprise. This usually involves:

(1) taking a comprehensive and realistic view of the organisation from various perspectives – the world market, competitors, long-term trends in technology and in society;
(2) assessing in comparative terms the business's overall perfor-

mance – its levels of costs, productivity, product quality, price, customer services;
(3) considering feasible alternative futures for the organisation – making established activities more efficient and more productive, developing new technologies and building new businesses.

PLANNING AS A POLITICAL PROCESS

A fourth approach to planning consists of a kind of *realpolitik* – a view which says that planning is essentially concerned not with logic, innovation or learning, but with *power*. Planning, after all, is a process which allocates resources. Planning decisions affect people's lives. Planning determines where investments are made and where businesses stop investing; where jobs are created and where employees are made redundant; which new projects go forward and which existing projects are terminated. Dividends, wages and salaries, promotion and advancement, recognition and status – this is what planning is about.

The Philosophy

The supporters of this idea share the view that life is a struggle for survival, a continual battle between competing groups.

In the political analyst's eyes, society is made up of organisations and interest groups which are continually competing for support from the public, from politicians and from other decision-makers in public and private organisations. Various groups in society are engaged in a struggle for power. Sometimes the opposing lines are drawn up according to social level in a type of class conflict. On other occasions, or on other issues, they may be arranged by nationality, by religious creed, by race or by sex.

Each political party or pressure group also consists of warring factions all clamouring for the attention of those in power. The business, too, is seen not as a homogeneous unit, a hierarchy led by the Board, or a single culture with a common purpose. Instead the firm is conceived as a model or miniature of society itself in which department vies with department, region with region and product division with product division, to gain a greater share of the firm's resources and the power which goes with them.

A major danger with this political game is that it can take everyone's eyes off the business of creating wealth. In their own interests and in the interests of society, managers and employees should be mainly concerned with building businesses: introducing new products, increasing productivity and expanding markets at home and abroad. If the political battle inside and outside the firm becomes too intense, then the energies of business leaders and trade-union officials can become absorbed in continual in-fighting and negotiation. Too much effort is spent in dividing the cake and too little time is left for the battle to keep ahead of international competition.

The Changing Political Environment

Nevertheless, the businessman has much to learn from politicians, trade unionists and the leaders of political pressure groups when it comes to influencing public opinion and using the media.

Management's authority is continually being challenged by trade unions and groups of workers, by government agencies and by pressure groups acting on behalf of consumers, conservationists, women's liberation and various ethnic minorities. Inside and outside the business, the objectives, strategies and plans of management are being questioned. Groups of employees, local politicians and social action groups are rejecting or vetoing the plans of management, demanding the right to be informed or consulted – or to participate in the planning process.

These interest groups are, in effect, asking: 'Whose objectives?' 'Whose plans?'. They oppose the idea of unilateral planning by management and claim the right to employee participation or public participation. Trade unions, committees of shop stewards, and action committees working on behalf of local communities are also putting forward their own Alternative Plans and requesting government assistance in putting their case.

The process of planning in the political arena needs to be studied by management. A number of key elements are clear:

(1) *Group Action* Planning in the public arena takes place largely *between* organisations, and the groups which are most successful are those which are well organised. In many cases businesses

must forget their traditional animosities in working for their common good – to influence government, or to make a case when challenged by social action groups.

(2) *Influence and Coercion* In the public arena it is rarely possible for one party to control the activities of another. Each group has to operate by influence and persuasion; and occasionally by threatening sanctions.

(3) *Communications* It becomes essential, therefore, for management to put their case in plain terms to company staff at all levels, to local communities, to particular interest groups, to national governments and to the general public.

(4) *Building Networks* Another central activity of the top management team is to deal with the external relations or foreign policy of the firm. This means carrying on a diplomatic campaign: maintaining liaison within professional and industrial associations, making contacts with political and social interest groups and forming alliances within the industries and in the regions where the business operates.

(5) *Liaison with the Media* Continuing contact with the press, radio and television is vital. Demonstrations, protests, marches, petitions – these are the stock-in-trade of the political activist. Industry has to be prepared to put its case like other interest groups through policy statements, manifestos, national conferences, surveys and reports.

(6) *Contacts with Governments* Links with government bodies need to be established on a continuing basis, directly in the case of a large firm, indirectly via a trade association for a smaller business. In either case it is essential to know how decisions will be made, who are the decision-makers, and who will influence the decisions. Also it is necessary to identify key social and political issues which are important to the company, and to put forward porposals which are constructive and politically feasible – if possible, speaking not just for one firm but on behalf of a sector or sub-sector of industry, or a region.

(7) *Contact with Trade Unions* Employee organisations need to be studied in the same way as government agencies, to determine the political strength of various groups, the framework of regulations and practices, the arrangements for electing officials, the ambitions and policies of various individuals, etc. Also it is necessary to establish communications with trade-union

officials outside the process of wage bargaining, if possible in normal times, so that an effective relationship can become established without the pressure of a crisis.

FUTURES RESEARCH

The futures movement grew up in the late 1960s, but planning in terms of 'alternative futures' only became fashionable in large companies in the late 1970s.[12] Managers in business and administrators in government are now using scenarios and other futures research techniques to try to cope with what they perceive as discontinuities. The year of the oil crisis, 1974, is seen as a watershed marking the end of an era of relative stability and affluence and the beginning of a period of turbulence and economic stagnation. In this new environment a number of trends – political, social, economic and technological – seem to be gathering momentum and interacting to create a business environment which is highly volatile.

Scenario Planning

As management witnessed successive plans being rendered obsolete by unforeseen changes, they began to doubt the value of traditional forecasting and planning techniques based on extrapolation and budgeting, and looked for other approaches better suited to a complex and turbulent environment. They were also convinced of the need to expand their planning and forecasting procedures to cover not only economic and market trends, but also social and political changes which might be reflected in legislation and in the activities of trade unions and social pressure groups.

The result was a spate of experiments in the use of modern forecasting techniques: Delphi Studies, Cross Impact Analyses, Trend Impact Analyses, etc. Also there was an increase in the use of simple financial models aimed at examining the sensitivity of company plans to changes in assumptions, about prices, levels of sales, costs of raw materials, wages and salaries, interest rates, etc. And companies began to make tentative contingency plans – confidentially and informally, to provide for major risks such as a strike, action by a social pressure group, a change of government, a new piece of legislation, the shortage or non-availability of a key raw material or component, or a substantial delay in the construction of a new facility.

However, the most impressive of these changes in planning techniques has been the increasing use of scenarios. In the late 1960s, Herman Kahn and Anthony Wiener defined scenarios as 'hypothetical sequences of events constructed for the purpose of focusing attention on causal processes and decision points.'[13] As used in business, scenarios usually take the form of 'qualitative descriptions of the situation of a company, an industry, a nation or a region at some specified time in the future'.[14]

Coping with an Uncertain Environment

Scenario planning has been criticised on the grounds that it is 'a practice without a discipline'; that scenarios lack the exactness of traditional economic forecasting techniques and there is no proof of their effectiveness. On the other hand, it is the very precision and the bogus authority of conventional approaches to forecasting that have led operating managers and those involved in forecasting to search for other methods which reflect the real uncertainty in the environment. The supporters of scenarios assert that 'it is better to be approximately right than precisely wrong'. To quote Alvin Toffler: 'Linear extrapolation, otherwise known as straight-line thinking is extremely useful and it can tell us many important things. But it works best between revolutionary periods, not in them.'[15]

Scenarios are not intended to predict the future. They are designed to help executives to deal with a highly uncertain environment: to assist the executive who is used to extrapolative forecasting and budgeting in coping with the unexpected. Scenarios are not supposed to provide an accurate picture of the future; they are designed to challenge the imagination: to encourage managers to plan, not just for the most likely future but also for other alternative futures which are less likely. Scenario planning should help managers to be more flexible in various ways:

(1) *Environmental Scanning* It should stimulate managers to scan

the business environment for 'weak signals', especially social and political changes, which might foreshadow a crisis.

(2) *Robust Plans* It should encourage executives to produce plans which are 'robust', i.e. which may not be optimal but would keep the business profitable under a wide range of conditions.

(3) *Contingency Planning* It should prompt managers to be prepared for contingencies: for example, strikes, revolutions or a slump in demand.

(4) *Awareness of Risk* It should make decision-makers more realistic about the risks to their business – social, political, technological and competitive – and persuade them to minimise the risk to the business from overdependence on any one source – a customer group, a technology, a range of products, a national or regional market.

(5) *Concern with Flexibility* Scenario planning also invites businessmen to consider the advantages of building flexibility into their operations, i.e.:
   – designing facilities which can be used in different ways
   – training staff for a broad range of tasks
   – consciously carrying 'slack resources' (skilled staff, extra stocks, back-up generators, etc.) in case of a crisis or a new opportunity
   – diversifying one's operations so as to have businesses, suppliers, production facilities, stock-holding or computers in more than one country or region.

A possible danger of scenario planning is that managers may become too preoccupied with uncertainty and risk – which is inseparable from business. As a result they may play safe while their less-sophisticated competitors are taking new initiatives, accepting or ignoring the risks and capitalising on opportunities for profit and growth.

Planning without Information

Futures research is a way of helping managers to think creatively about the future. This is especially important in a business where a technology, a market or the socio-political situation is changing quickly. In such an environment, the management have little useful information. They are planning in a vacuum. Often there is no historical data – the technology could develop in several directions; the market may not exist – the regulatory framework may not yet have been developed. Today, a surprisingly large number of businesses face this type of situation in relation to new technologies: biotechnology, cable television, telecommunications, the next generation of computers, etc.; and also in international markets such as Brazil, Mexico, Nigeria, Hong Kong and the Middle East. In these cases the only sensible way of 'planning' seems to be in terms of alternative futures.

The Construction of Scenarios

The writing of scenarios typically involves using a number of futures research techniques. For example, the approach recommended by the General Electric Company shown in Table 1.2 includes the use of a Delphi Study, Trend Analysis, Trend Extrapolation, Trend Impact Analysis and Cross Impact Analysis.

TABLE 1.2   *Constructing scenarios for an industrial sector (General Electric USA)*

1
Prepare background
Assess environmental factors – social, regulatory, technological, economic and competitive.
Develop crude 'systems' model of the industry.

2
Select critical indicators
Key indicators (trends).
Future events affecting key indicators (literature search).
Delphi panel to evaluate industry's future.

3
Establish past behaviour for each indicator
Historical performance.
Reasons for past behaviour of each trend.
Delphi questionnaire.

4
Verify potential future events
Delphi panel.
Past trends, future events, impact/probability, future trends.
Assumptions for forecasts, rationale for future trends.

5
Forecast each indicator
Range of future values for each indicator.
Results from literature search and Delphi study.
Trend Impact Analysis and Cross Impact Analysis.

6
Write scenarios
Guidelines for Strategic Business Units.
Annual revision.

Based on: Rochelle O'Connor, *Planning Under Uncertainty*, Conference Board, New York, 1978, p. 8.

A number of the techniques most commonly used in the development of scenarios are listed below:–

(1) *Trend Analysis* This involves scanning and analysing publications and other sources of information on a regular basis to plot long-term trends.

(2) *Computer Simulation* This entails building a computer model of an enterprise or an industry and making projections on different assumptions.

(3) *Decision Analysis* Using this technique, the analyst creates a 'road map' of decisions relating to a particular issue or project. At each step he plots the alternatives available to the 'decision-maker', the estimated payoff or loss for each course of action and the probability of success or failure. The technique is useful to determine the broad dimensions of a decision and as a means of keeping various options open. In analysing real decisions, however, the range of alternatives available is often far too wide for a planner to carry out a comprehensive quantitative analysis.

(4) *Sensitivity Analysis* One of the commonest ways to explore alternative futures is by analysing the sensitivity of a plan to variations in the assumptions. For this purpose it is helpful to

have access to a simple computer model. Thus the planner can produce an operating statement, a cash flow analysis or a balance sheet based on different assumptions about investments, sales, costs, prices, interest rates, etc. Many companies require their subsidiaries or divisions to explore the effects of a 10 per cent or 15 per cent increase or decrease in the major assumptions underpinning any major new project.

(5) *Delphi Study* This is a systematic way of carrying out a poll among experts. The experts are asked a series of questions, usually concerning the likelihood of certain events taking place. Then the results are fed back to the panel and they are asked a further set of questions. Experience to date suggests that the technique is valuable in eliciting the opinion of specialists on a narrow subject such as the probability of a breakthrough in a particular technology which they know well. It seems to be less useful in exploring social and political issues which are much less structured and where there are fewer experts. However, General Electric (USA) have used this technique to explore likely trends in population, employment, education, etc.

(6) *Impact Analysis* This implies setting up a matrix of events which are likely to affect other events (Cross Impact Analysis), or exploring the various impacts that a particular trend may have (Trend Impact Analysis). These techniques involve weighing the likely effects and then assessing which are the most important, and the most urgent.

SUMMARY

In the modern business corporation today, strategic planning is a widespread and highly diverse activity.

(1) Conventional budgeting is being supplemented by a 'funds allocation' procedure, based on a systematic evaluation of each business, its general environment, its competitive situation, and its strategy for the future. Also, instead of operating as a simple financial holding company, the top management of multi-industry, multi-national businesses are setting out to manage their investments as a 'portfolio of businesses'.

(2) It is being recognised that the process of corporate develop-

ment – improving the competitive performance of existing businesses generating new products, penetrating new markets, expanding internationally, and creating or acquiring new businesses – is a prime task of top management and needs to be fostered and managed with separate budgets, plans, project teams, task forces, etc.

(3) In businesses which have to cope with a great deal of uncertainty – for example, in new and growing technologies, in countries which are politically unstable, or in fluctuating international markets – managers have been forced to 'plan' in terms of alternative futures, using simulations, scenarios and contingency plans, rather than traditional forecasting based on extrapolation.

(4) The managements of most large business corporations now find themselves in a continual dialogue with governments, international agencies, trade unions, social pressure groups and the media. To handle this socio-political area they now have public affairs' departments and external consultants who monitor social trends, forecast emerging socio-political issues and formulate action programmes to safeguard the interests of the business and to help to contribute to the solution of social problems, such as unemployment and the decline of city centres.

(5) Executives who have tried to implement these kinds of changes have found that it is often not enough to set demanding targets, and ask for new strategies. It is a major problem to recruit and train managers who have the capacity to 'think strategically'. Usually a team of managers needs to work together over a period of time. They have to develop a new information system which relates to strategic issues rather than operational problems. Often the organisation structure has to be changed to pull out the separate businesses, or to co-ordinate strategies internationally in worldwide product divisions. The way managers are appraised and rewarded also needs to be adjusted to demonstrate that the development of new strategies and new businesses is just as important as the achievement of this year's targets.

Dealing with Crises

The strategic planning processes all take time to put into operation. But what about the firm that is in crisis? Often the company that is in a turnaround situation is there because its top management have not been able to think strategically, to anticipate international competition or the appearance of a new technology, and to develop new products or enter new markets in good time.

Their most urgent need is usually to improve the cash flow and buy time by closing loss-making businesses, cutting overheads, reducing staff, selling off assets, etc. But the next step should be to produce a strategy for the future, and to buy or build new businesses. It is interesting to note that in these crisis situations, top managers in such firms as Fisons, the Burton Group, Scandinavian Airlines and Electrolux have discovered that strategic thinking or strategic management is extremely effective without the usual apparatus of five-year planning, portfolio analysis, scenarios, etc.

NOTES AND REFERENCES

1. For a list of the publications in each of these schools of thought, see: B. Taylor, 'New Dimensions in Corporate Planning', *Long Range Planning*, December 1976.
2. Robert N. Antony, *Planning and Control Systems – A Framework for Analysis* (Cambridge, Mass.: Harvard University Press, 1965) p. 67.
3. Joseph Bower, *Managing the Resource Allocation Process* (Cambridge, Mass.: Harvard University Press, 1970) p. 54.
4. Peter F. Drucker, *Landmarks of Tomorrow* (London, Heinemann: 1959).
5. John W. Gardner, *Self Renewal – The Individual and the Innovative Society* (New York: Harper & Row, 1963) p. 5.
6. Boston Consulting Group, *Strategy Alternatives for the British Motorcycle Industry* (2 vols) Department of Industry (London: HMSO, 1975).
7. Donald A. Schon, *Beyond the Stable State* (London: Temple Smith, 1971) p. 67.
8. Peter F. Drucker, 'Entrepreneurship in Business Enterprise', *Journal of Business Policy*, 1 (1) (Autumn 1970).
9. Donald A. Schon, *Beyond the Stable State* (London: Temple Smith, 1971) p. 30.
10. Donald N. Michael, *On Learning to Plan and Planning to Learn* (London: Jossey-Bass, 1973) p. 19.

11. J. Friedman, 'The Future of Comprehensive Urban Planning: A Critique', *Public Administration Review*, 31 (3) (1971) p. 325.
12. See Rochelle O'Connor, *Planning Under Uncertainty: Multiple Scenarios and Contingency Planning* (New York: Conference Board, 1978).
13. Herman Kahn and Anthony Wiener, *The Year 2000* (New York: Macmillan, 1967) p. 6.
14. Recent scenarios developed in the UK cover, for example, the British economy, unemployment, supply and demand for energy, banking, the chemical industry, television, the world pharmaceutical industry and the future for Japan.
15. *Choosing Our Environment: Can We Anticipate the Future*, Senate Committee Report, Washington (1976).

2 Strategic Planning in the Nationalised Industries

JOHN GRIEVE SMITH

State ownership is only one of a number of factors determining the content and methods of strategic planning in the nationalised industries. In many cases the problems of planning in these organisations are very much akin to those experienced in large firms in the private sector operating in the same or similar fields. Planning in British Steel or British Airways is, for example, very similar to planning in any large steel company or airline. The distinctive factors underlying planning in the large public corporations, which we refer to as 'nationalised industries', are only partly a consequence of state ownership; they also reflect the characteristics of the industries involved.

The nationalised industries or public corporations in the UK may be regarded as falling into two main groups:

(1) public utilities with strong monopolistic tendencies (for example, electricity, gas, telecommunications, railways, airports);
(2) industries operating in competitive international markets (for example, steel, shipbuilding, aerospace, airlines).

(Coal essentially comes into the second group, but could be regarded as occupying an intermediate position by virtue of its protection from international competition.) The public utilities came into public ownership on the assumption that they constituted local or national monopolies and that public ownership constituted the most effective form of public regulation. The second group consisted of 'problem industries' with a long history of state involvement of one kind or another in this and other countries (as the existence of the European Coal and Steel Community bears witness in the case of these two industries).

The original nationalisation acts and subsequent framework of control tended to be dominated by the monopolistic nature of the public utility corporations: the various White Papers on the control of the nationalised industries with their emphasis on public utility pricing policies are typical in this respect. Successive governments have never really come to terms with the problems of those public corporations which operate in a regime of intense international competition.

The American progenitors of corporate strategy, such as Ansoff, placed almost exclusive emphasis on the 'product/market mix', i.e. the question of what products the corporation should sell and in what markets. This reflected their preoccupation with the strategic problems of conglomerates or highly diversified companies. For the public utility type of public corporation while there are some important problems of product/market mix in the public utility sector (a possible example is British Rail, where there is considerable strategic choice as to what services to provide, both in terms of route and standard and frequency of service), for the most part the answer to this question is more or less predetermined: the products which they are to produce are laid down by statute and their market is basically the total British market. Their strategic questions are, rather, how much should they plan to produce, and how? Subsequent chapters of this book, for example, discuss such essential questions to these industries as future electricity generating capacity and the quantity and type of the nuclear component within this total.

In the corporations operating in competitive world markets, however, the question of which markets to enter and with what products is as fundamental as for their private sector counterparts.

Recent concern with the problems of uncertainty, and differing methods of coping with it, are as important to nationalised industries as their private counterparts. So too is the growing emphasis on adapting organisations to live with change. Indeed this raises particularly interesting points for the public sector, because the nationalisation of traditional industries like coal and steel has to some extent increased the resistance to change by trade unions and public pressure, without correspondingly developing new means of adaptation and redeployment. (The British Steel Corporation's initiatives to provide alternative employment for redundant steel-workers through BSC Industry Ltd represents an interesting attempt to deal with this problem.)

PLANNING IN THE LARGE INTEGRATED ENTERPRISE

From the point of view of methods and techniques, the problems of planning in a nationalised industry are those of any large integrated enterprise operating predominantly in one industry, whether in the public or private sector. By 'integrated' we mean that the operation of the parts is interconnected. Three characteristics – size, integration and concentration in one industry – are all significant determinants of the nature of the planning process.

Size is important in that it affects both the nature of the problems and the means of tackling them. Large firms require a more elaborate and formalised planning mechanism than do small ones, and are in a position to employ specialised staff to operate it. The major nationalised industries all fall into the category of large enterprises with formal planning machinery.

The distinction between the predominantly *single industry firm* and *conglomerate* is a key factor in determining the approach to strategic planning. A conglomerate can be defined for this purpose as a firm producing a series of unrelated products, as against a single industry firm producing a series of closely related products. In the extreme case the conglomerate is buying and selling enterprises with little detailed interference in their management. It thus verges on an investment institution holding a portfolio of investments; the main difference is that it controls the companies in which it has invested and can replace management and dictate strategy. On the other hand, in large integrated concerns like oil companies, airlines, chemical producers, the different activities are closely interrelated; and the central management make decisions about the direction of the company's own managerial effort on new investment, development of new markets, etc. Strategic decision-making in these companies is more closely bound up with the human and physical means of achieving them. The fact that the nationalised industries all fall into the category of large integrated enterprises rather than conglomerates has important implications for the appropriate techniques to be adopted in planning. In particular, the 'portfolio approach' is of limited application.

In a large firm with some form of divisional structure, planning must be conducted on at least two levels: corporation-wide and divisional. These plans must be consistent, so there has to be a formal hierarchy of plans and a co-ordinated timetable for their preparation. This timetable has to meet not only the internal management needs of the corporation itself, but also any requirement to use the plans in dealing with the government.

Organisations of this type tend to have strong Head Office functional departments (Finance, Commercial, Personnel, Technical, etc.), and there is a problem as to how far the functional aspects of planning are tackled by Divisions and how far at Head Office. The resolution of this will tend to reflect the relative balance of power within the organisation. But the Corporate Plan is likely to have both a Divisional and a Functional dimension.

By the nature of the fact that they are complex, interrelated systems, all attempts at organisational breakdown are in some respects unsatisfactory. If Divisions are geographical, there are problems of product co-ordination; if they are product-based, there are problems of parallel management in a given geographical area. Divisions are never as self-sufficient as might be hoped, and the current reaction against large organisations tends to lead to constant reorganisation chasing the will-o-the-wisp of an organisational structure where the sub-units are virtually self-contained. The implication for planning is that there are bound to be major planning problems cutting across organisational structure; and a major task of the planners is to create and service *ad hoc* working parties to tackle such problems.

Hierarchy of Plans

The type of planning exercise undertaken varies both between corporations and at different times within each corporation according to the circumstances and personalities of the moment. But a fairly general hierarchy of plans would be as follows:

(1) a long-term strategic plan, looking forward anything from five to twenty or more years ahead;
(2) a medium-term plan covering around five years;
(3) an annual operating plan or budget, covering the year ahead.

In parallel there would be:

(4) the investment programme, which in the nationalised industries would cover three to five years.

The relationship between the investment programme and the medium-term plan is frequently misunderstood. The investment programme is primarily determined by the long-term plan, in that the major new projects in it will not generally make their full impact until the period of the plan is completed. The case for the projects in the investment programme and their impact on the profitability of the corporation is a major issue in the long-term plan. What the medium-term plan does is to highlight the financing issues by forecasting profits (or the lack of them) during the period in which the investment expenditure is taking place. While the format of the government's Public Expenditure Surveys has tended to create a demand for medium-term plans, the natural division for planning purposes is between:

(1) a short-term operating plan covering the period during which the organisation's capacity depends primarily on decisions already taken; and
(2) a longer-term plan concerned with the period in which plant configurations or the products available can be changed by new investment decisions.

While a major objective is to provide the analysis to assist in making major decisions about the direction of the business, it must also be remembered that another important function of the plan in a large organisation is co-ordination, and creating order out of what would otherwise be chaos.

System Approach

Industries like electricity generation and distribution, gas distribution, and telecommunications, which are physically interlinked, are easily seen as integrated systems. But similar considerations apply in an industry like steel, where different works have an overlapping product-mix, sell to the same customers, purchase materials and fuel from the same sources, and in some cases transfer semi-finished products from one works to another: here, too, the interactions between the different parts of the business mean that it needs to be regarded as an integrated system.

A key feature of planning in such integrated organisations is the need to adopt a 'system approach': that is, to consider the impact of a decision in one part of the system or organisation on the system or organisation as a whole. This means making decisions in particular works or divisions in the light of their effect on the profitability of the corporation as a whole. While this may in a sense seem obvious, it is in practice often inherently difficult. The advantages or disadvantages to one works may differ drastically from those for the corporation as a whole. Thus additional sales from one works may come at the expense of a similar or the same product at another works, with little or no benefit to the organisation as a whole. In the extreme case an individual works may be earning enough revenue to cover its costs, but the profitability of the corporation would be improved by shutting it down and increasing the load on under-utilised plant elsewhere.

What constitutes the relevant 'system' for examining such repercussions varies from case to case. Sometimes it is necessary to look at the corporation as a whole. In other instances it is sufficient to look at a system comprising certain parts of the corporation in order to identify any significant repercussions. Clearly the task of analysis is simplified if the system is defined in such a way as to be as small as necessary for the job in hand. Thus, taking steel as an example, a decision on a new multi-product works will normally have to be considered in the context of a system comprising all the works within the corporation, but a decision on new sheet-finishing facilities can be considered in the context of a system covering only sheet production.

Use of Models

The need for system analysis makes planning in an integrated enterprise a fertile field for the use of computer models (see Chapter 10). The investment in time and money required is, however, generally considerable, and the case for building planning models is generally strongest where there are continual exercises covering the same ground.

The primary purpose of constructing such models is to establish a rapid and efficient way of doing extended calculations, hence making it possible to consider the effects of varying the assumptions, and to examine alternatives. But one of the unintended advantages (and sometimes disadvantages!) is that the model is a hard task-master demanding a rigorous and disciplined approach to both the collection of data and the method of calculation.

There are, however, certain disadvantages which tend to limit the use of models. Not only is the initial investment in time and effort high, but a great deal of managerial time is required to reach agreement with the various interested parties on the provision of data and construction of the model. In my experience this is much the most difficult part of the whole operation. Allied to this is the fact that the model cannot be kept in regular use without updating the cost, capacity, sales information etc. which it embodies. Unless an agreed mechanism exists to do this, the model will quickly go out of use.

The other major managerial hurdle is to overcome the 'black box' effect: i.e. the idea that a lot of data is being thrown into the calculations without anyone other than the model-builders being clear as to how the results are arrived at. Very often the mere fact that the results are being obtained via a computer (quite rightly) raises doubts on this score, even though similar calculations (say of the profitability of different alternatives) if undertaken by hand would be accepted without proper understanding of the rules of the game. It is essential that all concerned, and particularly those making decisions in the light of such evaluations, should be clear as to the rules under which the model is operating.

Moreover, while the model is set up to embody the main quantitative factors to be taken into account in arriving at the decision, it is important not to create the impression that the alternative that comes out best in the calculations is automatically the right one. Apart from the inherent uncertainties in the forecasts, there is frequently more than one way of analysing a problem, and a decision may, in retrospect, turn out to have been misguided because some key element did not enter into the calculation: for example, to take an actual case, the evaluation may have shown the best site for a piece of finishing equipment without considering whether at some later date it would restrict the ability of the corporation to reduce the number of works making that particular product.

These are all fairly familiar points. They do not, to my mind, fully account for the resistance to the use of models. A less-familiar factor which seems important is the fact that the use of computer models tends to affect the balance of power within the organisation, and those who realise (consciously or subconsciously) that their power is likely to be diminished tend to resist the arrangements for collecting the data and constructing the model. For example, in the absence of a corporation model, the Divisional accountants will control the cost information supplied and probably have considerable discretion in the way in which, say, the effects on the profitability of their Division is calculated. With a corporation-wide model, they are reduced to supplying information in accordance with strictly defined guidelines; the execution of the calculations, the knowledge as to how they are turning out and the presentation of the results lie elsewhere. It is perhaps not surprising that the planners' enthusiasm for building models cutting across organisational frontiers is not generally shared by Divisional and Functional staff. It requires either an extremely autocratic organisation or an extremely co-operative one to overcome these problems.

PLANNING IN THE PUBLIC SECTOR

Long-term planning in one form or another has been a feature of management in the nationalised industries since their formation, well before corporate planning became fashionable in the private sector. This stemmed from the fact that long-term planning in *physical* terms was essential, both because of the long lead times involved in new investment in industries such as electricity or coal, and because of the size and complexity of these undertakings. In particular, investment planning has always been well developed, partly in response to internal management requirements, and partly to the statutory obligation to submit programmes of future investment to the government. Forecasting demand and estimating future capacity requirements five to ten years ahead have been basic planning tasks in most of these industries from the start.

The development of 'corporate planning' (in the sense familiar in the private sector) has evolved in many of these industries from their original, largely physical, planning process. One factor has been the government requirement for profit forecasts for up to five years ahead for Public Expenditure Survey purposes which has stimulated the development of medium-term financial plans. More fundamental has been the growing emphasis on the need for financial evaluation of different options. It may seem obvious to the outsider that decisions should be taken after the evaluation of the profitability both of the project or initiative in question and of the main alternatives, in particular the alternative of carrying on as at present. But anyone who has worked in this field will know that it is not always easy to ensure that such evaluations are made as often as they should be, or that they precede rather than follow the essential decision. There are a number of factors militating against thorough financial evaluation. One is the sheer time and effort involved, and in particular the reluctance of engineers and accountants to spend time in costing alternatives. The other is the uncertainty of the forecasts of demand, prices, costs, etc. on which such financial evaluations are based. Nevertheless there has undoubtedly been a gradual raising of standards in this direction over the years.

The second way in which physical planning has developed in the direction of 'corporate' planning has been a broadening of the planning process to cover all the main functions of the corporation: financial, commercial, technical, personnel, supplies and transport, etc. This has tended to lead to the creation of separate planning departments, neutral between the major functions, but with the corollary that the weight they carry within the organisation depends very much on their relationship with the chairman or chief executive.

As with other management activities, planning in the nationalised industries has certain characteristics and preoccupations which arise from state ownership *per se* rather than the nature of the industries. These arise mainly from the relationship between the corporations and the government (aspects of which are discussed in more detail in other chapters). The close government control to which the corporations are subject is a reflection of their statutory position, their financial dependence on government and, very often, their political sensitivity. It means that their planning is frequently geared as much to the dictates of government/industry relations as to the internal management needs of the corporations themselves.

This creates special problems which do not appear to have a parallel in similar enterprises in the private sector.

There is always, of course, some organisational bias in planning exercises within a large organisation, in that individual works or divisions want to place as favourable an aspect as possible on their own activities and hence their claims for additional resources. But the corporate nature of the exercise, and the scope for mutual criticism, make it possible to arrive at a fairly objective assessment – at any rate as between competing claims within the organisation are concerned. But serious difficulties arise where the corporation's plan becomes an instrument for extracting money from the government, or even merely for convincing the government that top management have the situation satisfactorily under control. Then the overriding pressure is to present a plan which shows a sufficiently favourable financial forecast to justify further invest-ment or financial support. The natural predilection of top manage-ment to overstate their case in this situation is frequently reinforced by the reluctance of Ministers and officials to accept a realistic forecast or plan where it is unpalatable, particularly for public consumption. Hence plans which are being prepared as a basis for policy discussions with the government frequently tend to be less realistic than those prepared primarily for internal use. Where the main impetus for planning has come as a means of impressing the government, rather than as an aid to internal decision-making, it very often tends not to be taken seriously within the organisation and may hinder rather than help the establishment of effective strategic planning.

The same difficulty does not seem to arise in the private sector because strategic plans are not often used as prospectuses for raising money from financial institutions.

Constraints on the Nationalised Industries

One of the features of the statutory corporations as compared with large enterprises in the private sector is the fact that their room for manoeuvre is much more highly constrained. The nationalised industries were set up to produce coal or steel or provide air travel, and they are not free to drop the production of these goods and switch to something else if the prospects for their original products are poor. Thus in considering product/market strategy they are mainly limited to products within their statutory field and to the UK as their primary market. (The major exception to this in the public sector was the National Enterprise Board which was free to operate in virtually any field.)

Product strategy remains important – for example, whether British Steel should supply submarine pipe-line for the North Sea, and whether British Airways should institute a shuttle service to Brussels. But the range of choice is narrower.

Strategic questions as to which markets to enter are also important, particularly for those industries operating on an international plane, like steel. But the scope for producing in other countries tends to be limited. British Steel at its formation inherited a number of subsidiaries of the former steel companies which produced or distributed steel, almost entirely in Commonwealth countries. These have now largely been sold off. Sole ownership of production facilities in other countries is difficult for state-owned enterprises, and proposals for joint ventures in steel in other countries have hitherto come to naught.

When it comes to the choice of technology the nationalised industries are not constrained by any statutory limitations, and frequently have the advantage of access to investment funds on a scale that would be difficult or impossible for the same type of industry in the private sector. Strategic questions bound up with the introduction of new technology quite often become a major issue. Thus in steel, the BSC's plans in the 1970s were dominated by the need to replace open-hearth steelmaking by oxygen steelmaking. This not only required heavy investment in new plant, but a major rationalisation reducing the number of steel plants (other than electric ones) from over thirty to give major sites. This severe rationalisation raised major social problems with the closure of smaller plants in traditional steel towns like Ebbw Vale.

Again the major strategic issue facing the Central Electricity Generating Board is the development of nuclear power both in terms of scale and choice of reactor. Here also social or ecological issues are a major factor to be taken into account.

On the railways, electrification remains a strategic issue, complicated not by external repercussions, but by the interrelation with working practices and productivity negotiations with the railway unions.

In most of the nationalised industries, manpower policy and relations with unions have been major strategic issues, particularly (but not exclusively) where the industries are labour intensive: for example, in coal and on the railways. There seems little doubt that in many nationalised industries such questions bulk larger than in the private sector.

Quantitative Planning

It is inevitable in many of the nationalised industries that long-term planning should be highly quantitative, since it is concerned with decisions about plant capacity based on forecasts of future sales (for example, electricity). There is no real escape from this even though quantitative forecasting has become unfashionable in recent years. More fundamentally any analysis of the impact of alternative strategies or plans in terms of their effects on the profitability of the enterprise involve quantitative forecasting. Attention tends to be directed primarily towards the uncertainties involved in forecasting demand, but selling-prices and the prices of inputs also have to be forecast to make any evaluation of future profitability, and are also highly uncertain. But it is not just such external factors that create uncertainty: future operating standards and efficiency, while subject to management influence are in fact variables that also have to be forecast.

Future sales for widely used commodities like energy or steel depend primarily on macro-economic developments. All economic forecasting has come under fire since the early 1970s, because the oil crisis and its aftermath were not foreseen. More recently, however, most errors in macro-economic and hence business forecasting have not been due to failure to foresee any such sudden, revolutionary change, but due to an expectation that a combination of government counter-measures and natural recovery would come into play before the recession became a major depression.

The problem now is not so much to discern any sudden changes in direction, but to judge how long the world economy will continue its present state. The nationalised industries face a particular dilemma here because of their size and importance in the national economy, in that if they plan for a continuation of present levels of unemployment and under-utilisation of national resources, they will in a measure contribute to that situation. But if they plan for a transformation which does not come about, their finances will suffer and they will come under criticism for over-optimism.

If there were no uncertainty, there would be no forecasting. The problem is to recognise the various degrees of uncertainty affecting the different variables and to explore the possible impact of these variations thoroughly and with an open mind. The greatest practical difficulty facing the planner and forecaster is the way communication problems create intense pressure for 'one set of figures' and the frequent reluctance of those who are most sceptical of the forecasting process to consider more than one outcome. With a kind of perverse logic, those who have least faith in forecasts often prefer to consider one forecast to several.

The key point about planning for uncertainty remains the simple one, that it is essential to consider a variety of outcomes. It is generally not practical to assign probabilities to different forecasts; but it is always possible to consider a number of 'scenarios', in the limited sense of a range of possible outcomes, and then to employ 'sensitivity analysis' to analyse the effects of these differing scenarios on the profitability of the investment or strategy under consideration. The intelligent use of such techniques remains the basic tool for dealing with uncertainty.

The immediate need is not so much to disseminate knowledge of current techniques among those operating at a professional level in the industries, as to engender an atmosphere at board level and in discussions with government more amenable to the consideration of a wider series of projections than the traditional one 'best guess'.

Role of Investment

Investment constitutes a major factor in strategic decision-making, since long-term changes tend to revolve around new plant, new processes or new products. This is particularly true in many of the nationalised industries because of their capital intensity. Investment plans are also a sensitive issue between the corporations and the government, in that the government is the sole source of outside finance for investment and exercises specific control over the investment programme and major projects. Successive White Papers on control of the nationalised industries have placed particular emphasis on means of controlling investment. They have, however, tended to take a rather simple view of investment decision-making in regarding it as giving a Yes/No decision to a project with a known financial return. The actual problem is considerably more complex.

Large investment projects require months, and in most cases years, of preparatory work, involving a high cost in terms of the time of engineering and technical staff before being put out to tender. The initial decision to start such work has to be taken against a background of limited or very approximate estimates of costs. When a certain amount of work has been done it is possible to get a much more reliable estimate of cost, probably based on 'budget estimates' from suppliers. A further decision, generally the key one, to give planning approval to the project may be taken at this stage. But more work is still required to arrive at contractual arrangements and the decision to give financial sanction. Even at this stage the cost is still not finally known; there will probably be escalation clauses in the contracts to allow for inflation. In addition, there may be scope for changes and delays, both of which will add to the real cost.

The original concept of the project is determined by the broad strategy the corporation is following. This strategy should be (but is not always) based on evaluations of alternatives using the best estimates of costs, and market forecasts available for the purpose. Such strategic planning studies are perhaps the most important of all the exercises undertaken by planning staffs. But the strategic concept of top management, however formed, is the key to the type of investment project that comes forward. Whether the projects are successful or unsuccessful depends essentially on the validity of the basic strategy. The second point which is generally ignored is that the most important and constructive element in the work of investment analysis and evaluation is its role in influencing the detailed formulation of the project: its size, location, timing, design features, etc. The influence of investment analysis on these factors helps to determine how good or bad the project will be. It should also kill off any uneconomic projects before too much design effort has been put in them.

The final Yes/No decision at the Planning Committee or Corporation Board meeting (which commands most attention) is in a sense the least important part of the decision-making process. By that stage the detailed features of the project are virtually frozen and the project will have been sufficiently vetted within the organisation to make its approval extremely probable.

Concept of Strategy

Much of these industries' planning activity is inevitably 'strategic', in the sense that it is concerned with major long-term objectives and the means of achieving them. But there are nevertheless a number of pressures at work limiting the extent to which the planning process is a wide-ranging look at strategic alternatives that are open to the enterprise. These pressures arise from the composition of the boards, their political involvement with the government, and the nature of the problems.

The concept of strategy is bound up with that of a clearly defined objective to be achieved; indeed it is generally taken for granted that in business, as in war, the definition of objectives is an essential feature of determining a strategy and making strategic decisions. In an autocratic or military style organisation the formulation of objectives presents no inherent difficulty. But in an organisation where the ultimate decisions are made collectively and those making them have conflicting or at least differing interests and approaches, reaching agreement on major long-term objectives may raise serious difficulties. Boards of nationalised industries and their government masters fall into this category. It is frequently possible to reach a sufficient degree of agreement to take individual decisions, while being virtually impossible to reach agreement on a common long-term objective; this applies particularly if the field where agreement is sought is extended to cover the trade unions. For example, it may be possible to agree on a decision to close a particular works (or pit), but not on a strategy and objective involving a programme of works' closures.

The government may be particularly reluctant to commit itself to any specific strategy, either because it fears unpopularity or because it involves commitment to future expenditure: generally one or other of these factors is sufficiently pressing to make it difficult to get agreement with the government on either a retrenchment or an expansionary strategy. The nationalised industries are not, however, unique in having to operate amid a welter of outside pressures and influences in addition to those of the market. In Chapter 1, Bernard Taylor calls attention to the way in which top management of the large American co-operation now increasingly sees a key part of its job as dealing with outside bodies, apart from customers, and there have been a number of references to the new cult of 'political management'. Against this background it is unrealistic for management in such key industries to believe that a return to the private sector would remove all these complications.

The most important factor in the long-term development of the public corporations (as in their private sector counterparts) is the nature of their strategy and whether it is appropriate to the problems and opportunities they face. The fact that different interests have different objectives and that the future is fraught with uncertainty makes it difficult to establish stable strategies for many of these industries, but the more difficult the task, the greater the need. To operate in circumstances where there are inevitable conflicts of objectives and unavoidable uncertainty, the establishment of basic agreement on a broad strategy is essential to the effective management of such organisations. 'Strategy' for this purpose covers the general policy governing future action in broad enough terms not to need revising from year to year, let alone month to month. While this may seem an inflexible concept in a changing world, it must be realised that most major strategic decisions have a long lead time before yielding results. Examples of this type of decision are the choice of reactor system for future nuclear power stations, railway electrification, the development of steel distribution or manufacturing in other countries. Unless such policies can be maintained intact for several years, chaos and paralysis will result. Effective strategic planning must aim to ensure that such strategies are based on the best possible analysis and forecasts and command sufficient agreement among the parties involved to provide the necessary degree of stability.

Part II
Control and Structure

3 The Framework of Government Control

I. C. R. BYATT*

> The efficient allocation of resources . . . subject to social and several considerations.
>
> (Cmnd 7131)

As the nationalised industries are very diverse and have a wide range of social obligations, any framework of control has inevitably to be either very general so as to be applicable to all the industries, or differentiated between industries and tailored to the particular circumstances of each. In practice the framework adopted has been of the former kind. It has, by and large, been a financial framework, but one that has evolved over the years, from an obligation to break even 'taking one year with another' to a complex mechanism involving short-term external financing limits (EFLs), medium-term financial targets and performance aims. It is likely to develop further in the coming years.

Successive governments – or perhaps one should say successive Treasuries – have seen the overall control of nationalised industries as being concerned with three main objectives:

(1) ensuring that nationalised industries conform to macro-economic policy objectives, in particular that they do not pre-empt too much of the nation's savings and investment;
(2) ensuring that nationalised industries contribute to the efficient allocation of resources, in particular that their pricing polices

---

* The views expressed are not necessarily those of the Treasury. But I am grateful to Treasury colleagues for valuable suggestions for improving my text.

are properly related to their costs and they earn an adequate return on investment;

(3) ensuring that nationalised industries are internally efficient, and provide adequate services while keeping their costs low.

These objectives are obviously linked. What constitutes the 'correct' allocation of investment resources to nationalised industries depends on the return achieved, which in turn depends on prices and costs. In principle, it is possible to have a set of instruments which can be used to pursue these objectives in a coherent and consistent way. But, in practice, differing emphasis has been placed on the macro-economic, resource allocation and internal efficiency objectives at different periods of time. Hence the differing emphasis given to different instruments.

THE EVOLVING SYSTEM

This section sets out, in broad terms, how the system of government control has developed, under the three objectives. The strengths and weaknesses of the system and pointers to further developments are discussed in the next section.

(i) Macro-economic Issues

Much of the writing on nationalised industries adopts a micro-economic approach. But the control framework cannot be understood unless it is related to macro-economic issues. In part this results from the dominance of macro-economic policy in the post-war period. Also the importance of the nationalised industries in the national economy makes it impractical to imagine that they will not play a rather different role in macro-economic policy than do large corporations in the private sector.

The focus of interest has changed over the years, with changes in the focus of policy. In the 1950s the main concern was with the nationalised industries' call on investment resources, especially for electricity. This was associated with relatively low prices and hence reliance on borrowing, initially directly from the capital market and, after 1956, from the government. It is against this background that the first of the three nationalised industry White Papers, that of 1961, is to be understood.[1]

In the 1960s the emphasis shifted as macro-economic policy switched towards the direct encouragement of economic growth. Nationalised industry investment totals were planned within total public expenditure, but regarded, alongside private investment and net exports, as a prior claim on the growth of national income before considering the split between public and private consumption. In the period of the National Plan,[2] the investment policies of the nationalised industries were explicitly linked with the growth target for the economy. Despite the tone of the 1967 White Paper,[3] that relationship was a macro-economic one, depending more on an overall statistical relationship between investment and output (the incremental capital:output ratio) than on the appraisal of individual investment projects.

As rapid inflation developed in the early 1970s, it was not surprising to find the nationalised industries asked to make their contribution to counter-inflation policy. Nationalised industry prices could no more fail to respond to the CBI 5 per cent limit on price increases than could their investment programmes fail to respond to the growth targets of the national Plan. In both cases, they found themselves on their own, leading to results which were as bad *ex post* as the cynics had predicted *ex ante*.

As the deficits mounted, and investment, encouraged by low prices, surged ahead, macro-economic alarm bells began to ring. In 1975–6, when the Public Sector Borrowing Requirement (PSBR) rose to an unsustainable level, about one-third of it was accounted for by the public corporations. 'Self-financing' once more became fashionable; hence the efforts to raise nationalised industry prices in the years 1976–8. Counter-inflation policy remained an objective, but was thought to be more appropriately pursued by limiting deficits than by limiting prices.

The period from 1972 to 1976 also saw an increase in government intervention in the economy in an attempt to combat rising unemployment and flagging growth. As part of this policy, shipbuilding and aerospace were nationalised, and Rolls-Royce and British Leyland became dependent on the government for their survival. The National Enterprise Board (NEB) was established with a remit to develop mixed ownership by state participation in private companies. But Rolls-Royce and Leyland absorbed most of the NEB's financial and management resources.

During the second half of the 1970s, macro-economic policy switched away from direct concern with output and employment towards the establishment of intermediate targets such as the money supply, expressed in nominal rather than real terms. Consistent with this, the treatment of nationalised industries in the Public Expenditure Survey (PES) was changed, shifting away from investment towards the external financing of such investment. Just as public expenditure programmes were expected to keep within their cash limits, nationalised industries were expected to live within external financing limits (EFLs). As these EFLs were part of the PSBR they had to conform to macro-economic policy.

The establishment of EFL's soon led to the argument that nationalised industries should be 'taken out of the PSBR'. Many of the industries felt that there was a danger that investment would be reduced below the amounts justified on micro-economic criteria. Problems of statistical definition apart, the arguments amounted to a plea for (some) nationalised industries to be allowed direct access to the capital market. For macro-economic reasons, the government rejected arguments for direct borrowing from the market, arguing that such borrowing would increase either interest rates or prices and so 'crowd out' some private expenditure – although not necessarily by an equivalent amount. The issue was examined by the Parliamentary Committee on the Treasury and Civil Service Department,[4] who came down against direct market borrowing by the industry. However, the possibility of direct borrowing was left open if it could be shown that this would be likely to improve micro-economic efficiency. This last question was investigated by the government, The National Economic Development Council, and the City, but practical progress has proved elusive. The British Telecom bond was one idea of this kind. But 'Buzby bonds' were soon overtaken by a decision to privatise BT.

(ii) Resource Allocation

For those industries with some power over their prices there are two, inevitably overlapping, key issues. First, how should national-ised industry prices be set if costs, including the opportunity cost of capital, are to be met? Second, how should the structure of prices be related to the structure of costs, i.e. how much cross-subsidisation should there be? For the industries operating in competitive markets, the 'price takers', resource allocation issues are focused on the level of output, and so on the scale of existing operations and on the volume of investment.

In considering these matters, resource allocation economics should not be divorced from accounting considerations. But the relationships between accounting and economic considerations are both confused and confusing.

Most nationalised industries began life with an obligation to break even. Subsequent experience has revealed the inadequacy of this obligation. The most obvious problems have arisen in relation to borrowing and investment. The interest on government or government-guaranteed loans has only a limited relationship to any calculation of the 'opportunity cost' of capital – that is, what the resources would have earned in other uses. In most circumstances, debt interest is likely to be significantly below the opportunity cost of capital; over most of the post-war period, although not at the moment, real interest rates have been low by historical standards.

The government's response was to devise an 'appropriate' rate of return on investment. The 1961 White Paper raised the issue of comparable returns in private and public industry, concentrating on the point that nationalised industries should cover supplementary depreciation, provide for replacement of assets, and should achieve a degree of self-financing. The 1967 White Paper argued that nationalised industries should make a return on capital broadly comparable to that sought in the private sector, and a test discount rate (TDR) for the appraisal of investment projects was established. This was set initially at 8 per cent in real terms, and subsequently raised to 10 per cent. The 1978 White Paper[5] reaffirmed the need to earn the opportunity cost of capital and introduced a required rate of return (RRR) of 5 per cent in real terms on an industry's investment programme as a whole.

These approaches implied a financial target which would take precedence over the break-even requirement. But because such targets usually do not have a statutory basis, they are agreed with an industry and not imposed on it. They have usually been set as a required return on assets as a whole. Some translation from a return on investment to a return on capital employed has therefore been required. This has not been easy to determine in practice.

Financial targets have also been used to accommodate situations where a nationalised industry is in a position to earn economic rent, or has loss-making social obligations. The 1978 White Paper argued that targets should be related to a whole set of objectives, but in practice this has not been done in any detail.

The 1967 White Paper was noteworthy in advocating marginal cost pricing. It carefully pointed out that the 'relevant' marginal cost would vary with circumstances, and left the development of operational rules to the industries aided by the National Board for Prices and Incomes (NBPI), which was given a new remit to conduct efficiency studies in the nationalised industries. Initially things seemed to be going well. But the abolition of the NBPI and the policy of price restraint set the clock back.

Progress has varied between the industries. In the case of electricity, where considerations of marginal cost go back to the Hopkinson tariff of 1892, much high-quality work has been carried out using systems models. But even so, broad-brush approximations have been used to estimate the capital element in the bulk supply tariff. In the other industries much less analytical work has been done although there has been some progress with systems modelling.

The 1976 report by the National Economic Development Office (NEDO)[6] pointed out the difficulties in calculating marginal cost, casting a good deal of doubt on it as an operational concept. The 1978 White Paper sought to reinstate it by developing the RRR as a broad-brush measure of (long-run) marginal cost, which could be calculated from information derived in the course of corporate planning. But progress in developing the RRR as a determinant of the financial target has been hesitant.

Traditionally, cross-subsidisation has been an important element in the operation of public utilities. The White Papers of 1967 and 1978 spoke out against the practice. But little seems to have changed. It is difficult for those outside the industries to know the extent of cross-subsidisation, partly because of conceptual difficulties, partly because little information is available on the (marginal) costs of individual activities. But casual observation suggests that there is quite a lot.

(iii) Internal Efficiency

Over the last two decades, concern with the level of nationalised industry costs for a given level of service output seems to have grown. The 1961 White Paper contented itself with pointing out that costs would be affected by the extent of commercially unprofitable activities. The 1967 White Paper had a whole section on costs, drawing attention to the need to look for cost savings, especially labour savings, and to increase efficiency. It referred to the strengthening of the NBPI to enable it to make inquiries into the efficiency of industries whose proposals for price increases were referred to it. It stressed the need to develop performance indicators, which would be used in the course of the annual Investment Review discussions with the industries.

But little happened. The NBPI was abolished. A system of performance indicators was not forthcoming. In its 1976 report, NEDO reiterated the arguments for performance targets as well as financial targets for the nationalised industries. The 1978 White Paper took up the challenge and asked the industries to include suitable cost and service aims in their reports and accounts. This time there has been some progress. Performance targets have been agreed with some industries and results monitored.

By 1980, the Price Commission has been given powers to investigate nationalised industry efficiency. Since then it in turn has been abolished, and powers to investigate nationalised industry efficiency vested in the Monopolies and Mergers Commission (MMC). Nationalised industries are also encouraged to initiate their own efficiency audits.

The privatisation programme, in so far as it opens up the industries to greater competition, can add a major new dimension to the search for ways to increase the pressure to reduce costs and improve services. But in areas where there is a natural monopoly, privatisation will not automatically lead to cost reduction.

Decision-Taking; the IFR and Corporate Planning

The focus of the present control system is the annual Investment and Financing Review (IFR). The industries submit their investment plans with their proposals for financing them. These are discussed with the sponsor Departments and the Treasury and then brought together in the IFR. The IFR, which is as much concerned with the total call by nationalised industries for external finance as with the claims of an individual industry, is an element in the Public Expenditure Survey (PES) where the case for external finance for the nationalised industries can be set against the claims of the other public sector programmes. The IFR, which covers the three years of the PES, is done in cash terms – in line with the emphasis on mominal magnitudes in macro-economic policy. Before the mid-1970s, the process was concerned with nationalised industries investment, not external finance, and was done in real terms to fit in with the real resource planning of the PES and the economy.

Underlying the IFR, recent years have seen increasing emphasis on corporate planning as a process for improving resource allocation and raising the efficiency of nationalised industry operations. The 1976 NEDO report argued the need for the government and the industries to agree on a business strategy, and recommended the establishment of 'Policy Councils' to carry this out. The 1978 White Paper preferred to increase the importance given to discussions between the government and the industry of each industry's corporate plan within existing institutional arrangements. The 1979 Conservative government took this process further. It began a process of agreeing objectives with the industries, and instituted collective Ministerial consideration both of forward-looking Corporate Plans and of backward-looking Performance Reviews.

Progress will not, however, be easy. The objectives of the nationalised industries are not identical with those of the government. This is not only because business objectives and political objectives differ and because of the different timescales that are involved. The nationalised industries often behave as though they had their own social objectives. This is reflected in cross-subsidisation and arguments about 'national needs'. The government for its part has not simply set social objectives; it has involved itself in issues such as the investment appraisal and the operating efficiency of the industries, which many would argue are matters of business not politics.

TABLE 3.1   *Macro-economic indicators of UK public corporations*

	Percentage share in output[1]	Percentage share in investment[2]	Overall surplus/deficit(−) as a percentage of GDP[3]	Budgetary burden as a percentage of GDP[4]
1946–49 ...	11.0	−0.7 (−0.8)	0.5
1950–53 ...	21.5	−1.7 (−1.7)	0.3
1954–57 ...	22.4	−2.2 (−2.2)	1.4
1958–61 ...	21.3	−2.2 (−2.5)	2.0
1962–65 10.3	19.8	−1.7 (−2.2)	1.3
1966–69 10.4	20.1	−1.9 (−2.3)	1.7
1970–73 10.0	16.3	−1.7 (−2.1)	0.8
1974–77 11.3	18.7	−1.9 (−3.0)	1.3
1978–81 10.9	17.0	−1.0 (−1.8)	1.2

[1] Share of public corporations' GDP in total GDP at factor cost.
[2] Share of public corporations' Gross Fixed Capital Formation in total Gross Fixed Capital Formation.
[3] Overall surplus/deficit is defined as the difference between (i) revenue plus receipts of current transfers and non-government capital transfers; and (ii) current plus capital expenditure. Figures in brackets exclude receipts of government current transfers.
[4] Budgetary burden defined as government subsidies, transfers, and net lending to public corporations less dividends and interest payments to government.

SOURCE Short, 'The Role of Public Enterprises: An International Statistical Comparison', IMF Working Paper DM/83/34. (Figures taken from NI Blue Book.)

Financial Performance

Table 3.1 indicates the macro-economic position of the public corporations over the post-war period. It shows their relative capital intensity. It also shows a sector of the economy which drew relatively heavily on external resources during the second half of the 1950s, but whose call has since declined. But this was more because investment fell then because profits rose. The public corporations return on capital has, however, deteriorated since the 1960s, and it is fairly clear that the public corporations are not achieving a rate of return commensurate with the opportunity cost of their capital.

CONTROL INSTRUMENTS: THE ANALYTIC ISSUES

This section surveys the analytic issues and discusses the main control techniques used by successive governments. Four main areas of concern stand out – pricing, investment, financial performance, and cost reduction. They are looked at in turn. But they cannot be isolated from the wider context, whose salient features are:

(1) Most nationalised industries inevitably have some political status. They supply basic goods directly to a large number of customers. They are major employers of a declining labour force. Some of them have natural monopoly power. Most are seen by the public to have social obligations which private sector firms do not.

(2) There are severe limits on how far it is possible to go in systematising the relationship between the industries and the government. The 'arm's length' relationship is a pipe-dream. The 'holding company' analogy provides some insights, but has limitations. The 'banker/client' model is again only part of the story. In principle it is possible to have sufficient clarity about objectives to work out a full and systematic relationship, but the different philosophies, styles and timescales of the political and business worlds would make this extremely difficult to achieve in practice.

(3) Information is scarce and the environment uncertain, both at the macro-economic and the industry level. Doubtless the situation could be improved, but this would still leave a very large number of decisions to be based on informed judgements – with a high probability that those judgements can only be generally right and, more often than not, will be precisely wrong.

Pricing in Public Utilities

The message of successive White Papers has been that prices must be reasonably related to marginal cost and that accounting costs must be covered. The potential conflicts have long been recognised and the two-part tariff offered as a form of squaring the circle. But while White Papers have stressed economic pricing, in practice concepts of accounting cost have, I judge, played a larger role – although without assuring prices that always covered costs.

Those who, like me, have been brought up on marginal cost

doctrines, are naturally disappointed to see them so little used. But in their present form they are deficient as operational guides. First, it is not possible to calculate a unique number, or set of numbers, for marginal cost. Second, because all marginal cost calculations contain a subjective element, agreement about marginal cost involves compromise. Third, a soundly based compromise requires that all parties have adequate information. If they do not, the results can be biased. Fourth, even if they do, compromise is difficult when the parties have different objectives.

The first point is the key one, because it underlies all the others. What increase in output are we talking about? To estimate long-run marginal cost (LRMC) involves long-term forecasting of a large number of both economic and technological variables and judging a hypothetical situation compared with what would otherwise have happened. The best anyone could hope for is to estimate LRMC as a range. With present information it is often more accurate to describe LRMC estimates as points on a wide spectrum.

In any case it is not always right to base all prices on LRMC. In a world of shocks, mistakes, myopia and fluctuations in output, it often makes sense to optimise over a shorter timescale. How short depends on a whole variety of factors which it is not possible fully to settle *ab initio*. Very often it only proves possible to settle the 'right' time scale in the course of the analysis of a particular problem.

A further difficulty, which perhaps deserves more analytical attention, is the issue of consumer expectations in responding to pricing signals. If, for example, marginal cost is changing through time, resource allocation theory requires consumers, especially when investment decisions are involved, to take account of future prices, i.e. of future marginal costs as well as current ones. But how can pricing signals be used to help consumers form the right expectations? Should changes in marginal cost be anticipated in prices? If so, how far ahead?

Practical men may be able to make sensible decisions about these matters in particular situations, when they can take account of wider considerations. But there are no set rules. It is not, as Arthur Young said of the work of the States-General in 1789, 'as though a constitution were a pudding to be made out of a recipe'.

With the exception of electricity, the nationalised industries themselves have not set much store by marginal cost concepts. They doubtless have their reasons. But if the industries do not calculate marginal cost, what can those concerned with resource allocation, either in the government or outside it, do? Are they to offend canons of good management by second-guessing? Or are they to accept whatever they are told?

It would be wrong to conclude from these arguments that marginal cost concepts should not be used in considering the allocation of national resources in this area. Decisions about the future must be related to estimates concerning the future. But those arguing for marginal cost pricing should beware of putting too much weight on it. Estimates must be broad-brush, both because of the limitations of our knowledge of the future and because of the political context. If they are to carry conviction, forward estimates must be more than pure forecasts of the future.

One of the objectives lying behind the introduction of the RRR was to provide a broad-brush estimate of LRMC using corporate planning data. Corporate plans which showed estimates of output growth and of the investment needed to achieve it could be used to calculate the incremental costs of that extra output. The estimates of the future would be related to the past through the process of constructing a corporate plan which would take the organisation from its historical position into the future. As corporate planning developed, and was complemented by a review process, the data would get progressively better; 'hockey-stick' planning, where the unfavourable trends of the past are miraculously linked to a golden future, would be controlled if not completely eliminated. Corporate planning information would, of course, be common to the government and the industry.

But in practice things have not worked out as envisaged in Cmnd 7131. Increments of output have not been costed in corporate plans. Only where such increments have been large in relation to existing supply, and have therefore required considerable investment, has it proved possible to calculate incremental costs from information set out in the corporate plan. Nationalised industries sometimes provide other estimates of marginal cost, but the basis of these calculations has not always been clear.

Five years on, it may be worth considering a more explicit accounting approach. In a steady-state situation, in the absence of shocks and mistakes, LRMC would be reasonably well proxied by a projection of running costs plus the mark-up required to cover economic depreciation and the RRR on existing assets when adjusted for inflation. But the steady state is an abstraction. Depreciation as calculated in the accounts, even when done on a Current Cost Accounting (CCA) basis, is often an imperfect approximation to economic depreciation. CCA asset values often fail to allow explicitly for the shocks, mistakes, etc. which people the real world.

Despite this, accounting costs (in contrast to planning estimates of marginal cost) have the merit that they are grounded on costs actually incurred. The more the industries' accountants are able to make explicit adjustments to allow for changed circumstances, the more accounting costs and forward-looking marginal cost estimates will be brought closer together. The key requirement is to ensure that, where assets need to be replaced if the business is to continue to operate in the longer term, they are entered in the balance sheet at their current replacement cost.

Carsberg and Lumby[7] have shown how an accounting approach can be used to meet the objectives of Cmnd 7131. But, in practice, accounting and planning approaches to marginal cost will not necessarily produce the same number, so compromise would still be necessary when setting prices. But such a process would involve useful iteration between the two sets of estimates, one based on planning models looking to the future, and one based in accounting costs, grounded in the past, to the benefit of both. Adjusting the accounts to allow for shocks, mistakes, etc. would concentrate the mind of management, and where appropriate that of the government, on what had gone wrong compared with past expectations. Ensuring that forward-looking estimates were explicitly linked to accounting performance would improve the process of monitoring of performance against expectations.

It is often necessary to go below the level of the whole industry. Better resource allocation also depends on how far it proves possible to relate the structure or prices to the structure of costs. The presence of massive cross-subsidisation within an industry can be fatal to any attempt to improve resource allocation.

But there is no generally agreed definition of what constitutes undesirable cross-subsidisation. Even cross-subsidisation itself is difficult to define. Should prices be related to average costs? Or should cross-subsidisation refer to divergence between the structure of prices and the structure of LRMC? Or are short-run marginal costs also relevant? These distinctions are important ones and there are no universal answers. Professions vary in their approaches. Accountants traditionally tend to have an average-cost philosophy; economists dislike attempts to allocate 'overheads'. Again the need is to bring them closer together. It is also necessary to recognise the rather different objectives of the government and the nationalised industries. The government is mainly concerned to avoid medium- to long-term (i.e. LRMC) cross-subsidisation. Yet industries with significant joint costs, facing different demand elasticities, may be more interested in relating the structure of their prices to relative SRMC than to relative LRMC.

If the aim is to reduce divergences between LRMC and price for different elements of a nationalised industry's business, several approaches are possible. Where different operations or activities are involved, separate profit centres (or separate businesses) with separate accounting systems can be developed. But it is not always possible to take this very far. Completely separable activities are rare among nationalised industries, and where they exist privatisation is already well advanced. In an integrated systems industry, cost allocation poses problems, but difficulties with common costs can too often deter the assembly of costing information that could help with decisions. Different industries have given different degrees of priority to cost disaggregation; progress by British Rail shows, however, that useful improvements can be made.[8] Generally speaking, there is a strong case for more and better disaggregated costing information, partly from public policy reasons (the need to avoid 'discrimination') and partly for business purposes. Again Carsberg and Lumby are helpful.[7]

Where operations or activities are integrated, such as the production of peak and off-peak electricity, separate profit centres cannot be established and costs cannot be disaggregated. In these cases, the best structure of prices will be that which is consistent with multi-period output and investment optimisation.

Investment

The 1967 White Paper set the tone for investment appraisal, not only in nationalised industries, but across the whole public sector. But its application was inadequate on three counts. First, not all elements in an investment programme were seen as requiring appraisal by those concerned with the determination of the whole programme: some schemes were said to be for essential replacement, some needed for safety, some to meet statutory requirements to supply. Second, and the two points merge, the TDR did not affect prices; it was more concerned with the composition of investment and the choice of techniques than with the size of the programme. Third, the TDR test was very strict by comparison with the revenue required to cover interest on any associated borrowing from the National Loans Fund (NLF). Projects not yielding the TDR could still pay off in financial terms; those that met the TDR yielded large cash surpluses.

The 1978 White Paper attempted to deal with the first two points by developing the RRR, which was designed to apply to the whole investment programme and to be one of the elements determining the financial target. But it was recognised that there were difficulties in doing the latter. An investment programme yields returns over the long term; it is not easy to identify the return during the period of a medium-term financial target sufficiently clearly for tight monitoring to be possible.

But the switch to a 5 per cent RRR did little, if anything, to deal with the third problem. Because the RRR at 5 per cent in real terms exceeds the real rate of interest on NLF loans, and because inflation during the 1970s greatly reduced the real value of nationalised industry debt, a nationalised industry which earned its RRR on the assets would make a large post-interest surplus. Such surpluses would naturally be used to pay off its debt or be retained as capital for new investment on which it would not have to pay interest. As nationalised industries become progressively less dependent on external borrowing this is likely further to reduce the incentives they have to earn the 'opportunity cost of capital'.

The problem, to which the Public Accounts Committee has drawn attention,[9] could be dealt with within the existing framework if the nationalised industries were to make payments to the government which were related to the return on their investment rather than to the interest on their outstanding debt. There are several ways that this could be done. They would all involve a hard look at the liabilities side of the balance sheet and the role of interest payments. Carsberg and Lumby have shown the relationship between cost estimates, including the cost of capital, financial targets and 'dividend' payments, and have set out proposals which would bring together accounting and economic principles and so achieve a closer relationship between an industries return on capital and its financial target on the one hand, and between its payments to its owner, the government and its cost of capital on the other.

It has sometimes been argued that rather than give nationalised industries access to the NLF, they should be allowed, or forced, to borrow directly from the market. But as any nationalised industry borrowing is virtually guaranteed by the government, implicitly if not explicitly, the interest rate paid would remain advantageous compared with the cost of capital to the private sector.

Financial Targets

All three of the post-war White Papers recognised the need for financial objectives – although only in the case of the water authorities is there statutory provision for one. But practice has been less satisfactory. Many years have gone by when no targets have been in operation. While it is right in principle to stress medium-term (3–5 year) targets, this does reduce the pressure to make some return on capital, even in bad years. Although there are good arguments for basing the financial target on a 'wide range of factors', it makes monitoring difficult.

The 1978 White Paper preserved the formal position by saying that when announcing a target, the government would 'indicate the main assumptions on which it was based', so that 'Parliament and the public' could 'subsequently judge the industry's performance against the target'. But for a number of reasons it seems unreasonable to expect any very precise relationship between the target and the various factors lying behind it, and susbequent history tends to bear this out.

Where an industry is judged to have extensive social obligations or to be a beneficiary of substantial economic rent, it is often better to take explicit account of this, as in the case of Public Service Obligation for the railways, or the Gas Levy. There is a case for extending the concept of explicit subsidies or levies more widely, and in some cases such a move could naturally accompany the reduction of cross-subsidisation. But some 'looseness' in the target, especially in relation to 'social and sectoral considerations', is inevitable.

The arguments for more emphasis on annual EFLs do not, therefore, derive solely from considerations of macro-economic policy. Provided they are consistent with the medium-term target, they also have a valuable resource allocation role. Also financial control is a necessary element in achieving internal efficiency. If macro-economic objectives were to play an *additional* role, the policies underlying EFLs could have taxation as well as resource allocation implications. But the financial performance of the nationalised industry sector as a whole – which is what is relevant for the macro-economic aspects of EFLs – does not suggest that taxation elements have been of quantitative significance. On the contrary: in addition to explicit subsidies there have been implicit subsidies resulting from failure to achieve a return on capital comparable to the private sector.

Cost Reduction

The need to maintain pressures on nationalised industry costs is well recognised. But tools for the job are not easy to find. EFLs have undoubtably had some effect, but they cannot be a precision instrument. Advocates of cost and service measures and targets make a powerful case for them. But should they be aggregative measures, such as labour costs per unit of output for the industry as a whole, or should they be concerned with the detailed operations of a part of the business? Perhaps the government should concentrate on asking the industries to agree and to monitor general performance indicators, leaving them to decide how best to translate general indicators into specific indicators for elements of their businesses.

But regular performance measures need to be backed up by periodic examinations of efficiency by a body such as the MMC. How frequent such investigations should be must, however, depend as much on specific as on general considerations.

A completely new element has now been introduced by the privatisation programme. Initially the emphasis was on opening up the industries to the disciplines of the capital market. Some of the issues involved have already been touched on in this chapter. But in making proposals for direct borrowing, advocates also argued that micro-economic benefits could be achieved if direct lending were linked to a specific project, so that the return to the lender would depend on the success of the project, and thus that lenders would be concerned with its design and investment appraisal, and possibly with its subsequent management. But so far it has proved impossible to find separable projects where lenders were prepared to be involved on terms that would involve them in significant risk.

But the debate is now shifting towards the role which competition could play in product markets through privatisation. Privatisation can meet a number of objectives, of which increased competition is only one. Beesley and Littlechild[10] have recently stressed this dimension, which is clearly a very important one. As they point out, the introduction of greater competition would involve disentangling the natural monopoly elements of nationalised industries from elements that could operate in competitive markets. This would imply an analysis of what structural changes might be desirable in order to maximise the exposure to competition. It would also imply consideration of the best way to treat the residual natural monopoly elements. If so, it would be for consideration whether the framework of control developed to date for the nationalised industries would apply to those natural monopoly elements or whether new approaches were desirable. Moving in such a direction thus opens up a large new policy – and research – agenda.

SUMMARY AND CONCLUSIONS

The basic framework of government control of nationalised industries is a financial one. The industries have statutory obligations to break even. From time to time statutory or non-statutory medium-term financial targets have been set, or agreed. Since the mid-1950s nationalised industries have been unable to borrow medium or long term direct from the domestic capital market. Since the mid-1970s annual limits have been set on their use of external finance.

On top of this framework the government has, in the course of the White Papers of 1961, 1967 and 1978, put a layer of non-statutory guidance. This has involved the issues of supplementary depreciation and an adequate contribution to the nation's savings (1961), investment appraisal, marginal cost pricing and financial targets (1967), and corporate planning, the required rate of return on investment and overall profitability (1978).

The government's concern with nationalised industries has covered both macro- and micro-economic issues. The industries have been expected to play a role in macro-economic policy throughout the post-war period. The focus has shifted from control of total investment programmes to control of external borrowing, and from a concern with price restraint to a concern with the PSBR. The focus may shift in the future as macro-economic policy develops. But while the nationalised industry sector is large, this macro-economic concern will persist.

At the micro-economic level the focus has been on pricing and investment. Economic pricing has been defined as marginal cost pricing, subject to the need to cover accounting costs. At the disaggregated level, White Papers have argued that the structure of prices should reflect the structure of (marginal) costs. The direction of government prescription has been against cross-subsidisation and in favour of explicit rather than implicit subsidies. Investment was covered in rather different ways in successive White Papers. The 1961 White Paper concentrated on the effect of prices on the demand for investment and the need for more self-financing. The 1967 White Paper concentrated on project appraisal and the achievement of comparability with the private sector. The 1978 White Paper returned to the influence of the 'opportunity cost of capital' on the determination of total investment and focused on *ex post* achievement rather than *ex ante* appraisal.

It is not easy to characterise the relationship between the government and the nationalised industries. The 'arm's length', the 'holding company' and the 'banker/client' analogies illustrate part of the relationship, although none of them is wholly right. Perhaps the political context of the relationship inevitably involves both fuzziness and conflict. In recent years attempts have been made to improve the relationship in the context of corporate planning. This offers a more flexible model where a common process may be able to accommodate different policies.

A key factor in nationalised industry policy is the need for cost reductions. This is difficult to achieve in industries which either have natural monopoly power or are seen to have non-economic obligations. It is also difficult where cost reductions involve shedding labour and where unions are strong. Financial targets, however necessary, do not guarantee success in this area. The White Papers have therefore advocated performance and service

measures. External investigations of nationalised industry efficiency began with references to the NBPI and the Price Commission
and are now in the hands of the MMC. In so far as the privatisation
programme can be used to increase competition, it will provide a
major new tool of cost control.

There is much unfinished business in government:nationalised-
industry relations. Much of it is concerned with specific industries
and specific policy areas. But at the aggregate level, the following
interrelated issues stand out:

(1) What role should the break-even requirement play? How
    should this be defined in current conditions? How should it
    relate to medium-term financial targets?
(2) What should be the relationship between forward-looking
    concepts, such as marginal cost, and an industry's accounting
    framework?
(3) How can economic pricing be made operationally useful (a) at
    the level of the whole industry, and (b) in relation to the
    different products of an industry?
(4) How can cross-subsidisation be made explicit and be control-
    led? How far should cost allocation go? What are the respective
    roles of the economist and the accountant?
(5) How can a requirement to earn a rate of return comparable to
    that in the private sector be made compatible with the
    nationalised industries' debt structure?
(6) How can the need to earn a satisfactory return on investment be
    linked to an industry's medium-term financial targets?
(7) How can pressures to reduce costs be best put on industries
    with natural monopoly power or social obligations? What is the
    role of performance measures and external and internal
    efficiency audits?
(8) How can the privatisation programme be best used to increase
    efficiency and reduce costs? Is it right to think in terms of
    separating elements which could operate in competitive mar-
    kets from those with irreducible natural monopoly power? If
    so, how would those residual elements be best controlled? Is a
    regulated private monopoly to be preferred to a public
    monopoly? How can competition be introduced into areas
    where social obligations loom large? Is franchising[11] a possible
    answer?

NOTES AND REFERENCES

1. Cmnd 1337, *The Financial and Economic Obligations of the Nationalised Industries* (London: HMSO, 1961).
2. Cmnd 2764, *The National Plan* (London: HMSO, 1965).
3. Cmnd 3437, *Nationalised Industries: a Review of Economic and Financial Objectives* (London: HMSO, 1967).
4. Treasury and Civil Service Committee, *Financing of the Nationalised Industries*, House of Commons (London: HMSO, 1981).
5. Cmnd 7131, *The Nationalised Industries* (London: HMSO, 1978). See also, I. C. R. Byatt *et al.*, 'The Test Discount Rate and the Required Rate of Return on Investment', Government Economic Service Working Paper No. 22 (London, 1979).
6. National Economic Development Office, *A Study of UK Nationalised Industries* (London: HMSO, 1976).
7. Carsberg and Lumby, *The Evaluation of Financial Performance in the Water Industry – The Role of Current Cost Accounting* (London: Chartered Institute of Public Finance and Accountancy, 1983).
8. British Railways Board, *Measuring Cost and Profitability in British Rail* (London: British Railways Board, 1978).
9. House of Commons Session 1980–81, *15th Report from the Committee of Public Accounts* (London: HMSO, 1981).
10. Beesley and Littlechild, 'Privatisation: Principles, Problems and Priorities', *Lloyds Bank Review*, no. 149 (July 1983).
11. Gretton and Harrison (eds), *Franchising in the Public Sector* (London: Public Money, 1983).

4 The Impact of Financial Constraints

ANDREW LIKIERMAN

Uneasiness about the financial aspects of the relationship between the nationalised industries and the government has existed ever since the industries were brought into public ownership.[1] Current preoccupations about cash constraints and the impact of other financial problems are therefore no more than the latest chapter in the long-running saga of complaints, charges and counter-charges. But these preoccupations are only one manifestion of much wider problems in the relationship between the industries and the government of the kind outlined in other chapters (particularly those by Byatt, Grieve Smith, Harrison and Richardson) and which have been the subject of debate for many years. There have been no less than five major attempts in the last sixteen years to resolve these problems.[2] The continuingly high level of voluble dissatisfaction about the relationship indicates that none has laid the matter to rest.

This chapter will examine the case that financial constraints make strategic planning in the nationalised industries much more difficult than in the private sector. It will argue that while there are grounds for believing that there are some special problems for nationalised industries, the case is by no means proven. It will also argue that, far from being able to blame the government for making life difficult through short-term twists and turns in policy, the industries need to reassess their assumptions about how much freedom of action it is reasonable for them to expect. It may well be that it is their expectations which are unrealistic. Finally, the chapter will argue that the position is quite different for the industries privatised by the Conservative government since 1979 but where the government retains a significant shareholding. For these industries, the problems are real enough.

Before discussing the arguments, it is necessary to clarify what will be covered by 'financial'. For the nationalised industries, as for the private sector, the two primary financial measures are those of profit and cash. For profit, the current basis is a 3 to 5 year target, with the level:

decided industry by industry. It will take account of a wide range of factors. These will include the return from effective, cost-conscious management of existing and new assets; market prospects; the scope for improved productivity and efficiency; the opportunity cost of capital; the implications for the public sector borrowing requirement; counter inflation policy; and social or sectoral objectives for e.g., the energy and transport industries.[3]

In the case of cash, annual limits to borrowing (or target repayment figures), now called external financing limits or EFLs, have been set since 1976. The White Paper setting up the system[4] was ambiguous about the relationship between annual cash planning and longer-term plans, stating only that the intention was 'to relate cash control to estimates of their financing needs to be met by loans, grants and public divided capital'. It is worth noting that measurement of both profit and cash is against a target. In the private sector, while a generally similar system of cash constraints or target cash generation tends to operate, it is profit growth rather than profitability against target which is a more common measure of performance. This does not mean that strategic planning becomes nessarily more difficult. But for nationalised industries it may well alter the relationship between strategic planning and profit performance. On the one hand the relationship may be made closer than in the private sector because of the need to provide a series of plans of varying length. On the other hand it may make it more difficult to integrate plans if targets are susceptible to frequent change. (Throughout this chapter, any reference specifically to 'financial target' will be to the 3–5 year target alone, not to the combination of financial target and EFL.)

THE PROBLEM AS SEEN BY THE INDUSTRIES

Statements by chairmen and ex-chairmen of nationalised industries are redolent with complaints about the way in which financial framework inhibits successful management of an industry.[5] Four of the major complaints in relation to strategic planning are outlined below.

(1) *Meeting financial performance criteria may be incompatible with meeting other objectives which are central to a strategic plan.* The difficulties of operating with apparently incompatible criteria are dealt with in other chapters and have been discussed elsewhere.[6] The argument that there are incompatible criteria depends on two possible bases. One is that while individual targets and objectives may be agreed, they do not combine together to make an internally consistent strategic plan. The second is that while the individual parts of the government financial control mechanism – target, EFL and so on – are compatible with each other, they are not, together, compatible with the strategic plan. This may be, for example, because the resources available are insufficient to finance the investment required, or because achievement of financial targets means that non-financial objectives cannot be met.

(2) *The timescale under which the financial targets and cash constraints are set makes strategic planning almost impossible.* The majority of nationalised industries have a long lead time for decisions on purchasing major fixed assets, both in terms of ordering and of delivery, as Grieve Smith's chapter shows. The assets themselves, such as steel mills, power stations, rail electrification or airport runways, then generally have very long lives. Juxtaposing these timescales against those provided for financial and cash targets, it appears as if there are likely to be incompatibilities with the longer timescales required for strategic planning.[7]

(3) *Changes of government and changes of policy by government provide an unfavourable climate for strategic planning.* There can be little doubt that there have been major changes in policy towards the nationalised industries as a result of party political changes and also as a result of changing priorities by successive governments within their term of office.[8] There are certainly enough occasions for them to implement the desired changes. Openly this may come about through announcements about policy changes required to fine-tune the economy through mini-budgets or other short-term measures. Discreet pressure can also be exercised through the annual discussions on corporate plans, on the investment and

financing review, or by means of a quiet lunch between minister and nationalised industry chairman.

(4) *In some cases, governments do not even provide financial targets for the industries.* Again, this is not a matter of dispute (as is shown in Tables 4.3 and 4.4). In some cases there have been delays in setting financial targets, although there is no evidence from published sources as to why this is so and whether the industries themselves are in some way responsible for any delay.

Before discussing these arguments, it is worth noting that ministers in recent governments would not disagree with most of them. Successive Treasury ministers have argued that the industries cannot expect to be shielded from the macro-economic forces which necessitate policy changes and determine the financial framework within which the government itself has to operate. On this basis they would argue that it is unreasonable for the industries not to have to suffer the effects of policy changes. As Byatt puts it in his chapter, the importance of nationalised industries 'makes it impractical to imagine that they will not play a rather different role in macro-economic policy than do large corporations in the private sector'. In practice this has undoubtedly meant that it is those industries most dependent on government funding which have been subject to the most pressure. Desire to free themselves from what they see as the shackles of Treasury control must be a powerful incentive for an industry requiring constant injections of government cash.

ARE THE PROBLEMS AS SIGNIFICANT AS THEY SEEM?

At first sight the complaints outlined above appear to carry considerable weight, even on the basis of the evidence which is publicly available. An illustration that the thinking of which the industries are complaining is still very much in evidence is provided from a recent parliamentary reply on the objectives of the CEGB:

> The Board's plans for effective operation and cost reducing investment should be developed within the framework of a corporate plan for the industry which will be reviewed annually with the Government. They should take full account of the financial targets agreed with the Government and of the industry's external financing limit.[9]

TABLE 4.1 *Changes to nationalised industry EFLs*

	Revisions		Revised EFL	Outturn EFL	Outturn as % of	
	Numbers (all up)	Amount £m	£m	£m	Original EFL	Revised EFL
1976–7	1	74	3300	2243	70	68
1977–8	0	–	2721	1474	61	61
1978–9	1	49	2643	1946	75	74
1979–80[2]	3	320	2648	2389	103	90
1980–1	6	888	3214	3126	134	97
1981–2[1]	5	997	3380	3237	136	96

[1]Revised to give comparability.
[2]Based on reduced figures set in June 1979.

SOURCE A. Likierman, 'Monitoring the Credibility of Cash Limits', *Fiscal Studies*, vol. 4, no. 1 (April 1983).

This leaves it quite unclear as to how long-term planning can take place within a collection of short-term constraints.

An equally strong piece of evidence is the announcement made in 1983 by the Chancellor of the Exchequer as part of an emergency financial package, introduced because it was feared that public spending in total would exceed target: 'The total provision for the external financing limits of the nationalised industries will . . . be reduced by two per cent. This reduction will be allocated in proportion to their turnover.'[10] Such an arbitrary cut in EFLs, on a basis for applying the cut as apparently inappropriate as turnover, appears to justify complaints about potentially incompatible objectives and timescales as well as indicating the unfavourable climate for strategic planning. It certainly makes ironic reading against the passage on EFLs taken from the 1978 White Paper which was quoted earlier in the chapter.

But before strategic planning can be written off as being incompatible with the way in which governments either choose or are forced to operate, some of the basis of the complaints need to be questioned.

Missing from real understanding of what happens is any unbiased evidence. The information which *has* emerged is clearly an important element in a game which involves a good deal of political manoeuvring. The statements therefore have to be seen in the

TABLE 4.2 *EFL breaches*

	No. of blocks	Amount (£m)
1976–7	0	0
1977–8	0	0
1978–9	0	0
1979–80	1	5
1980–1	4	84
1981–2	5	252

SOURCE A. Likierman, 'Monitoring The Credibility of Cash Limits', *Fiscal Studies*, vol. 4, no. 1 (April 1983).

TABLE 4.3 *Performance against financial target 1982/3 (or 1982)*

	Achieved target?/On target trend?
British Airports Authority	NO
British Airways	YES
British Gas	YES
British National Oil Corporation	NO TARGET
British Rail	NO/UNCERTAIN/NO TARGET*
British Shipbuilders	NO
British Steel	NO
British Telecom	YES
British Waterways	NO TARGET
Electricity Council	YES
National Bus	YES
National Coal Board	NO TARGET
N.O.S.H.E.B.	NO TARGET
Post Office	YES
Scottish Transport	NO TARGET
S.S.E.B.	NO TARGET

NOTES: On trend = Target set for period of more than one year and industry's performance is on target to fulfill the trend.
No target = No *financial* target, although there may be a statutory target.
*British Rail – Intercity/Freight (from Annual Report)/other parts of British Rail.

context of a negotiating process between the industries, the government, Parliament and others.[11] Discreet arm-twisting in particular is hardly likely to be well documented unless one or other of the parties involved wishes to justify actions or exercise pressure.

At least superficially, based on the quotation from the 1978

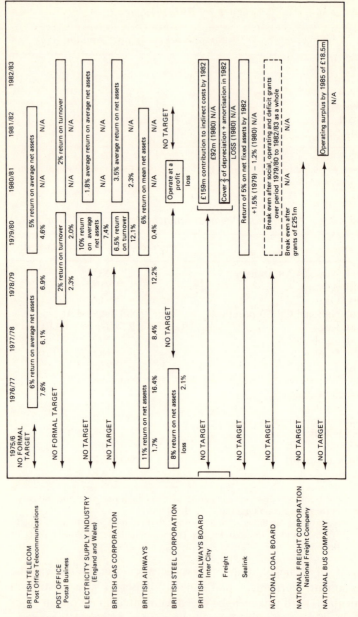

TABLE 4.4 *Nine major nationalised industries – financial targets established by government and related outturns*

SOURCE House of Commons Public Accounts Committee (1981, Annex B).

White Paper on the setting of financial targets, there is an understanding that there are potentially conflicting requirements which have to be taken into account in the process of discussion and negotiation. What is missing is evidence on how far this understanding has been turned into plans which provide a consistent framework. Such evidence would require an observer to the negotiating process – a requirement which is unlikely to be acceptable to the government. So the chance of obtaining the unbiased evidence seems slight. The analyst therefore has to fall back on public pronouncements or indiscretions by one of the negotiating parties – hardly the sort of evidence which inspires confidence. Taking, somewhat tongue-in-cheek, one rough-and-ready indicator – the number of chairmen complaining in the annual report – at least here there seems to have been a recent improvement. In 1983 only two were critical of the government's financial framework, a distinct improvement over earlier, more confrontational years. This may, of course, simply reflect the increasing number of chairmen appointed by the government.

A second important element for consideration is that the financial framework is by no means as rigid as many of the industries have claimed. Tables 4.1, 4.2, 4.3 and 4.4 show that failing to meet the target occurs frequently. The following extracts from the Annual Reports of the British Transport Docks Board indicate that, for one industry at least, 'failure' was hardly regarded very seriously.

. . . the return on capital improved from 15.5% to 16.8%. This represented a positive step towards the target of 20% return by ·1980 which was agreed with Government early in the year. (1977)

The return on capital was 16.9% (1977 16.8%). This was little advance towards the 'target' return of 20% agreed with Government for 1980: but the objective was established when trading conditions were expected to remain much better than they have proved to be. Nevertheless, a satisfactory step towards the 'target' would have been achieved but for industrial disputes arising from the Board's support of the fight against inflation and adherence to the Government's pay guidelines. (1978)

. . . the return on capital on this basis was 15.1% (1978 16.9%). The target agreed with Government when world trade was on an upward trend was 20% to be achieved by 1980. This objective cannot, of course, be achieved in the present economic climate particularly when the Board are increasingly subject to subsidised competition from other ports which are receiving subventions from Government and Local Authorities. (1979)

I reported last year that the quinquennial target (20% return on capital by 1980) agreed with Government when trade was on an upward trend could not, of course, be achieved in the then economic climate. In the succeeding 12 months the gap between the expectations of five years ago and the current situation has been widened. The effects of the deepening recession, including the collapse of the steel industry, have been exacerbated by competition from those ports which are receiving subvention and by the high costs and inflexibility of the National Dock Labour Scheme. The actual return of 9.9% is therefore a significant achievement in the ports industry in these times. (1980)

Together this evidence indicates that there is far more flexibility in the system of cash constraints and financial targets than many industries are prepared to admit.

To this evidence must be added consideration of the fact that very little is known about the sanctions which the government can apply against a recalcitrant chairman or board. On the surface, the chairman can be sacked, but it is hardly likely that this will even be discussed, until all other means have failed. ('Other means' probably include the government threatening to block investment plans, keep the industry short of cash, or withhold an honour from the chairman.)

The evidence quoted is not intended as even an implicit criticism of flexibility. It cannot be surprising to those who have had to manage any commercial organisation to know that conditions of uncertainty make it extremely difficult to meet targets set months or even years ahead. But since there clearly *is* flexibility within the system,[12] this implies that the financial constraints are not quite so rigid and that sufficient flexibility may be available to mean that long-term strategic plans may not necessarily be jeopardised.

A final factor worth considering is whether the relationship between financial constraints and strategic planning is so different from the private sector that it constitutes a special dimension to which different rules have to be applied. A well-run company in the private sector is likely to have financial objectives at the centre of its strategic plans. As is the case for nationalised industries, cash generation may be an objective, or it may be a constraint. And as is the case for the nationalised industries, profitability may or may not be the primary objective of the organisation. This means that the relationship between financial and other objectives may not be so different to that in the private sector. Furthermore, the private sector organisation, as Taylor's chapter shows, is likely to recognise that it lives in a world where very precise forecasting is not possible and that the strategic planning system will need to take account of uncertainties, including those arising from short-term changes in policy and changes in the political climate. Such changes will affect its profitability and its ability to generate or raise cash. There is at least a case, therefore, for suggesting that while there are undoubtedly differences from private sector practice and a different set of constraints, the industries do not live in a world which is so different as to make a completely new set of rules necessary.

'HYBRID' INDUSTRIES

A separate set of issues appears to arise in the case of 'hybrid' industries – those which the government has privatised by selling a bare majority of the shares to the private sector while retaining a significant percentage for itself. These industries appear to be in a quite different position in respect of their strategic planning to those industries remaining wholly publicly owned. The difference arises because the government has reserved some key powers for itself, while not indicating when and how it might use them. Taking three passages from the prospectus offering shares for sale in Associated British Ports (the renamed and privatised British Transport Docks Board):

> HM Government does not henceforth intend to exercise its right as a shareholder to elect directors to the Board, to intervene in the commercial decisions of the group, or to vote in opposition to a resolution supported by a majority of the directors. But HM Government will be prepared to use its voting rights as a shareholder in exceptional circumstances or when it considers the national interest may be involved.

HM Government does not consider it appropriate to attempt to lay down a detailed plan or framework for the operation and development of Britain's ports. Nevertheless, because of the important position of ports in the national infrastructure and their statutory responsibilities and obligations, HM Government cannot wholly divorce itself from the industry's longer-term development.

It is for port authorities to decide their own capital investment plans. However under the Harbours Act 1964, ministerial approval continues to be required for major port investment projects, currently those over £3 million.

The implication is that intervention will be unpredictable and could touch every part of the industry's planning process.

It is possible of course that nothing of the kind will occur. BP is regularly quoted as an example of an organisation where the government has maintained a significant shareholding for many years, but has not exercised any of the powers which have been available to it. But then questions such as 'Why have such a large shareholding if advantage is not taken of what it offers?' might reasonably be asked. The uncertainty is compounded by the fact that little is known about government reaction should an industry wish to act more like a private sector organisation by, for example, diversifying its activities or raising additional cash from its shareholders. If, as seems likely, the reaction will depend on short-term political and economic considerations at the time, the board will have some major problems in planning even in the medium-term. As for strategic planning, this will require accurate political as well as economic forecasting.

Time alone will show the government's intentions. It is possible that they will wish to sell off or run down shareholdings as soon as possible, so that the ambiguities will be only short term. Otherwise it cannot be long before some of the key questions need answering. While each hybrid industry is likely to have a different relationship to the government, reflecting its relative importance in the economy and how far its own plans fit government policy, more will have to emerge about how that policy will be exercised. The need to protect the rights of other shareholders in what, after all, is now a company governed by normal Stock Exchange regulations, will significantly influence whether the government wishes or is able to exercise the same kind of pressure as is applied to the wholly owned industries.

This will be one of the most interesting developments arising from the creation of the 'post-BP' generation of hybrid industries. The position as stated in the prospectus is messy for the board and must be confusing for any of the shareholders who bothered to read even the medium-sized print. For the hybrid industries, at any rate, there is a reasonable basis for contending that the process of strategic planning is potentially much more difficult than for their private sector counterparts.

CONCLUSION

The arguments above do not mean that the industries still wholly in the public sector have no possible grounds for complaint. Their problems are undoubtedly greater because ministers do not always exhibit as much understanding as is desirable about the impact of policy changes on the industry for which they are responsible. Indeed in some cases ministers show that they greatly enjoy trying to 'run' an industry themselves. But it is hardly proven that the problems are such that strategic planning is impossible, and it is worth considering whether nationalised industries (in common with many private sector organisations) delude themselves into believing that a golden age might exist. In such an age, government priorities would never change, or if they did, it would be very slowly and the world would stand still for long enough to allow them to plan free of the hurly-burly of short-term constraints.

There are evidently problems in reconciling the timescales under which government operate and those required by the strategic planners in nationalised industries. But these problems need not be insuperable if both sides recognise the problems and are willing to tackle them. A genuine doubt must, however, remain as to whether ministers *are* prepared to discuss how the problems might be overcome. Dudley and Richardson's chapter outlines some of the complexities of the political relationships, and on past performance ministers are likely to resist attempts to spell policies out too far in advance. The greater the ambiguity, the greater their freedom of manoeuvre in being able to implement the short-term economic or social policy changes which are such a consistent part of the British political scene. If this is accepted, it has to be assumed that it will be a normal element of the framework within which the industries have to operate. It may be that it is the expectations of nationalised industry chairmen which are out of line, rather than the actions of ministers.

NOTES AND REFERENCES

1. Sir N. Chester, *The Nationalisation of British Industry* (HMSO, 1975).
2. See HM Government, *Nationalised Industries: A Review of Economic and Financial Objectives*, Cmnd 3437 (HMSO, 1967); House of Commons, *Ministerial Control of the Nationalised Industries*, 1st Report of the Select Committee on Nationalised Industries, Session 1967/8, HC 371 (HMSO, 1968); National Economic Development Office, *A Study of the UK Nationalised Industries: Their Role in the Economy and Control in the Future* (NEDO, 1976); HM Government, *The Nationalised Industries*, Cmnd 7131 (HMSO, 1978); Central Policy Review Staff, unpublished (though reported) study of nationalised industries (1981).
3. HM Government, *The Nationalised Industries*.
4. HM Government, *Cash Limits*, Cmnd 6440 (HMSO, 1976).
5. As a forceful example, see Sir W. Barlow, 'The Problems of Managing Nationalised Industries', in *Allies or Adversaries* (RIPA, 1981). For most of the major arguments, see House of Commons Treasury and Civil Service Select Committee, 8th Report, Session 1980/1, *Financing of the Nationalised Industries*, HC 348 (HMSO, 1981); and House of Commons Treasury and Civil Service Committee, *Financing of the Nationalised Industries. Observations by HM Treasury*, 2nd Special Report, Session 1980/1, HC 496 (HMSO, 1981).
6. For example, D. Heald, 'The Economic and Financial Control of UK Nationalised Industries', *Economic Journal*, 90 (June 1980); and D. Heald and D. Steel, 'Nationalised Industries: The Search for Control', *Public Money*, June 1981.
7. Hundred Group of Chartered Accountants, *The Financing of State-Owned Industries* (1982).
8. See R. Pryke, *The Nationalised Industries. Policies and Performance Since 1968* (Oxford: Martin Robertson, 1981); House of Commons Treasury Committee, Session 1980/1, 8th Report, and 2nd Special Report; Sir A. Knight 'The Control of Nationalised Industries', *Political Quarterly*, vol. 53, no. 1. (January, 1982).
9. House of Commons, 'Nationalised Industries: Objectives': written reply by Mr Nigel Lawson to Sir William van Straubenzee, Hansard, col. 296, 18 March 1983.
10. HM Treasury, *Public Expenditure Adjustments*, Economic Progress Report no. 159 (August 1983).

11. See H. Heclo and A. Wildavsky, *The Private Government of Public Money*, 2nd edn (London: Macmillan, 1981); J. Barnett, *Inside the Treasury* (London: Andre Deutsch, 1982).
12. For a detailed analysis, see A. Likierman, 'Monitoring the Credibility of Cash Limits', *Fiscal Studies*, vol. 4, no. 1 (April 1983).

5   Monitoring Performance

A. J. HARRISON

THE CASE FOR EXTERNAL MONITORING

The case for external monitoring is simply put: nationalised industries, because they are not subject to commercial pressures and the fear of default, do not have strong incentives to be efficient. In the case of the monopolies, pressure exerted through EFLs runs the risk of pushing over on to prices; in the case of loss-makers, the pressures are considerable, but the management is inclined to politicise the relationship and concentrate on making the case for more grant, rather than getting on with the job of cutting costs. External efficiency audit is a proxy for market pressure.

When outside investigations into industry show that the operations could be more efficient, in the sense that they have not adopted the appropriate techniques, one might argue that this, in the case of such large enterprises, was simply par for the course. No industry could escape criticism entirely. On this view, clearly tenable only if the criticisms were limited in number and seriousness, any weaknesses could be attributed to the complexities of the enterprises, which in turn leads to the fact that not all parts of it can be scanned with equal vigour even by an energetic management. Such a management might even welcome the investigation since they would know that on the whole they would come out well, and they would welcome the extra resources the investigation would bring to bear. Such a benign view of the process might fit the Monopolies Commission investigation of the CEGB, and possibly one or two others.

But is such a benign view tenable? Why should we expect industries to heed the outcome of the assessments? If the audit reveals problems, why are they there? If the faults identified are sufficiently serious to suggest serious management weakness, are we led to the solution of replacing it? That might be the right solution; if people aren't right, nothing will be right, as the truism goes. But what if the people are right, and things are not? The conventional answer over the last fifteen years or so has been that management still need to know what it is they should do; what the policy is, what the criteria are.

CLARIFYING OBJECTIVES

It seems obvious that the objectives must be clear if performance is to be monitored. But the 'clarity of objectives' approach rests on three assumptions, none of which may hold: first, that objectives can be set with sufficient clarity; second, that if they are clearly set, the industries will 'obey' – they will, in other words, accept their subordinate status; third, that the objectives are attainable.

To illustrate the first point, take the case of British Rail and the London and South East commuting network in particular. The problem facing the Department came out before the Public Accounts Committee in 1983.[1] Although the Railways Board and the Department have had discussions over a period of years on the very question of objectives for this part of the rail network, Sir Peter Lazarus, Permanent Secretary at the Department of Transport had to admit to the Committee that there had been little progress.

If no one can set performance targets or objectives in quantifiable terms, then the right conclusion may be that the present view of what the relations should be between industry and department is wrong. Either it should, borrowing from Foster's categorisation,[2] be on the public trust model – in which the industries are 'allowed' to act politically on such matters as fare and service policies – or on the departmental model – where the Minister carries the political role explicitly. Put another way, it makes no sense to delegate a task you cannot define unless you are prepared to let the subordinate body make its own choices. But there may be criteria which can be brought to bear on the manner in which it discharges its delegated authority. For example if the subordinate body adopts good-practice techniques on, say management information, it could be deemed to be acting responsibly. There would be no criteria to judge the decisions themselves. External audit would be confined to technique, more or less as is the Commission's current practice.

The second point is whether the industry will obey the Minister. Suppose, as the public choice theorists would argue, the aim of any bureau (industry) is to maximise its budget (output), then how does it behave if it is responsible to a minister? The answer is of course that it plays it long, courts other power bases, such as the general public, and is obstructive in relation to information. Such behaviour may appear to be reprehensible, but it can be given the moral justification that is inherent in the public trust model. Those in the industry know the needs of the nation best, not ministers or civil servants, whose commitments lie elsewhere. In these circumstances it would be impossible to agree on objectives except in terms so broad they could not be monitored.

One might still wonder why enterprises should not carry out certain tasks efficiently, even if they do not know what their strategic objectives are. For example, errors of the kind the CEGB made in forecasting demand could not be attributed in their case to lack of clarity of objectives. But could the same be said about the Coal Board? Could the over-optimism that the Monopolies and Mergers Commission identified in their demand forecasts be attributed not to simple technical failure but to a wider weakness in the Board?

Though the Commission did not say this in terms, one interpretation of their report is that the NCB was an output-maximising organisation, at the top as well as lower down the hierarchy (where the Commission does identify the problem).

In those circumstances, repeated in other loss-making industries, it is not unlikely that the forecasting process would become corrupted just as it does in other organisations, including central government. If a figure has some probability attached to it, it will be seized upon as the truth. In other words, an apparently technical criticism could be a clue to a graver problem. But in that case, a purely technical critique will change nothing. The intellectual weakness will remain as long as the wider problem of divergent objectives remain.

The third question is whether the objective is attainable. The management may, for example, be in thrall to another power base, the unions. Thus if the Commission find, as they did in relation to the Inner London letter post, that the management had been too lax in relation to the unions, do we regard that as a technical failure, a failure of judgement, as Morris Garner expresses it,[3] or something more serious, that the industry itself cannot solve? If the latter, then again a 'technical' criticism is irrelevant unless the necessary political will to tackle the real problem can be mobilised round it.

LIMITS ON EXTERNAL MONITORING

To sum up so far, external monitoring of the kind we have hitherto experienced could well be more rigorous. But it may nevertheless be ineffective if the root problems do not lie in the field of management technique. Moreover, there are other reasons for arguing that more external monitoring would not be productive.

The chairmen of nationalised industries would argue that there is already too much monitoring for them to be able to run the businesses efficiently. That encapsulates their response to the proposals of the St John-Stevas Bill – as it did, fifteen years ago, when William Robson presented a paper to the Select Committee on Nationalised Industries on efficiency auditing. Now that such a system exists in the form of the Commission, alongside the stricter forms of financial control, which have been taking effect at more or less the same time, it is scarcely surprising that their reaction remains now what it was then. Different chairmen have put it in different ways, but the image used by Sir William Barlow of 'living in a goldfish bowl' is one that they would probably recognise.

Nevertheless that metaphor, if taken literally, is not quite what it seems; the characteristic of the bowl is that the outsider cannot easily grasp the fish. It looks accessible, but isn't. The transparency of the bowl is of little use if the fish itself is slippery and opaque. If it is to be caught and pinned down, some water has to be spilt.

But those responsible for the bowl – the departments – are reluctant to do that, and they do not in any case have the skill, it is argued,[4] to catch the fish. Yet the other monitors, it can be said, do little better. Public opinion, even expert opinion, is ill-informed, likewise parliament; user councils are impotent; the Commission, though useful, is sporadic and carries with it no sanctions. Into this large gap, the St John-Stevas Bill would have put the Exchequer and Audit Department. But one of the most telling arguments against the St John-Stevas Bill was that the Department was not geared up to the task.

Critics of the Exchequer and Audit Department, user councils, departments and, indeed, outside experts, have tended to emphasise how ill-equipped they are for their tasks. Even the Monopolies Commission with its relatively large resources is, it may be argued, inexpert in relation to the industries it investigates. And so proposals are developed for a stronger Commission, a better-staffed Exchequer and Audit Department, more professional or businesslike civil servants, better-resourced MPs and better-resourced user councils – not to forget a better-informed public opinion.

If we accept the criticism, this reaction is understandable. But if all the existing bodies were to become better at what they now do, what would happen? For one thing, there is little doubt that overlaps would occur, in large measure because of the very reasons why there is pressure for more monitoring – i.e. the blurring of the roles of ministers, departments and industries.

The recent Commission investigation into the NCB, as Morris Garner has pointed out, suggests the Holmesian diagnosis of the dog that did not bark. The Department of Energy scarcely gets a mention throughout, as though the NCB operated in a world of its own. Why that happened may be explained by deft footwork at the Department's and the industry's end, as a former member of the Commission has suggested.[5] Another explanation is that the Commission has tended to concentrate on issues of management information systems and similar technical matters, because that is a task that could be done on traditional audit lines. Thus, even though most industries have not published performance targets against which they could be monitored, they could reasonably be brought up against accepted professional or best-practice standards of management. Whatever the reason, the Commission could not confine itself to that kind of approach if it became larger and more expert.

Similarly, select committees, for example the Social Services Committee, have shown that they can ask very awkward questions about accountability, chains of command and management systems which, while starting at the broad policy end, finish up in management issues. There is little doubt that the specialist nationalised industry committee often suggested for reincarnation would do just that.

Even the user councils can finish up in the same area, as the recent initiatives of the London Electricity User Council has shown. Helped by the London Business School it has confronted the Board with an array of performance indicators many of which bear directly on management performance.

There are dangers even in 'better-equipped' departments. The experience in the late 1960s at the Ministry of Transport of employing a large number of economists, illustrates the potential for creating greater friction as much as better control.

If it does not seem profitable to go down the track of having more monitoring, and if there are inherent limits in the extent to which objectives are set, is there another way forward? Foster has suggested in a recent paper that there is.[6] Although he was an early supporter of the external efficiency audit notion, the arguments he puts forward in this paper tend to be sceptical about what it can achieve. His scepticism results from his experience in the Ministry of Transport in the late 1960s, and in private consultancy in applying, or helping to apply, pressures to make others efficient. In what follows, I re-state and amplify his arguments.

THE 'SELF-MONITORING' ALTERNATIVE

One possibility is that the industries should themselves determine the ground rules and criteria. Foster argues:

> The long term answer to the existence of a major divergence of interests [as between industry and Ministers/departments] is to devise procedures for generating information and controls which make possible inter-temporal checks on performance by a public body and for their use of resources to be monitored over time, given the objectives of that body and its prior forecasts. Ultimately such systems are pointless unless devised within the public body, are acceptable to it for its own internal management purposes and are part of its managerial equipment. In the public sector such a system will have objectives, economic and social, which will need to be discussed and agreed in outline with the sponsoring departments. Experience shows that Ministers and sponsoring departments are always reluctant to lay down precise objectives. The public body's best policy is to set its own precise objectives which should reflect what its statutes require modified

by its understanding of what ministers would wish. Such efficiency auditing will make it easier for a public body to give a reliable and convincing account of stewardship to any outside agency with the task of reporting on performance.

Put another way, we can argue as follows: nationalised industries have been set up precisely in order that they should in some measure enjoy independence and hence executive discretion. There are limits to which the extent of that discretion can be pinned down by purely financial criteria or even physical indicators. Once that is accepted – and the evidence of the last fifteen years could be used to support that proposition – then it follows that we have to look elsewhere for ways of delimiting that discretion – if we want to do so.

But can the self-monitoring approach be made to work? There appear to be several difficulties. First, is it technically feasible? The problem that British Rail and British Telecom and the other industries face in tracking the results of particular investments is very considerable because of the extent of interdependence and jointness in their internal economies. Second, at least some of the problems of the industries stem from persistent ministerial interference; could that be assumed away? Third, even if objectives are self-selected, does that make it any more likely they will be clear and verifiable – instance again the London and South East network. Fourth, in the case of the monopolies, how do departments ensure the objectives are not too easy? Fifth, what happens (cf. British Telecom's failure to meet its cost reduction target) if the self-appointed targets are not met? Sixth, in the case of deficit industries, how long should the financial rope be?

Most, though not all, of these difficulties exist now, but perhaps more important, if one was going down the 'self-monitoring' track, it would have to be a gradual process, during which time there may be scope for techniques to develop and attitudes to change. If we accept this for the moment, then is it possible to sketch out in more detail how self-monitoring might work?

TRANSPARENCY

At present, most British nationalised industries are, from an outsider's viewpoint, black boxes. To take one example, it is hard to think of a study of any of the existing industries comparable to, say, the study by John Meyer and his colleagues of the telecommunications industry in the USA.[7] Until the liberalisation debate created a number of instant experts in telecommunications, the industry may as well have been invisible as far as the academic world was concerned, as the bibliography of Richard Pryke's recent book shows.[8]

It is not unique in that. In part this stems from the drift of government policies over the last fifteen years. It has been remarked before that as governments have tried to make nationalised industries more like commercial companies, they have reacted by limiting the amount of information they published about themselves. Although annual reports by, for example, British Telecom may be useful within the confines of the balance sheet – and even win awards for presentation – they tell one very little about the business. We do not know, for example, what the extent of cross-subsidisation is between areas or between business (nor probably does British Telecom even yet).

Take another example: British Gas and the London Electricity Board, in defence of their showrooms, use non-financial arguments. In the latter case the distribution function is actually compensated for carrying out energy-saving but loss-making activities. But even though both have been investigated by the Commission there remain basic features of the internal accounting processes, even for these functions, that are obscure. The examples are easy to multiply.

If 'self-monitoring' is to work, the standard of reporting would have to be tough – much tougher than one of the current examples, the annual White Papers on the Roads Programme. For historical reasons the minister responsible has to present an annual account of his 'stewardship' but he decides the terms on which that is done. As I have argued in an article in *Public Money* (March 1983), that account is self-justificatory and inadequate in important respects. No outsider can put it right because those responsible for the programme have an effective monopoly on information, which will persist even after the new public enquiry documents are available.

Similarly, as the Electricity Users Council recently pointed out,[9] the performance indicators that the area boards are using hide more than they reveal. They require further information if they are to yield much.

What would a self-monitoring approach require from the industries? Foster mentions a more careful allocation of costs to objectives – an output budgeting approach essentially – and presumably to parts of each business. But if it is to have a chance of working – if, that is, we are to avoid the public relations approach of the Roads White Papers – we would have to go far beyond better accounting, though that would be a prerequisite, and more physical information, though that too is a *sine qua non*.

I would suggest three major additions, none of which are to do with targets or objectives:

(1) Major submissions, for example to the board plus ministers, to be published.
(2) (Selective) presentation of policy options.
(3) A much more precise statement of the assumptions being made in forward planning, *not* simply the forecasts themselves.

In other words, we would be looking for arguments and evidence as in judicial or similar hearings. The aim here is to reveal the actual, not the theoretical, quality of the information on which decisions are based, and hence the scope within which judgement – or discretion – is exercised.

CONCLUSION

Why should this approach be preferred to that of ever more rigorous external audit? There are two reasons: first, that by exposing people to 'peer review', professional talents would be harnessed to creative rather than defensive tasks; and second, it would put the wider public, experts in particular, in a position to be much more effective than they are now, simply because they would have so much more to go on.

As we noted above, there are severe problems to be overcome if ever this approach is to get off the ground. Perhaps the most severe is the position of ministers and Parliament. The public trust approach requires greater theoretical and practical recognition of the industries' independence and hence intervention becomes more difficult to justify. However, in the past, such intervention has always been easy to hide, because of the very lack of transparency the self-monitoring approach would aim to end.

Nevertheless, it would seem prudent, as Foster suggests, to retain some form of external audit – as a long-stop. The public trust concern rests, by definition, on a degree of trust. The industries at present don't enjoy it. The self-monitoring approach is one way in which they might earn it.

NOTES AND REFERENCES

1. Public Accounts Committee, Monitoring and Control Activities of Sponsor Departments of Nationalised Industries Session 1982/83, HC. 322.
2. C. D. Foster, *Politics, Finance and the Role of Economics* (London: Allen and Unwin, 1971).
3. M. Garner, 'Auditing the Efficiency of Nationalised Industries: Enter the Monopolies & Mergers Commission', *Public Administration*, vol. 60, no. 4, Winter 1982.
4. M. Garner, 'Nationalised Industries and Spending Departments', *Public Money*, September 1983.
5. See *Public Money*, September 1983, p. 5.
6. C. D. Foster, 'Some Observations on Accountability and Efficiency Auditing in the Public Sector', in 'Public Sector Accounting and Research', published by *Public Money* 1984, General Series No. 3.
7. J. R. Meyer *et al.*, *The Economics of Competition in the Telecommunications Industry* (Cambridge, Mass.: Oelgeschlager Gunn Hain, 1980).
8. R. Pryke, *The Nationalised Industries* (Oxford: Martin Robertson, 1981).
9. Electricity Users Council, *Measuring Area Board Performance* (The Council, 1983).

6 The Political Framework

G. F. DUDLEY and J. J. RICHARDSON*

POLITICAL VICTIMS

The seemingly endless political controversy which surrounds nearly all aspects of the work of the Nationalised Industries (NIs) inevitably gives observers of the scene considerable pause for thought. Surely, so the argument usually goes, there is a better way of conducting affairs? Should it not be possible for governments and the management of the NIs to form a more harmonious relationship? Cannot the management be given clearer guidelines by ministers and then be left 'to get on with the job'? Do the appointments and salaries of the NI Board Members have to be the subject of widespread political controversy? Cannot the NIs themselves devise some system of 'co-ordinated rationality' which could be to the benefit of all, rather than indulge in regular bouts of in-fighting and mutual recrimination? When will the trade unions realise that an efficient and productive NI is to the benefit of all the community, and that no lasting good can come from the maintenance of restrictive practices and an obdurate refusal to recognise the need for change? Is it not possible for the wishes and needs of the NIs' customers to be given greater consideration? When will the time come when interests such as those of the environmentalists can be integrated more successfully into the NIs' decision-making processes, without the need for interminable set-piece public inquiries which cost millions of pounds to stage?

Given this complex and politically 'messy' policy-making process, it would not be surprising if, in attempting to achieve a consensus on

* This process is part of a wider study of the UK policy process, funded by the Nuffield Foundation. The authors wish to thank Craig Pickering, John Grieve Smith, and David Steel for their comments on an earlier draft of this chapter.

112

policy, the management of an NI felt rather like a blindfolded man trying to unravel a long and tangled piece of string, while at the same time attempting to ride a bicycle along a tight-rope wire![1] In some cases, there is real confusion on the part of an NI chairman as to what objectives he should be seeking to achieve. Thus the Chairman of British Rail, Sir Peter Parker, asked the government to define for him: 'What is winning?' In Sir Peter's view, there were two prerequisites for a successful relationship between an NI and government:

> First, there should be complete trust between the Minister and the Board, in particular the Chairman . . . Secondly there must be agreed objectives – clear, attainable and understandable. Winning should be possible for a nationalised corporation, even if the prizes have not been glittering hitherto. Whatever the secrets of management success may be, they include stimulating incentives, morale and pride of achievement.[2]

Sir Peter's prerequisites for 'winning' appear rational enough, but to bring the various interests together in an agreement on how the policy-making process should proceed (sometimes known as metapolicymaking)[3] is usually an extremely difficult task, let alone achieving a consensus on concrete objectives. Interests such as government, NI management, trade unions, consumers and pressure groups such as those representing environmentalists, will each have an individual view of what, for it, constitutes 'winning'. This competition between interests can become so intense that each may transpose Sir Peter's question of 'What is winning?' into the more prosaic and pluralistic 'How can I win?'. In order to appreciate how these various interests fit into the political framework, we can analyse their relative strengths and weaknesses in the context of NI metapolicymaking. In turn this can tell us more about the strengths and weaknesses of the policy-making system itself.

THE POLITICAL POWER OF THE NATIONALISED INDUSTRIES

Expertise and the Arm's Length Relationship

The predominant position which the majority of the NIs occupy within their own sectors gives power not only over other interests in that sector, but also over government. Put at its most basic, government requires the co-operation of the NIs if policy is to be implemented successfully; for objectives are of little use if the means of obtaining them are neither administratively nor politically feasible. Linked to this element of performance of a task is the NIs' associated strength as a respository of expertise. Foster, writing in the early 1970s, described how in his experience as Director General of Economic planning in the Ministry of Transport, few major investment projects suggested by the public corporations were turned down by government. He considered that a prime explanation for this Departmental passivity was a basic lack of confidence on the part of either officials or ministers.[4] Although in recent times the government does appear to have developed a more sceptical approach to the transport industries – for example, British Rail electrification plans – governments still appear generally reluctant to challenge the judgement of the NIs. Consequently, the problem of developing the required level of expertise in the Departments to assess and monitor the work of the NIs remains acute. A recent report by the Comptroller and Auditor General (CAG) dealing with the appraisal of public investment projects (not in the NIs as such), severely criticised Departmental officials for a failure to apply Treasury guidelines, which he thought suggested an incomplete understanding of the required techniques.[5] Although appraisal of the NIs operates under different rules (and by different officials), the CAG report does illustrate a general weakness of the British civil service, and its vulnerability to the 'doctrine of superior knowledge' when operating in highly technical fields.

In addition to this Departmental weakness, the NIs are also in a strong position with regard to the interpretation of statutes. As Foster points out, precise expressions of policy tend not to appear in statutes, even though Parliament could be more precise if it wished. A White Paper will usually be introduced *before* legislation, but *after* legislation the exact interpretation of the statute will be left in the hands of the relevant public corporation.[6]

Thus it was said of Sir Monty Finniston, the former Chairman of the British Steel Corporation, that he slept with a copy of the Iron and Steel Act under his pillow. When Tony Benn, as Labour's Secretary of State for Industry, attempted to intervene to prevent the BSC closing a number of steelworks in 1975, Sir Monty used the provisions of the Act as a weapon to defend the autonomy of the Corporation. A useful by-product of the dispute was a detailed public discussion (including an exchange of letters) on what the wording of the Iron and Steel Act (which set out the powers and duties of the BSC) actually meant. A debate such as this is nevertheless very rare where the NIs are concerned, and ministers are usually reluctant to claim more authority for themselves by means of challenging a corporation's interpretation of a statute.

That there can be considerable doubt about the exact meaning of a statute was well illustrated by the example of the 1969 Transport Act, which placed the London Transport Executive under the control of the Greater London Council. When the GLC attempted to introduce its radical 'Fares Fair' policy in 1981, its right to do this was successfully challenged in the House of Lords by Bromley District Council, on the grounds that the 1969 Act did not allow the GLC this authority. Perhaps surprisingly, this process of policy-making by means of the judicial process has now become official government policy, for the 1983 Transport Act allows ratepayers to sue the GLC or a Metropolitan County where they consider that public transport subsidies have gone beyond a reasonable limit. It is perhaps unlikely that such legislation will become more widely fashionable as an indirect tool of government control over the NIs (for example, allowing British Rail to be sued for failing to make a profit),[7] but the London Transport example does illustrate that the relationship between government and NI can depend more on a mixture of custom, economic circumstances and political will than exact statutory interpretation.

The NIs as a Lobby

Despite the existence of clientelism, the NIs still feel themselves to be in need of allies. As Tivey points out, the political automony of the NIs allows them to form alliances in the interest group world. Thus the majority of NIs are members of the Confederation of British Industry, while two NI chairmen serve as members of the National Economic Development Council. In addition, an NI may join forces with trade unions and consumer councils in order to campaign for higher investment.[8] A watershed for the NIs, in the quest for recognition that they represented an individual interest, occurred in 1978, with the creation of the Nationalised Industries Chairmen's Group (NICG). Tivey succinctly puts the point in this way:

> It is now widely argued that the public service leaders do represent an obvious interest – their own. They argue and propagandise for 'their' industry or 'their' agency because their own affairs – prosperity or at any rate satisfactions – are bound up with it. Its expansion is therefore consciously or unconsciously part of their pursuit of their individual welfare just as much as that of any capitalist.[9]

The work of the NICG, although performed on a limited budget, has enabled the NIs to adopt a more open approach to lobbying, as well as allowing the Chairmen another channel of communication with government and in particular the Treasury.[10] In order to illustrate the type of subject which particularly interests the NICG, we will briefly examine two examples. In the first of these the Chairmen have achieved some success, while in the second there was a totally satisfactory outcome for the NICG.

First, during 1980–1 the NICG became increasingly concerned about what it considered to be the government's excessively restrictive attitude towards capital investment in the NIs. The Chairmen were worried that viable investment programmes were being held back by the government's obsession with the Public Sector Borrowing Requirement (PSBR), while the government (and in particular the Treasury) argued that increased investment by the NIs would put unwarranted pressure on public expenditure, and could also 'crowd out' investment by the private sector. The Treasury had set up its own Ryrie and Monck Committees (named after the officials who chaired them) during 1980–1 to investigate this problem in association with the NICG, but it had a powerful variety of interests ranged against it. The NICG itself commissioned a study, by the economist Michael Posner, into how a new code might be developed, whereby the External Financing Limits (EFLs) of the NIs might be more loosely and flexibly tied to the PSBR. The NICG had powerful allies for its case in the shape of both the CBI and the TUC, who were both aware of the strong interconnections between the public and private sectors, and hoped that new investment by the NIs could help the economy out of recession. It was also thought that several Departments, and in particular the Department of Industry, were sympathetic towards the Chairmen's arguments, and eventually the National Economic Development Office added its voice in support of the campaign.

The culmination of this pressure arrived in June 1981 at a meeting of the National Economic Development Council. The Chancellor of the Exchequer, Sir Geoffrey Howe, found himself in a tight corner, and so resorted to the tried and trusted British solution to problems of this type by suggesting the setting-up of a working party to consist of representatives from the government, the CBI, the TUC and the NIs (the NIs had apparently succeeded in creating quadripartism rather than tripartism). However, the working party was to be under the chairmanship of Bill Ryrie, the Treasury official who had in public argued the government's case that there was little scope for relaxing the NIs' financial constraints.

The Treasury seemed to be discomforted by the NIs' newly discovered resources of lobbying power, a fact well illustrated by the reply Leon Brittan, Chief Secretary to the Treasury, gave to a question on this subject in the House of Commons:

> Such campaigns are not only surprising, but deplorable. I do not believe that the money obtained by Nationalised Industries, from whatever source – whether through what they charge for their products or from elsewhere – ought to be spent in this way.[11]

When the working party reported in October 1981, it became clear that the NICG case in principle had been accepted, for it was recommended that the government should encourage the industries and their sponsoring Whitehall departments to identify schemes where private finance could be used, in addition to regular funding provided in annual public spending budgets. The first fruits of these recommendations were realised in March 1982, when the Treasury abandoned its objections to British Telecom's plan to raise £150 million of risk capital in the City. (In the event, when the government later announced its intention to privatise British Telecom, the bond idea was quietly dropped.) Several other NIs hoped to follow where British Telecom had (at least in principle) led, but the Treasury was determined that they would not find an easy way through to private sector finance. In June 1982 a joint report prepared by the Treasury and the NICG was presented to the

NEDC. This report was clearly heavily influenced by Treasury thinking, and stressed the several tests which NI investment plans involving finance from the private sector would have to take if they were to pass scrutiny by the Treasury. Thus it could be said that a process of agreement by accommodation had been reached, where the Treasury had conceded a major point of principle to the NIs, but was determined to maintain its own authority. The other important facet of the campaign was that the NICG had established its legitimacy as a lobbying interest, and had proved its ability to fight its corner.

The second example involved the NICG in a campaign where, ironically, it found itself on the same side as the Treasury. Backbench MPs have for some time been unhappy with their inability to scrutinise in detail the affairs of the NIs, and towards the end of 1982 a Private Members' Bill was introduced by the Conservative MP Norman St John-Stevas, which had the intention of greatly increasing the power of Parliament to audit the accounts of the NIs. The four principal clauses of the Bill included a proposal that the Comptroller and Auditor General's remit be extended to include all publicly owned bodies, including the NIs.

The government and the NICG joined forces to oppose the clause dealing with the NIs, chiefly on the grounds that it would have the effect of reducing the NIs' ability to operate commercially. Supporters of the Bill initially appeared to have a good chance of steering the clause dealing with the NIs through the Committee stage, and both the Treasury and the NICG immediately entered into discussions with the MPs involved. The CBI also opposed the Bill, as did many of the trade unions with workers in the NIs. The opposition of the unions was of particular political significance, for their sponsored Labour MPs gave a potential means of influencing the policy process.

After a series of negotiations, described by St John-Stevas as being of 'Byzantine complexity', a compromise was reached whereby it was proposed that the Comptroller and Auditor General would not be allowed access to the books of the NIs. Instead the Select Committee on Public Accounts would be involved with government-sponsored Monopolies and Mergers Commission inquiries into the NIs. In addition, commercial auditors would conduct value-for-money inquiries on behalf of Whitehall sponsoring Departments, the results of which would be made available to

the Public Accounts Committee and the relevant Select Committees. The NICG considered that it had negotiated the best deal it
could hope for, but in the event it achieved a bonus. The Commons
Committee voted ten to seven against the clause, and all reference
to the NIs was dropped from the Bill. In addition to its outright
opponents, the clause was also opposed by several MPs (both
Conservative and Labour) who were disappointed that St John-
Stevas had backed down as a result of pressure from the Treasury
and the NIs. As with the first example, the NICG has discovered
that with the right allies it could achieve considerable political
success.

Despite these successes for the NICG, there are inevitably limits
to the unity that the group can achieve. As Tivey comments, the
targets of pressure for several NIs, particularly in the energy sector,
are other NIs.[12] This point is endorsed by Richard Marsh who, when
taking on the job of Minister of Power during the 1960s, found that
the nationalised industry chairmen in the fuel industries were
engaged in the beginnings of a major war with each other.[13] Similar
levels of competition can also be found in the passenger transport
industries with competition between rail, bus and air services. In
addition there is a more oblique type of competition, in which one
NI may make profits at the expense of another: for example, the
British Steel Corporation (BSC) claims that excessive prices
charged by the National Coal Board (NCB), the Central Electricity
Generating Board (CEGB) and the British Gas Corporation (BG)
is one of the principal explanations for its financial problems. It is in
this sense that an NI with great power within its own sector, such as
the BSC, may consider itself to be vulnerable within the industrial
structure as a whole.[14] In a similar fashion all NIs will consider
themselves vulnerable to general market conditions, particularly in
time of recession. Ironically it is the oblique competition that also
exemplifies the interdependency of the NIs, for greater efficiency
and hence lower prices within one of them can benefit many of the
others. It is doubtful if the NICG has the means to facilitate this type
of co-ordination, but it is significant that when the Chairman of the
BSC, Ian MacGregor, switched jobs to become Chairman of the
NCB, he retained strong links with the BSC.

THE POWER-POINTS OF GOVERNMENT

The power to appoint Chairmen and Board members is one of the principal bases of government control over the NIs. Perhaps even more important, the Minister has the power to renew or not to renew these contracts and, as Tivey notes, it would be unrealistic to think that NI Chairmen do not have this potential threat to their futures in mind when they are lobbying government.[15] At the same time, Foster argues that, once appointed, it is almost impossible for an NI Chairman to be sacked, while in addition the dismissed Chairman's remarks might prove an embarrassment to the government, with the Minister probably accused of excessive meddling in the affairs of an NI.[16]

In reality, although it is highly unlikely that an NI Chairman would be sacked in the middle of his contract, it is common for a contract not to be renewed, by what on occasions might euphemistically be termed 'mutual consent'. It appears that Chairmen are often not keen to voluntarily submit themselves to another term in the 'goldfish bowl', and therefore leave the government with the difficult job of finding a replacement. Nevertheless, the government does on occasion decline to renew the contract of a Chairman willing to serve another term, the most recent notable example (in April 1982) being that of Glyn England, the Chairman of the CEGB. After his dismissal, England complained bitterly about what he considered to have been excessive government interference in his work, which he thought had made it much more difficult for the CEGB to be efficient. One example of this intervention occured in February 1981, when Ministers, under the threat of industrial unrest in the mining industry, asked the CEGB to reduce its imports of relatively cheap foreign coal to a minimum, in favour of more expensive UK supplies. This is of course a good example of the kind of oblique competition we referred to earlier, and in this case political trouble in one sector was averted by passing it on to another.

Although the departure of Glyn England from the CEGB might suggest that an NI Chairman who attacks government policy is unlikely to last long in his post, it is impossible to generalise on this point. The other side of the coin is represented by the case of Sir Denis Rooke, the Chairman of British Gas. During 1981 Sir Denis launched into a public and outspoken attack on government plans to sell off BG showrooms to the private sector. Yet at the height of the controversy, Sir Denis's contract was renewed for a further five years. Nevertheless, despite Rooke's survival, Tivey is probably correct in concluding that, with respect to the government's power to appoint a Chairman, NIs are in a position of *comparative* weakness.[17] In the case of Board appointments the position is somewhat different. These are usually made by the Minister after discussion with the Chairman, a right which is interpreted by most Chairmen as constituting a veto power on their part.

Related to the power of appointment is the ability of government to control the pay of NI Chairmen and Board Members. During the 1970s these salaries came under the ambit of the Top Salaries Review Body (TSRB) which consistently recommended substantial increases for the NIs, and equally consistently found their reports rejected by government on the grounds that they would destabilise pay policy. In 1981 it appeared that the NIs had been freed from this constriction when the Prime Minister decided that their salaries would no longer come under the TSRB, but would instead be decided by market forces. The hopes for this brave new world soon evaporated however, when the government decided later in 1981 that a pay norm of 7 per cent would be appropriate for NI Chairmen and Board Members. The government adopted a slightly more flexible attitude towards salary increases for 1982–3, but was determined that the Treasury should keep a keen watch out for Departments making 'excessive' awards. Like its predecessors, the government found itself torn between wishing to pay salaries at a sufficiently high level to attract top-class executives, and the need to maintain an incomes policy in the public sector. This government has been more innovative than its predecessors (for example, the complex remuneration 'package' negotiated with Ian MacGregor and the American merchant bank Lazard Freres), and it appears that in the future the government hopes to find a way past this problem by linking salaries to performance-related criteria.

Price control is another area traditionally associated with government intervention in the finances of the NIs. Throughout the 1970s, successive governments used NI prices as an integral part of prices and incomes policies, often to the frustration of management. The Conservative government of 1979–83 has been less obviously interventionist, preferring instead to exert indirect control of prices and incomes by means of cash limits. Nevertheless, even this government has been forced to take action on the thorny question of energy prices. With regard to gas, the government decided early in 1980 that, because of what it considered to be under-pricing by British Gas, each year for the following three years prices charged to consumers would rise by 10 per cent above the rate of inflation. Conversely, after extensive lobbying by industry, the 1981 budget introduced a freeze of gas prices to industrial and commercial users until the end of the year. A further freeze was imposed as a result of the 1982 budget, and was then extended to last until at least the end of 1983. In November 1982 the electricity supply industry agreed to freeze its prices for the whole of 1983.

Perhaps ironically, it was said that this stability in electricity prices had been made possible because of lower long-term forecasts in future demand, which had allowed the CEGB to reduce its provision for capital investment. Despite the NIs' long campaign to free themselves from the constrictions of the EFLs and PSBR, in November 1982 the Prime Minister wrote to the NICG in order to encourage its members to step up capital spending! For 1982–3 it was estimated that the NIs would show a shortfall of around £1.6 billion on the budgeted figure of £7.6 billion for investment in fixed assets. The position with regard to British Telecom (the organisation given permission to market its own bond) was so bad that the government threatened to reduce its EFL if it did not spend more. This anomalous situation on capital spending reminds us that, regardless of complex negotiations at the 'peak', general economic conditions and implementation problems will insist on intruding. Like British industry as a whole, the NIs found themselves having to modify their plans during a recession, but some of the NIs also attributed the shortfall to delays in deliveries and cheaper suppliers' prices. Thus government 'control' of the NIs by means of the EFLs can be somewhat illusory. In addition it can be said that where the financial state of an NI deteriorates rapidly, as has happened frequently in the case of the BSC, the government invariably raises the EFL to accommodate the crisis. In these cases the political costs of restricting the EFL are usually considered to be too high a price to pay.

RECENT POLICY INITIATIVES

The government's increasing awareness of its limited ability to control the NIs has led to several policy initiatives. First, the 1980 Competition Act made provision for the Monopolies and Mergers Commission to undertake regular efficiency audits of selected NIs.[18] Second, the government commissioned its Central Policy Review Staff (popularly known as the Think Tank) to investigate the relationship between the government and the NIs. On the whole, the Think Tank's recommendations were based on the premise that the expertise to be found in Whitehall with regard to the NIs required considerable strengthening. Thus new Cabinet Committees on the NIs were set up, the Treasury created a Public Enterprise Analytic Unit to monitor the industries, and more accountants and business executives were hired (with a mixed response from the Departments) to bolster the various Departments dealing with the NIs: for example, an executive from private industry was taken on to help run the Railways Directorate. In addition, all the NIs were to be set detailed strategic objectives.

Politically, it is likely that at least in the short term these developments will exacerbate the prickly relations between government and the NIs, for the latter will regard them as yet more unwelcome intrusions into their affairs. Yet in the long term, it could be argued, there is much to be gained from Whitehall being able to speak to the NIs on more equal terms: i.e. a debate between equals may engender a higher degree of mutual respect and rationality. On the other hand, if civil servants should come to regard improved expertise purely as a means of imposing more authoritarian control over the NIs, then an opportunity to improve communications will be lost. Thus there is always a danger that increased technical expertise on the part of civil servants will be used to convert what ministers see as political issues, and NI Boards see as managerial issues, into administrative issues to be resolved by civil servants.

In this section we have seen that government does have definite levers of control over the NIs, for example with regard to appointments, pay and the EFLs, but that there are also many constraints on its power. In a number of instances the present government's solution to these control problems has been to privatise several NIs. In recent years the government has sold majority shareholdings in a number of organisations, including British Aerospace, Cable and Wireless, and Britoil, and has completely privatised the National Freight Corporation. This may, however, be just the start of a new set of control problems. As Hogwood points out, political rhetoric may treat movements from the public to private sectors as being synonymous with movements from administrative to market allocation, but in some cases a firm in the private sector might be a monopoly and operate an administrative criterion, while one in the public sector may have many competitors and operate a market criterion.[19] Thus the government now plans to sell off its majority shareholding in British Telecom, but in order that BT does not abuse its monopoly position in the private sector the government has found it necessary to create a complex regulatory framework.

In contrast, when the government took the simple expedient of deregulating express bus services as part of the 1980 Transport Act (the particular effectiveness of this clause of the Act was that implementation could be secured without the agreement of the principal interests), it immediately had the effect of driving the state-owned National Bus Company (NBC) into a flurry of action, in which it reduced fares on many services and also took a large slice of the market off the private sector. Ironically, the government's answer to this policy development was a plan to denationalise NBC express services (now apparently abandoned in favour of denationalising NBC as a whole), a complex procedure which was unlikely to change anything in the real world. In this case, it is deregulation rather than denationalisation that is the government's more effective 'power tool' for policy implementation.

THE PLACE OF OTHER INTERESTS IN THE STRATEGIC PLANNING PROCESS

It is inevitable that the respective power of government and NIs, and the relationships between them, should form the chief focus of debate on the political framework surrounding the work of the NIs. These twin pillars are key supports for the entire structure, and the nature of the duopoly sets the shape and tone of each policy community. Decisions made at the central level – for example, on investment, prices and wages, rationalisation and regulation – will inevitably have a profound effect throughout the whole policy process, even if plans are eventually somewhat modified.

Traditionally, other interests, either through passivity on their part (for example, trade unions) or because of obstruction from the centre (for example, environmentalists) have found it difficult to break through into what might be described as the core policy-making process – i.e. the stage when policy options (and values) are first framed and then sifted out. At the same time, other interests can be potential agents of change in the policy-making process, and we can briefly examine the role that some of them play.

Parliament

Parliament itself is in a somewhat paradoxical position. Officially, it is the body to whom the NIs owe their existence and their authority, yet in reality its status has been that of an 'outsider' in the community. After several years of frustration over the relative unwillingness of ministers to answer questions on the NIs, Parliament has more recently attempted to take matters into its own hands. Yet as we have seen in the case of the St John-Stevas Bill, both the executive and the NIs are unwilling to allow Parliament a more integral role in the affairs of the NIs. The most significant development in recent years has been the creation of Departmental Select Committees in 1979. Previously, investigations into the NIs have been undertaken by the Select Committee on Nationalised Industries (SCNI). In some cases, the new more-specialised committees do appear to allow greater scope for continued and detailed investigations of the NIs (for example, the Industry and Trade Committees monitoring of BSC), but it could be argued that the abolition of the SCNI caused a discontinuity in expertise which is difficult to replace.

The Trade Unions

The interest with the most obvious ability to influence both government and NI management is represented by the trade unions. Indeed, as the National Union of Mineworkers demonstrated in 1974, a powerful trade union can potentially be instrumental in bringing down a government. In addition, the steel strike of 1980, and action taken by the train drivers in 1982, demonstrated that strikes in the NIs can have a generally disruptive effect (although significantly neither strike had the catastrophic results originally predicted). Yet in spite of (or perhaps because of) their potential power, the unions have usually been reluctant to become centrally involved in NI strategic planning. Their role is usually reactive rather than innovative (although during the 1970s the NUM did become more integrally involved in planning for the coal industry).

Union leaders have usually shied away from joining NI Boards, although several retired trade unionists are Board Members, while a union leader who did join a Board, Clive Jenkins of the Association of Scientific, Technical and Managerial Staffs, was removed from the British National Oil Corporation's (BNOC) Board in 1982 when he publicly protested at the government's plans to denationalise BNOC's oil exploration assets. In the case of the majority of union leaders, there is a fear that a full tripartite relationship with government and NI management might compromise their general negotiating position. Thus the sight of trade unionists sitting on NI Boards has largely been restricted to a few experiments. Probably the most notable of these has been the appointment of worker directors to BSC Boards. Worker directors have sat on BSC Divisional Boards since shortly after the birth of the Corporation in 1967, and have been present on the main Board since 1978. It cannot be said that this scheme has proved a success, for many of the worker directors have found themselves mistrusted by their own members and ignored by management.[20] Another experiment occurred in the Post Office in 1978 where the new Board included the Chairman, seven management and seven union members, and five independent members, but this new structure was abandoned after its two-year term by Conservative government.

Relatively rare examples of effective grassroots involvement in NI strategic planning occurred during the 1970s, when a number of action committees (largely autonomous from central union control) were set up to fight proposed steel works closures. These groups were effective for a time, but were obliterated when BSC management discovered a highly effective policy implementation tool. When unions and action committees were bypassed, and the workers received direct offers of high redundancy payments, a works closure could be secured quickly.[21] (Like the deregulation of express bus services, this policy had the political attraction of bypassing obstructionist interests.) The BSC has followed this up by the almost complete decentralisation of pay bargaining (linked to productivity agreements). In the NIs generally, if the trend towards local bargaining continues, national union leaders may wish to find a new role by becoming more integrally involved in the central strategic planning process.

Consumers

Another range of groups that has generally failed to become centrally involved in NI strategic planning is the consumer councils. These councils (forty-four of them) were set up in piecemeal fashion by the government, and nearly 1,000 ministerial appointments are involved. These close links with government and the NIs have led to charges that the consumer councils lack independence, and are thus unresponsive to the true needs of consumers. It could be argued that the NI consumer councils have played a part in at least reinforcing a climate of opinion leading to policy change – for example, holding down energy and postage prices – but their role has been rarely more than peripheral.

Early in the life of the present government the consumer councils' tenuous hold on central policy-making was further weakened. First, the Post Office Board experiment, which included two consumer representatives, was aborted. Second, it saw the end of the short-lived Energy Commission (created to advise the Secretary of State on the development of energy strategy) which consisted of a wide range of representative interests, including trade unions and consumers.

At the same time, the present government is sympathetic to the general concept of greater consumer pressure on the NIs, and in the long run this may benefit the consumer councils. In December 1981, the government produced a Green Paper which suggested as a possible policy option a considerable reduction in the number of consumer councils, with three broad industry groups for utilities, transport and communications. It was intended that this considerably rationalised system would improve communications between the consumer councils and create pools of staff with a high level of expertise.[22] The political attraction for the government in this plan was that it would achieve the twin policy objectives of reducing the number of quangos and also (hopefully) improving public scrutiny of the NIs.

This fundamental restructuring of the NIs' consumer councils appeared to be favoured by the government, but following consultations it was announced (in December 1982) that the radical approach had been ditched, chiefly because all the chief interests were against it! Instead, all the forty-four councils were to remain intact. Each consumer council was to be given guidelines on how it should operate, but significantly it was intended that the councils themselves (and not the government) would propose what these guidelines should be.[23] The consumer councils were therefore able to resist policy change in their own particular area, although they themselves have found it difficult to gain admittance to the central areas of NI strategic planning.

A contrasting view on how consumers might acquire more real power over the NIs is provided by Redwood, who puts forward the case for what might be termed the market model. In the opinion of Redwood, consumers will never be helped by institutional reform, but will only realise their full potential when the NIs are made more subject to market forces.[24] The deregulation of express bus services is a good example of this theory being put into practice, although in other cases (for example, the vast majority of local bus services which are not commercially viable) deregulation would bring with it a mixture of costs and benefits. The taxpayer would undoubtedly benefit, but traffic congestion could increase and, in rural areas, greater pressure would be placed on voluntary organisations.

Environmentalists

One interest which has succeeded in imposing itself with some political force in the realm of NI strategic planning is that represented by the environmentalists. They have achieved success not by becoming 'insider' groups within the central policy community, but by utilising public inquiry procedures to gain maximum impact for their own case and maximum discomfiture for the NIs. The environmental groups won a particularly notable success at the expense of the NCB in 1982 when the Secretary of State for Energy, after a lengthy planning inquiry in 1982, refused permission for mining in the Vale of Belvoir in Leicestershire.

Environmental groups such as Friends of the Earth, the Council for the Protection of Rural England and the Town and Country Planning Association have also challenged the development of nuclear power in the UK.[25] In 1977, at the hundred-day Windscale inquiry, they challenged British Nuclear Fuels Limited's (BNFL) plans to develop its nuclear reprocessing plant there. (In this case the government eventually made a decision in favour of BNFL.) A second example arose in 1983, in the public inquiry into the building of a Pressurised Water Reactor at Sizewell 'B' power station in Suffolk. Although the environmental groups are strongly represented at the Sizewell Inquiry, there is nevertheless a wide disparity between their own financial resources and those of the CEGB. A total of over £5 million was being spent by the CEGB to present its case, whereas an appeal for £500,000 by the environmental groups was terminated when only £8,000 had been raised.

Although they are of importance, financial resources are not necessarily decisive in deciding the success of environmental groups. The groups themselves have the powerful support of the coal industry in their opposition to nuclear power stations, and other groups have found that cultivating the right friendships can be vital. Thus Transport 2000, a group which campaigns for greater railway investment and also fights against many major road building plans, is a coalition of the rail unions and environmental groups.

A further example of this type was provided during the long debate on the siting of a third London Airport. The Wing Airport Resistance Association (an example of what might be termed a 'not here' environmental group, formed to fight a particular campaign) shrewdly enlisted the support of a wide cross-section of MPs, so that when the Roskill Commission in 1971 recommended the inland Wing/Cublington as the site for the airport, this opposition was immediately mobilised by WARA with the result that the government decided against any of the inland sites proposed.[26] As the NICG later discovered, the creation of alliances can be the most effective form of political action in the typical British policy process.

ORDER OUT OF CHAOS?

We have seen that government and the NIs do have particular political levers of control and influence over each other. There is a notable contrast between the nature of these levers, which must affect the tone of the debate. In the case of the Minister, his controls are of the more direct and wholesale kind: for example, the decision not to reappoint a chairman, the remuneration 'package' offered to a chairman, a determination to haul back an EFL, and selling off profitable sections of an NI. On the part of an NI, its strengths are somewhat more implicit and intangible: for example, the authority bestowed on those with specialised expertise, the knowledge that a government relies on the NI to secure successful implementation of policy, the ability of an NI to embarrass a Minister by discreetly circulating stories to the media about his proclivity for 'interference'. Thus the bargaining between the government and an NI is rather like a duel between someone wielding a broadsword, and an opponent holding a rapier (with the blood usually being spilled behind closed doors).

The reality of the relationship is certainly very far from the original Morrisonian doctrine of the 'arm's length relationship'. At its worst the relationship can at times appear quite chaotic, with policy outcomes unpredictable and with considerable problems in securing effective accountability. Decisions are reached by a 'messy' process of bargaining in which both sides have particular strengths and weaknesses. The balance of strengths and weaknesses is itself unpredictable.

PRIVATISATION

Under Mrs Thatcher's government, the very strong impetus given to privatisation has at least the potential for radical policy change in the relationship between government and the nationalised industries. At the time of writing the pace of privatisation is increasing and the nationalised industry 'map' could look radically different by the next election. Space does not permit a proper discussion of either the motives or the potential effects of privatisation. Cynics see privatisation as a mixture of ideology and a pragmatic need to raise funds in order to reduce the public sector borrowing requirement. We have yet to see the full effects of the total privatisation programme. It seems reasonably certain that privatisation itself will not remove political problems. The government is likely to find itself exchanging one set of political problems for another (although that is not to say that the balance of advantage does not lie with privatisation). The privatised industries will still remain key industries in the context of the British economy, and government will remain a very substantial shareholder in many of them. It will be unable to escape the responsibility which falls upon such a large shareholder, or the responsibility, as a government, for a fair and efficient regulatory framework for many of the industries.

It seems likely, therefore, that the problem of achieving a workable relationship between government and these industries (be they wholly or partly owned by the state) will remain. It would be naive to believe that there is an arrangement (government department; public corporation; partially privatised; fully privatised) which can 'squeeze the politics out' of the system. As a result some observers see bringing the industries more fully into government, as departments, as the only respectable and defensible solution. Even private sector companies are finding it necessary to move closer to government and to become more involved in the political process. British companies are now following the American pattern of greater awareness of the importance of 'politics' to their activities.[27] We can at best hope that it might be possible to simplify and clarify relationships, while accepting that the NIs will be subject to political direction.

REVIEW BODIES

The question of *expertise* remains the most fundamental issue to be resolved. If a satisfactory balance in expertise can be achieved, then there is at least the possibility of a more orderly and stable relationship. It is in this area – essentially the degree to which governments can and should 'second guess' the NIs – that the present government may be groping towards a more workable system of control. Its use of the Monopolies and Mergers Commission (MMC), *ad hoc* inquiries, and private consultants, suggests a recognition that Whitehall is still short on relevant expertise in relation to the industries themselves. Amid the confusion, resulting from failed attempts to make the Morrisonian doctrine work, there are the seeds of a more effective system. The difficulty with the increased use of the MMC and outside consultants is that the review arrangements are either intermittent or *ad hoc*.

There is an understandable lack of enthusiasm for major institutional reform, reflecting a weariness with a long history based on a belief that institutional reform will provide workable solutions. There is particularly strong resistance from the NIs to any proposals which threaten to add yet more layers of control, when they feel that they are already subject to too much control. Yet there appears to be a recognition by the NIs that they can 'learn to live with' genuinely *expert* external review bodies. The Price Commission, before being abolished by the Heath government had begun to earn the respect of the NIs for the quality of its work. The MMC has also begun to establish itself as a well-informed and expert analyst of the NIs, though doubts remain as to whether it is quite the appropriate body for such reviews. Greater doubts are held concerning the quality of other *ad hoc* reviews, such as Serpell and some recent private consultant's reports which have been conducted at breakneck speed and are, as a result, extremely vulnerable to the 'doctrine of the superior knowledge'.

A rationalisation of the current search for more effective external and independent review procedures might assist in the creation of a more lasting and effective relationship. Thus the review process could be institutionalised through the creation of a range of permanent, independent review bodies, modelled on the MMC or Price Commission.[28] If such bodies were genuinely independent of both government and the industries (British public administration has many such independent bodies), they would earn the respect and co-operation of the industries and would act as an alternative source of expertise to whom government could turn for advice. They need to be permanent in order to develop the necessary expertise and might act as a buffer between government and the industries. They might also shed light on the rather grey and confusing world which we have described in this chapter.

NOTES AND REFERENCES

1. For a comment see Sir William Barlow, 'The Problems of Managing Nationalised Industries', in *Allies or Adversaries?* (London: Royal Institute of Public Administration, 1981) p. 36.
2. *The Times*, 16 May 1980.
3. Dror defines metapolicy as the problem of how to make policy about making policy. See Y. Dror, *Public Policymaking Reexamined* (Bedford: Leonard Hill, 1973) p. 8.

4. C. D. Foster, *Politics, Finance and the Role of Economics* (London: George Allen & Unwin, 1971) p. 61.

5. *H.M. Treasury Property Services Agency. The Use of Investment Appraisal in Straightforward Spending Divisions by Government Departments*, 28th Report from the Public Accounts Committee, HC417, 1981/82.

6. Foster, *Politics, Finance*, pp. 23–5.

7. For a detailed discussion of this concept, see A. Dunsire, 'Central Control over Local Authorities: A Cybernetic Approach', *Public Administration*, 59 (1981) pp. 173–88.

8. L. Tivey, 'Nationalised Industries as Organised Interests', *Public Administration*, 60 (1981) pp. 45–6.

9. Ibid, p. 49.

10. Ibid, p. 44.

11. Hansard, 2 July 1981, col. 989.

12. Tivey, 'Nationalised Industries as Organised Interests', p. 44.

13. R. Marsh, *Off the Rails* (London: Weidenfeld & Nicolson, 1978) p. 101.

14. See J. J. Richardson and G. F. Dudley, 'Steel Policy in the UK: The Politics of Industrial Decline', in Y. Meny and V. Wright, *The Local Management of National Industrial Problems: The Case of Steel in the 1970s* (Walter de Gruyter (Berlin) and European University Institute (Florence), 1984) and a shortened version, under the same title published in *Strathclyde Papers on Government and Politics*, no. 10, October 1983.

15. Tivey, 'Nationalised Industries as Organised Interests', p. 47.

16. Foster, *Politics, Finance and the Role of Economics*, pp. 75–6.

17. Tivey, 'Nationalised Industries as Organised Interests', p. 47.

18. For a detailed discussion of this development, see M. R. Garner, 'Auditing the Efficiency of Nationalised Industries: Enter the Monopolies and Mergers Commission', *Public Administration*, 60 (1982) pp. 409–28.

19. B. W. Hogwood, 'The Instruments of Desire'. How British Government Attempts to Regulate and Influence Industry', *Public Administration Bulletin*, special issue on regulation and de-regulation, Summer 1983.

20. See P. Brannen, E. Batstone, D. Fatchett and P. White, *The Worker Directors* (London: Hutchinson, 1976).

21. G. F. Dudley, 'Pluralism, Policy-Making and Implementation: The Evolution of the British Steel Corporation's Development Strategy', *Public Administration*, 57 (1979) pp. 253–70.

22. *Consumer Interests and the Nationalised Industries* (London: Department of Trade, 1981).

23. *The Nationalised Industry Consumer Councils: A Strategy for Reform* (London: Department of Trade, 1982).

24. J. Redwood, *Public Enterprise in Crisis* (Oxford: Blackwell, 1980).

25. For a discussion of these environmental campaigns, see H. Ward, 'The

Anti-Nuclear Lobby: An Unequal Struggle?', in D. Marsh (ed.), *Pressure Politics* (London: Junction, 1983) pp. 182–211.

26. R. H. Kimber and J. J. Richardson, 'The Roskillers: Cublington fights the Airport', in R. H. Kimber and J. J. Richardson (eds), *Campaigning for the Environment* (London: Routledge & Kegan Paul, 1974) pp. 165–211.

27. See B. Taylor, this volume; and J. J. Richardson, The Development of Corporate Responsibility in the UK, Strathclyde Papers on Government and Politics, no. 1, 1983, Politics Department, University of Strathclyde.

28. For a discussion of an example of such a body, the Norwegian Petroleum Directorate, see J. J. Richardson, 'Problems of Controlling Public Sector Agencies: The Case of Norwegian Oil Policy', *Political Studies*, vol. XXIX, no. 1 (March 1981) pp. 35–50.

7 The Role of Market Forces

M. E. BEESLEY and P. GIST

INTRODUCTION

This chapter will consider the role which increasing competition may play in influencing the behaviour of nationalised industries, and the implications for the design of government policy to achieve it.

We regard increasing competition as one possible way of influencing the behaviour of these industries. We take this influence to have been an underlying reason for nationalisation in the first place, and to be the ambition of all governments in their current dealings with the industries. In the UK, successive governments have departed from the original means of doing this. The framework conceived by Herbert Morrison within which national-ised industries would operate was a system of social control by exception. The public interest in the industries' day-to-day conduct was to be ensured by a broadly representative Board, in which concerns such as better labour conditions were to be kept in view not by direct representation, but by an appropriate voice (for example, a prominent trade unionist not belonging to the industry in question). In effect, the public interest was the Board; its decisions involved agreement on social aims, and appropriate conduct was accordingly implied. The funds necessary for providing socially desirable services were to be raised through the industries' monopoly power. Ministers would intervene only in exceptional circumstances, or to set constraints derived from overriding national interests, such as defence. Thus government influence would stem from the appointment of the Board, and the parties' duties as laid down in initial Acts of Parliament. Financial integrity was to be ensured by a duty to break even.

The reasons for the overall retreat from this model are only too well known. The relations between the parties – arms of government and nationalised industries – were increasingly those of negotiating from separate premises.

A series of *ad hoc* instruments was devised to meet unforeseen contingencies. Each attempted to alter conduct thought to be inappropriate. For example, in 1961 the failure of some nationalised industries to cover costs and make sufficient provisions for investment prompted proposals for closer scrutiny of capital expenditure plans.[1] In 1967 more rules for investment and pricing were introduced, the Test Discount Rate and the use of Social Cost Benefit analyses to justify non-commercial projects.[2] In the interests of allocative efficiency the aim of setting prices equal to long-run marginal costs was established, with provisos ensuring further *ad hoc* intervention. *Ex ante* financial targets were specified for each industry.

Beginning in the early 1970s, greater emphasis was placed on the corporate plan as the focus of the government's means of influencing behaviour. Later, in 1978, alongside renewed interest in corporate plans, investment planning moved from the *ex ante* appraisal mechanism of the Test Discount Rate to an *ex post* Required Rate of Return.[3] Financial targets were set for between three and five years, and performance indicators were now to play a greater role in influencing the non-price aspects of service provision.

Strategic planning in nationalised industries is, we would argue, yet another instrument of influence which can potentially affect the continuing negotiations between government and nationalised industry. Nationalised industries are both politically and economically orientated; emphasis on one mode of influence or another tends to reflect the current state of the continuing negotiation between the chief parties concerned, the industry, the sponsoring department and the Treasury – the last two representing the partly co-operating, partly contending, faces of government. As seen in its current political and administrative context, this is likely to be favourable to increasing competition, or more broadly, market influences, for some time ahead. In this chapter we focus on the economic orientation of the industries.

The history of moves to influence nationalised industry conduct indicates clearly the importance of the market conditions in a particular industry, and the degree to which public money is involved. These two are, of course, related. One of the main reasons for the decline of the Morrisonian model was increasing need for Treasury intervention as a condition for maintaining social objectives. Financial weakness was largely market weakness. Market structure must therefore be a leading element in our own analysis of a (relatively) fresh instrument, introducing competition, and this is seen below. It is a curious fact, however, that discussions about nationalised industries' relations with government have been singularly opaque to the differences made by underlying market structures.[4]

In practice, of course, the extent to which the different means of influence have been brought to bear has reflected the varied circumstances of each industry, including the amount of competition which each faced. Thus, means of limiting price increases through requirements for the approval of ministers and consumer bodies, and measures of performance, have been more important for those nationalised industries which also have substantial statutory monopoly power. The measures have been intended to stand as proxies for the effects of competition in the final goods and services markets. What we want to consider is the scope for substituting market forces themselves for other means of influence.

In principle this could be achieved either with or without the sale of the public corporations, i.e. so-called 'privatisation'. We wish to focus here on the question of how far it is reasonable to expect that a useful role for competition may be achieved without also moving altogether from a context of public ownership. We conceive of two ways in which this form of increased competition might be achieved:

(1) by relaxing restrictions on the entry of new firms to the markets served by nationalised industries (i.e. where public corporations are also statutory monopolies); and
(2) by methods of splitting the public organisations into separate autonomous parts, but without changing from the public ownership form.

We seek first to establish the significance of distinguishing demand and supply conditions in guiding attempts to increase market pressures, and then discuss what might be done without privatisation. Our own recent experience in this area has been mainly in telecoms. We use this to illustrate, later in this chapter, some of the issues involved in carrying through an intention of this kind. We see that, to judge by the telecom example, there may well be a conflict between privatisation and what we regard as the more fundamental objective of increasing competitive forces.

The benefits from increasing competition we take to be those usually associated with it; greater incentives to innovate in processes of production and in products themselves, and pressure to keep prices down and to expand markets. In this process, the commercial reaction of incumbent firms to rivalry from newcomers will make an important contribution to the benefits realised.

THE UNDERLYING DEMAND AND SUPPLY CONDITIONS

It is necessary to base suggestions for increasing market pressure on an analysis of the demand and supply conditions that public enterprises face, for these govern what is feasible and useful to suggest by way of relaxing entry to the market and changing the organisational scope of the existing corporation.

Following Beesley and Littlechild, we describe the market characteristics of the industries in which public corporations operate as a 2 × 2 matrix.[5] On the demand side are described current underlying trends, either as 'good', i.e. buoyant, or 'bad', i.e. static or declining. In general, more scope exists for increasing competition where prospects are good, for there competitive firms will be attracted to produce. 'Supply' conditions describe the inherent tendency of the industry to single or multiple ownership – i.e. describe what we think would result were market forces given full rein: a single firm or several independently owned firms. This distinction between 'sustainable' or 'non-sustainable' monopoly is founded on underlying cost characteristics, at any given time a function of the technology available to producers and the prices of factors of production. Thus the matrix (Table 7.1) sets out what it would be possible (not necessarily desirable) to achieve in terms of industrial structure.

The theory of sustainability of monopoly has recently received renewed attention in the literature from William Baumol, Elizabeth

Bailey and others.[6] It bears on our placing of the industries in the matrix as follows. In the theory, three characteristics of costs (as opposed to nationalised industries' rights) are conducive to sustainable monopoly. First, with only one good or service produced, economies of scale are conducive to sustainability. Second, with multiproduct or service production, the presence of substantial elements of joint costs will have the same result. Third, the fact that the incumbent is already in production, whereas the potential entrant is not, will give the incumbent cost advantages over the entrant irrespective of whether economies of scale or joint costs are also present. Sunk costs are likely to be the most important aspect of this cost advantage: i.e. any outlays which cannot be recovered by sale of the assets for which they were originally incurred. To the incumbent they are bygones, but have yet to be faced by the potential entrant. Other differential cost advantages may also accrue to the incumbent – such as lower costs of capital than the entrant because of an established track record on which to raise finances, and lower costs of marketing because of access to better information. Here we emphasise the importance of these differential cost characteristics for sustainability, and especially those arising from sunk costs. Thus we emphasise the relation between an existing producer, the incumbent, whom we can identify with a nationalised industry, and potential entrants. The appendix to this chapter treats in more detail the connection between these elements and the consequent market structure.

In the matrix, those sectors of the nationalised industries would be sustainable against competition are suggested, and those that would not. Of all the elements in sustainability just described, we would assign most importance to sunk costs. As seen in the matrix, with some industries (for example telecommunications and gas) elements of both sustainable monopoly and non-sustainable monopoly are currently present. These industries are therefore placed in more than one quadrant of the matrix.

A policy of relaxing restraints on entry to markets in which public corporations operate would be especially relevant where the current legislation grants monopoly or some restricted form of monopoly, and where the public corporation is not already subject to a substantial degree of competition in the domestic market – for example, from foreign competitors. Relaxation of entry restrictions would therefore be particularly relevant for the industries listed in

TABLE 7.1 *Classification of the industries in which public corporations operate*

		Demand prospects	
		Good	Bad
	Single	(A) Electricity distribution (each area board and grid) Telecommunications (each local network) Gas distribution (each local network) Airports (each airport)	(B) Rail Post Waterways
Supply prospects given unrestricted competition	Multiple	(C) Electricity (excluding grid) Telecommunications (excluding local networks) Gas production Coal Aviation	(D) Steel Motor vehicle manufacture Ship building Bus services

quadrants (A) and (C), rather than those in (B) and (D). As pointed out in Beesley and Littlechild, in the latter quadrants the public corporations operate to a greater extent in environments already subject to competition, both from abroad and from other domestic producers (including both public and private sector corporations).[7] To consider the effects of a policy of lifting entry restrictions we therefore concentrate our attention on industries in quadrants (A) and (C).

If entry into these markets were permitted, the extent of entry which occurred would in theory follow the lines we have suggested. Some sections of the industries would remain as monopolies, those in quadrant (A), while others would function as competitive environments, those in (C). For those industries in quadrant (A) or sections of them, where there is little prospect of sustainable new entrants, we must concentrate on the other form of introducing

market forces here, i.e. through changing organisational boundaries. This occupies our next section.

However, even if a policy of lifting entry restrictions has the
potential to create a competitive market structure in important
parts of the existing nationalised industries, as the matrix suggests,
there is a further difficulty associated with it.

Because any policy has to bear upon market situations at a
particular time, we have in effect a fourth element to consider in the
account of sustainability, namely the starting market share which
the incumbent enjoys. The likely emergence of competition is not
unaffected by this starting position even where parts of the
incumbent's present operation are non-sustainable. This is not
emphasised by the theory and does not affect our placing of the
industries in the matrix, because it concerns the question not of the
underlying possibility of achieving a competitive structure, but
rather the path from the present organisation to that structure. The
point is, of course, that in the process of establishing competition,
the incumbent may be able to use his strong market position in some
parts of the business to secure differential advantages in the area
more subject to entry, in which a very high market share is inherited
from statutory monopoly days. The higher the overall initial market
share, the more important is this likely to be.

Unless, therefore, specific account is taken of this in pursuing a
policy of encouraging entry, the potential may not be realised. In
practice, this means devising rules of competitive behaviour between the incumbent and would-be entrants. Experience with
telecoms is very relevant to this and we consider the problems later
in the chapter.

CHANGING ORGANISATIONAL BOUNDARIES

Some incumbents are, in effect, a collection of individually sustainable monopolies. Increasing market pressures could be accomp-
lished either by creating independent enterprises within the present
governmental style of ownership, or by involving a different basis
for public enterprise. In the UK case, such a policy of basing public
ownership on local or regional authority rather than central
government would have precedents in nationalised industries'
history – for example, municipal supply of electricity, telecoms and

gas – all of which in whole or part preceded nationalisation. Some of these enterprises were very large organisations for their day – one thinks of Birmingham's municipalisation of water and gas. At least one interesting example of municipal public enterprise in these industries persists even now – Hull's independent telephone system.

Ownership can be divided vertically or horizontally. There are considerable opportunities for vertical disintegration. The present scope of ownership in UK nationalised industries is largely a matter of historical accident in the degree of vertical integration of preceding companies. For example, the CEGB is a distinctive part of the rest of the electricity industry even though in the same 'ownership', because its roots go back to 1926. At this time production was a much more local affair, and so was final distribution; the key was organising the national grid.

To the extent that so-called economies of scope (arising from joint costs) and scale are not sacrificed, it is perfectly reasonable to divide public enterprises. This is most obviously true of separate activities such as posts and telephones, which happen, in most countries, to be (historically) linked. In general, one has to be extremely sceptical of claims for these 'economies', either horizontally or vertically. Real vertical economies require rather special conditions, such as heat saving in steel, or other manifestations of very important transport cost savings. Horizontal economies often turn out in real terms to be illusory. In analysing nationalised industries, gains from monopoly power are too often mistaken for real (resource saving) gains.

Examination of the economies would indicate several successor organisations. If these can be based in separate public owners, it is easy to imagine their effective independent operation. Each Board would be locally appointed or elected with truly separate accounts, and draw on government guarantees for financial purposes subject to central rules. Locational separation is indeed the key in horizontal reform. Apart from utilities, the outstanding possible examples occur in transport, notably in airports and railways. These are both eminently suitable to division below the national level.

What benefits can one expect from this? First, on general grounds, the more separate organisations there are in a given type of activity, the more the effective competition for career advancement, and the more likely the skilled are to rise. Second, rule-making at the centre – for example, by government departments –

will be more feasible where there are more separate enterprises. The key point about successful influence (a more accurate word than 'control') on the set of public enterprises is the using of evidence coming from relevant comparisons, as far as possible comparing like with like to monitor performance. With single public enterprises in a given activity, the evidence is necessarily confined to time series observations, often difficult to interpret in themselves because of changing external circumstances. Creating, perhaps only a few, separate organisations in effect adds cross-section comparisons, based on genuinely independent observations. This adds greatly to the stock of information useful for interpretation and prediction. In turn, it also adds more point to external comparisons (for example, with other countries' experience) and in general to harnessing the various ways in which what might be called the professional guilt mechanisms can be enlisted to back up central influence.[8]

Will the separated public organisations be 'truly' independent, especially where owned by central government? Clearly not as much as if they were privatised. But the fact of separate accounting must be encouraging. Cross-subsidy as between what were formerly parts of one entity is made much more difficult. Judging by the remarkable persistence of pre-nationalisation divisions (in attitudes as well as practices) in the UK nationalised industries, the prospects for generating independent views are reasonable. But if more diverse industries are thus created, one cannot expect that the problem of securing greater economic efficiency and openness to innovation is solved. Quadrant (A) industries in particular will still have considerable monopoly power in the separate organisations. The big gains from division are likely to arise from these organisations' rivalry in securing suppliers, bidding for scarce talent, etc.

Monopoly power could be curbed by regulation by government, as it has in the past, but, we would argue, the opportunities for independent innovation would be forgone. Alternatively, power could be curbed by encouraging entry where possible, i.e. ensuring that the sustainable monopoly element is tested and thus confined, and devising some other means of curbing monopoly power in the remaining sustainable part.

THE PROBLEMS OF ENSURING ENTRY

A policy of lifting restrictions on entry into an industry where the incumbent enjoys a high market share and where sustainable monopoly elements are also present, must ensure that the incumbents' use of this existing market power, both as a supplier of services to customers and purchaser of factors of production, does not deter entry. It is useful to consider the policy needs here under three headings: industry ownership patterns, the use of purchasing power, and specific competitive acts.

Industry Ownership Patterns

The incumbent's commitment to an existing technology may induce it to seek joint ventures with or acquisition of entrants for the purpose of suppressing innovation, i.e. where the entrant would appear to have access to a better technology and the incumbent does not. A prohibition on extensions of ownership rights from those areas in which the incumbent has invested considerable sums in sunk costs would appear to be the solution here.

Use of Purchasing Power

The incumbent's long-established relations with suppliers of equipment, for whom the incumbent may remain the most important customer after restrictions on entry are lifted, may be used to bring pressure to bear on new competitors. The overseer of competition must ensure that competitors' choices of supply remain as wide as possible. Thus there should be no restrictions on imports, or where there are, the incumbent producer and domestic suppliers must be prevented from colluding to the detriment of potential competitors. Backward integration by the incumbent into sources of supply should be prohibited.

Specific Competitive Acts

Potentially, obstructions to increasing competition may arise from predatory conduct by the incumbent, or from collusion. 'Predatory conduct' describes a pattern of behaviour designed to make life difficult for a specific competitor, as opposed to competitors in general. Collusion describes a situation in which two or more parties act jointly to create and then exploit a monopoly position.

The incumbent's interest in preventing entry or its consolidation is clear; it has a greater chance of benefiting from future market and cost changes the fewer the number of effective rivals. The initial very high market share provides the opportunity to pursue this policy. When a policy of increasing competition in a nationalised industry begins, competitive effort by the incumbent is very likely to focus on a specific competitor. As the two recent examinations of restrictive practices policy conclude, the common characteristic of all potentially anti-competitive practices such as tie-in sales, loyalty bonuses and exclusive dealing contracts, is that to be effective in restricting competition those who practise them must already have some degree of market power.[9] *A fortiori* the danger of these practices occurring must be higher in the context of 100 per cent or near 100 per cent market share, as in the case of some nationalised industries. The term 'predatory conduct' is commonly identified with pricing competitive products or services below costs. But identifying such conduct on cost grounds is in practice particularly difficult where firms produce a range of products or services and many costs are 'joint'. Allocations of total costs between individual products is then arbitrary, and a variety of prices may be said to be 'cost based'. When this is the case, the firm may choose where in the markets in which it competes to cover total cost and make its profits. It will be able to derive a greater contribution to joint costs from those products subject to lower degrees of potential competition. The scope for predatory conduct, attacking a specific competitor, is thus greater when a portfolio of products is produced and costs are joint, and also more difficult for an outsider to detect on grounds of 'cost based' prices.

The policy to combat predatory conduct, we would suggest, should rely upon a strong presumption against discrimination on the part of the incumbent, together with the effective separation of competitive and non-competitive markets i.e. divestiture. Non-discrimination would ensure that at least all customers (irrespective of whether they are the potential customers of a competitor) would be offered the same terms. The dominant producer, the incumbent, is then forced to consider the impact on all of his businesses of selecting the particular form of contract to offer. This would to a certain extent constrain the incumbent to diverge from the course of conduct that best serves its own interests, and may not result in prices that considerations of economic efficiency in a static sense would indicate. However, for the sake of encouraging entry and the gains to dynamic efficiency from innovation these sacrifices may be necessary.

A policy of divesting monopoly from competitive services will be necessary to combat predatory pricing, where revenues from monopoly services are used to subsidise competitive ones. We do not think that attempts to assess whether prices for particular services are truly 'cost based' or prices are below marginal costs can be successful – especially where substantial joint costs are present.

Further rules will be required to back up the use of a policy of non-discrimination. First, publication of prices and terms will help the adjudicator of competition policy (whoever it may be, the Office of Fair Trading, Monopolies and Mergers Commission or some new body) to decide whether reported conduct is in any sense discriminatory. Second, because all relevant information will reside with the incumbent (until such time as successful entry occurs, and the adjudicator of policy can refer to other sources of information), it may be necessary to shift the burden of proof in such cases on to the incumbent.[10] Thus he would be asked to demonstrate that a case of discrimination, established on prima-facie grounds, was unfounded.

The existing provisions for dealing with collusion in restrictive practices legislation should be sufficient in circumstances where the number of competitors has grown such that implicit collusion is difficult for them to achieve. Where only two competitors exist, and implicit collusion is likely, little can be done. Thus, dangers of collusion can only effectively be circumvented by more competition in the long run.

THE EXPERIENCE WITH TELECOMMUNICATIONS

The most important attempt so far to introduce competition to a nationalised industry with important sustainable monopoly elements has been in telecommunications. When the government embarked on a programme of freeing entry to telecommunications markets they did so with no clear idea that privatisation of the public corporation would follow. The first moves to liberalise telecoms markets began in 1980–1 when the Beesley report on the commercial uses to which BT's network could be put by its customers, so called 'resale', was commissioned.[11] The announcement that privatisation would also follow was not made until July 1982.[12] The intervening period saw attempts to combine more freedom to enter with the continuance of traditional controls over a nationalised industry. Indeed, in many ways, British Telecom, after it was formed by the 1981 British Telecommunications Act, resembled more closely the typical Morrisonian-style public corporation than other corporations. It inherited from the Post Office its 'exclusive privilege' to run telecommunications systems in the UK and its exemption from legal proceedings against it. As had been the case before its separation from the postal business it continued to operate with highly delegated responsibilities from its sponsor ministry. The principal way in which the regime after the 1981 Act differed from the one before was in the powers conferred on the Secretary of State to license other telecommunications systems, either through BT or independently, and to approve apparatus to be attached to the public telephone network for commercial supply. Before 1981 the Post Office alone had permitted other companies to infringe its statutory monopoly, an activity which by European standards it undertook with relative liberality.[13]

The 1983 Telecommunications Bill, before Parliament at the time of writing, makes provision for establishing a Director General of Telecommunications (DGTel) to oversee competition in the industry, and lays the ground rules for the competitive environment. The Bill also transfers the licensing function wholly to the Secretary of State, and ends BT's exclusive privilege in telecommunications, repealing the extension of that power granted by the 1981 Act. BT itself will thus require a licence once the Act is passed. The Bill also makes provision for the privatisation of BT.

The principal issue for us is the design of policy to increase competition in a context of public ownership. Although the Bill, which also provides for privatisation, simultaneously formulates provisions for this, the two aspects of the Bill are essentially separate. We will therefore discuss the telecoms experience with increasing competition by first considering the events leading up to the Bill and the provisions of the Bill designed to solve the issues which have arisen. While our critique of these provisions is necessarily specific to this Bill, several points of principle emerge. Choosing the path of increasing competition has led, as we shall see, to the problems of transition foreshadowed earlier. There has also emerged a practical issue of maintaining 'social' services, which influences the way the incumbent is dealt with. In the light of this experience, we pose in the conclusions to this chapter the question of how far privatisation works against the ambition of increasing competition.

In pursuing its policy, the government has – at least to date – not elected to alter the organisational boundaries of the incumbent. Although the 1981 Act split the Post Office into two corporations – effectively increasing the scope for market forces by permitting competition between them in certain services (for example, electronic mail) – this has not been extended in the 1983 Bill. Instead, competition has been increased through selectively raising entry restrictions in parts of BT's market through the licensing of competitors. The Secretary of State has so far exercised licensing powers in the following ways.

First, a system for establishing technical standards for competitively produced apparatus was put in hand. Second, 'resale' was established in only a limited form in order to protect BT's revenue from trunk telephone calls, arguably used to cross-subsidise local services and social services. Third, the Government licensed an alternative network to BT, the 'Mercury' network, which would be permitted to compete in all telecommunications markets, and Racal, a company which will compete with BT in providing mobile radio services. Also, following the recommendations of the Hunt Committee on cable TV,[14] some competition in building local cable networks and in providing services on them will be permitted.[15]

In the supply of attachments, the scope for competition in attachments has widened since the first restrictions were lifted – for example, BT's right to install and maintain the first telephone connected to a telephone line has now been abolished. But the slowness in setting standards and approving equipment remains a constraint on competition. On the resale issue, Beesley[11] had recommended that no market restrictions should be placed on the use to which circuits, hired from BT, could be put. The report argued that if innovation in service offerings was to be encouraged then competitors should be permitted to offer any services. Voice services, i.e. telephony, constituted by far the major market and therefore scope for building business, while technical distinctions between types of message transmitted made less sense as technology developed. Opponents of resale, BT included, argued that resellers would link major cities in Britain with BT circuits connected to local telephone exchanges and cream off BT's revenues from trunk calls. The arbitrage possible for resellers in the existing relationship between trunk-call prices, local-call prices and prices for leased lines – itself determined by requirements for cross-subsidy – would encourage this. BT's response to competition would have to be higher leased-circuit charges, and lower trunk charges, but at the expense of higher local-call charges. In the event, the criteria for resale services which the government introduced defined a category of services as 'value added network services' or 'VANS'.[16] This criteria essentially limited the markets in which resellers could compete with BT to exclude telephone services. During this period there was little evidence of a rush to secure licences to offer 'VANS' services. In October 1982 a general licence for 'VANS' was issued in which the criteria for 'VANS' services were widened to include conference calls.[17] Thus, a limited amount of voice competition has been permitted. In February 1983 an announcement was made to the effect that the government supported the view that restrictions on resale should be lifted further,[18] and in Novement 1983 the Minister for Information Technology announced the intention to investigate permitting the group use of leased circuits.[19] So far no proposals for this have materialised. At the time of writing approximately fifty licences for 'VANS' have been granted, but no progress had been made on the central issue to open up competition in voice markets.

In network competition, no effective entry has yet occurred. The Mercury network, which received much publicity initially, began to lay plans for its operation. It opened negotiations with British Rail to lay optical fibres beside the railway, and started discussions with BT to interconnect with local exchanges and with other organisations who could provide means of access to customers' premises in city centres – for example, London Transport. Its experiences in requiring interconnection with BT's local networks in order to offer an effectively competitive service, confirm the sustainable monopoly characteristics of local networks which we identify in Figure 7.1. Since its initial announcements, however, little actual competition has arisen in the intercity sectors of telecoms transmission. BT's own responses to Mercury's potential competition may have had something to do with this. BT's prices on so-called 'low cost' trunk routes, essentially the ones in which Mercury had announced it would compete, were lowered. Also new digital high-speed transmission services have been introduced, using radio technology, which compete directly with the service Mercury had proposed to offer on its optical fibre network. In local cable networks, the government has announced that any interactive voice services, and the linking of local systems, will be provided by BT or Mercury.[15] Potential competition here has therefore been restricted to non-voice interactive services, i.e. data services.

In sum, therefore, the extent to which entry restrictions have so far been lifted in the telecoms industry is limited. The widest scope for entry now exists, in principle, in attachments supply; but the slow pace in establishing standards and approving competitors' apparatus acts as a constraint. In resale, competition is essentially limited to non-voice telephony services, a small percentage of the potential market. In networks, two competitors have been licensed to date, but as yet no actual competition has emerged.

Competition Rules

We suggested earlier in the chapter that rules to foster competition should include provisions to prohibit the extension of monopoly power through acquisition of, or joint ventures with, competitors, integration with suppliers, predatory conduct or collusion. The cornerstones of such a policy might include prohibitions on acquisitions, a strong presumption against discrimination, and the structural division of BT into monopoly and competitive companies. To aid the regulator, the non-discrimination policy should be backed up by publication of terms and charges for services, and by shifting the burden of proof in cases of alleged predatory conduct onto the incumbent. Dangers of collusion, we argued, would in the long run only be prevented by more competition.

On the dangers of extension of monopoly power via acquisition and joint ventures, no steps have been taken to prohibit such action in areas connected with monopoly power, such as local networks. It is intended merely that such ventures should be referred to the DGTel who may require an MMC reference. Indeed here, the reverse, rather, has been true. The opportunity to encourage competition via licensing of independent interactive local cable networks to provide voice telephony has been foreclosed.

Proposals for competition rules bearing on predatory conduct are contained in the draft BT licence of 25 October 1983[20] and the 1983 Bill.[21] Although the draft licence explicitly prohibits such anti-competitive practices as exclusive dealing and tying sales by BT (licence conditions 35 and 36), and requires publication of standard charges, terms and conditions (licence condition 16), other provisions in the licence and the Bill increase in scope for predation and foreclosure. The draft licence fails to require BT to establish separate subsidiaries for its businesses, except for equipment manufacture. The most important distinction between the sustainable monopoly in local networks and other, potentially competitive areas, is not made. Although cross-subsidising between parts of its business is expressly forbidden (licence condition 18), the scope for doing so undetected is much greater without separate companies. Also, instead of prohibiting discrimination in terms and charges by BT, the company will be required by the licence not to exercise 'undue discrimination' or 'undue preference' (conditions 17 and 22). These terms repeat the wording of the Bill. The implication that in certain circumstances discrimination or preference would be permissible, again increases the scope for predatory or foreclosing behaviour. The draft licence does nothing to shift the burden of proof in cases of alleged anti-competitive behaviour on to the incumbent.

The powers of the DGTel to monitor and prevent anti-competitive practices are derived from the existing legislation with respect to monopoly situations and anti-competitive practices. Thus the powers of the Office of Fair Trading under the relevant sections of the 1973 Fair Trading Act and 1980 Competition Act have been transferred to the DGTel's office, and he may make references to the Monopolies and Mergers Commission where he sees fit.[22] The DGTel may also make modifications to licence conditions, subject to consultation with the licensee, or if a question of the public interest arises refer the question of whether licence conditions should be modified directly to the Monopolies and Mergers Commission.[23] Whatever shortcomings there are in the existing MMC's treatment of abuse of dominant power, these are thus transferred to the new system – and the MMC has not been notable for its robust approach to, or significant impact on, the behaviour of the subject firms. But in the telecoms case the prospect is even worse because of the criteria loaded upon the DGTel and the MMC. Clause 3 of the Bill described these. Subsection 1 enshrines the concept of 'universal service' and the Secretary of State's and DGTel's duties to secure it. Subsection 1 states:

> The Secretary of State and the Director shall each have a duty to exercise the functions assigned or transferred to him . . . in the manner which he considers is best calculated –
>
> (a) to secure that there are provided throughout the United Kingdom, save in so far as the provision thereof is impracticable or not reasonably practicable, such telecommunications services as satisfy all reasonable demands for them including, in particular, emergency service, public call box services, ship-to-shore services and services in rural areas; and
> (b) without prejudice to the generality of paragraph (a) above, to secure that any person by whom any such services fall to be provided is able to finance the provision of those services.[24]

This takes precedence over all other duties listed in subsection 2, which are, in order; promoting the interests of consumers; maintaining and promoting effective competition; promoting efficiency and economy; promoting research and development; enabling 'such persons' as are engaged in telecoms activities to establish and maintain a leading position in the field of telecommunications; to encourage foreign businesses using telecommunications to settle in the UK; to promote the provision of international transit services in telecommunications in the UK; and to promote outside the UK competitive activity by those persons producing telecoms services within the UK.[25]

All this might be more acceptable if licence conditions themselves contained clear and explicit rules for the behaviour of licensees, but the draft licence for BT indicates that this will not be the case. Also, the spirit of the clause, by giving priority to a vague expression of universal service and placing the other duties clearly in second place, will inhibit the Secretary of State in granting further licences. An important aim of the Bill and the draft licence is to secure continued provision of social services. These are listed in the draft licence as services to rural areas, public emergency call services, public call boxes, and apparatus and services for the blind and disabled. Clause 3 of the Bill places a duty on the DGTel to ensure that the operator does not make a loss in providing them. The licence provides for a non-discriminatory tax on competing systems which interconnect with BT, and on BT's own trunk network in order to fund these services (termed an 'access charge'). The Bill provides explicitly for local authorities to contribute to the financing of services which they consider 'would be for the benefit of the whole or any part of their area'.[26] These provisions are laudable as an attempt to make explicit provision for the funding of social services rather than to rely solely, as in the past, on implicit cross-subsidy between parts of a public corporation's business, a process inhibiting to the introduction of competition. However, the principle that competition issues and funding of social services are separate should be more firmly established. For example, in determining the size of the losses to be recovered through 'access charges' it would be preferable to insist on reference to future losses in terms of cash flows which could demonstrate that BT's financial position would improve were the services withdrawn.

Thus, as provisions now stand, there are at least two further sources of possible confusion between social services and competition issues. First there is the general duty in clause 3 to provide universal service. Second, what is deemed to be 'due' discrimination may well be connected with provision of the social services. The effect of these will be to distract the DGTel from what ought to be his principal function – promoting competition by preventing predatory practices by the incumbent producer.

CONCLUSIONS

We have argued that an increased role for market forces may be found with continued public ownership, but that the nature of that ownership may have to alter. However, the incumbent's response to increased competition will make an important contribution to the benefits which competition can bring, and the flexibility of his response may be curtailed by continuance of public ownership. With public ownership, the freedom to enter new market areas or leave old ones is constrained by statute. The benefits of the disciplines of the capital market, where past successes determine future borrowing, are forgone, and substituted by budgets subject to change for reasons often nothing to do with the industry as such.

But, as Beesley and Littlechild have argued recently, the form which privatisation takes is itself crucial. Privatising a statutory monopoly, in conjunction with lifting restrictions on entry to the industry, may do nothing to increase competition unless the other policies, which we have outlined, are also adopted. The structure of the privatised company will be especially important. A possible danger arises because government may see the needs of privatisation *per se* and the requirements of a policy designed to increase the role for market forces, as opposed: i.e. that the market will be prepared to pay more for a privatised monopoly than for a company against whom greater competition will prevail. The recent history of the telecoms industry shows clearly a reluctance to increase competition in the face of a prospective privatisation. This fear would be well founded if market size were static; but entry itself, we argue, increases the size of the market. Also the privatised incumbent will be in a strong position to increase his market share in the competitive environment.

The Secretary of State made it clear on 29 June 1983, when the Telecommunications Bill was published, that BT would be floated as a single company.[27] But, we have argued, the provisions of the Bill are insufficient to guard against predatory behaviour. BT, as a private company, will have every incentive to exploit monopoly positions and extend its monopoly power to potentially competitive markets. We suggest therefore that the history we have recounted shows that although the liberalisation process may have started with the intention of increasing competition, the priorities associated with a programme of privatisation seem to have substantially reduced the pace of liberalisation.

APPENDIX – SUSTAINABILITY AND MARKET STRUCTURE

Following the line of argument on sustainability in the text, what happens if a statutory monopoly is abandoned?

First, let us consider the opposite of sustainable monopoly, namely non-sustainable monopoly. In circumstances in which technology is freely available to all producers, in which there are no (or small) economies of scale or scope (joint costs) and no sunk costs (which arise by the facts of historical development), the incumbent's market position cannot be sustained. Both the incumbent and potential entrants can produce market output as cheaply as it can be produced. If statutory restrictions on entry are lifted, the incumbent will have to price at a level less than costs to prevent entry. Bankruptcy will result. Any attempt to raise prices will attract new firms into the market. The incumbent may survive, but not as a monopolist. His market share (and that of others) is indeterminate. The freedom for firms to enter ensures that any available economies are passed on to consumers. However, now suppose that with only one good or service produced, economies of scale are present, or if there is multiple product or service production, joint costs exist. Again, we assume that technology and factors of production are equally available to incumbent and potential entrants and no sunk costs exist. The incumbent's position may be sustainable, although one cannot be sure. It will definitely be non-sustainable, as before, if the 'economies of scale' or joint costs are not big, relative to the size of the markets in question. But where they are substantial, sustainability is possible.

To enter the market the potential entrant must produce at large volume to get costs down to a level competitive with the incumbent where economies of scale are present, and for a full range of competitive products where joint costs are also substantial. His addition to total market output will depress prices. If the incumbent is already meeting market demand at average costs then prices will fall below this. Whether some form of market sharing will result, with each producer serving part of the market at higher than minimum costs, or whether the entrant will be deterred by the prospect of ensuing price falls and leave the market to the incumbent, is not clear. But, a sustainable position for the incumbent is at least a possibility.

However, it is unrealistic to consider 'sustainability' in abstraction from the possibly different costs facing entrants and incumbents, even if all parties would have equal access to technology, and hence opportunities to produce at least cost, once they are in production.

In the first place, simply because he is there first, the incumbent has made commitments in the past that the entrant has to face for the first time if he enters. Hence the incumbent can price at his avoidable costs, enjoying a positive cash flow, until such time as items included in sunk costs have to be renewed (if they do at all). On the other hand, were entry to occur at the level permitting the reaping of economies of scale (or joint costs) this would, *ex hypothesi*, add substantially to market output unless the incumbent obligingly cuts output to compensate. Hence the incumbent can effectively raise the cost of entry by an actual or latent threat to impose extra financial outlays.

These characteristics of sustainability imply a degree of freedom to the incumbent to raise prices, restrict output and make monopoly profit. This could, in principle, outweigh the potential benefits consumers might otherwise enjoy via economies of scale.

A further consideration is, of course, that incumbents and potential entrants may not have equal access to technology, or, equally important in practice, may not have the same ability to find and create markets. This obviously affects sustainability also. The greater the advantages, if any, enjoyed by the potential entrants, the less sustainable is the incumbent's position. If entry then occurs, the consequent market structure depends on the nature of the advantages enjoyed. If an entrant himself has the sustainable advantages, one monopoly incumbent is substituted by another. On the other hand, the incoming technology or market skills may not be conducive to sustainability, and then the structure will consist of many firms.

These views are somewhat different from those expressed by the recent proponents of the theory of sustainability, although we draw heavily on them. The earlier articles by Panzar and Willig, and Baumol, Bailey and Willig,[6] were concerned with identifying the circumstances in which free entry into a regulated industry might be inefficient, in the sense that production of the initial vector of market outputs by more than one firm might be more costly than with only one. The efficient single-firm industry they defined as a 'natural monopoly', and identified the circumstances in which, in the absence of regulatory restrictions on competition, the initial output vector would not be sustainable against entry. Our own, admittedly crude, examination of cost characteristics in telecommunications, in relation to market size, leads us to the conclusion that the argument for restricting entry into telecommunications markets on the basis that 'natural monopoly' advantages would be forgone, is a highly esoteric one. More recently, the same authors (Baumol, Baumol and Willig, Bailey[6]) have concerned themselves with sustainability as such (rather than sustainable or non-sustainable 'natural' monopoly), and the importance of factors such as sunk costs, which prevent the incumbent's position being challenged. They argue that where sunk costs are *not* present then markets are 'contestable'. The ability for firms to enter if the incumbent raises prices in an attempt to exploit, prevents him doing so. Therefore, where markets *are* contestable, a policy of free entry is an effective influence on behaviour. The actual market structure which results may of course be competitive (in the sense that more than one firm produces), or oligopolistic. Here potential competition may be as effective an influence on the incumbent's behaviour as actual competition.

While the effects that sunk costs have are acknowledged, our interpretation of this analysis and the policy prescriptions which are made from it, is that not enough emphasis is placed on the effects of sunk costs as a protector of the incumbent's position, especially when, as in telecommunications, the incumbent starts with 100 per cent market share in both sustainable and potential non-sustainable markets. The practical problem for regulators is then devising policies which will actively encourage entry in the non-sustainable markets. Lifting a restriction on entry will not by itself guarantee that entry occurs or that potential entry is an effective discipline on behaviour.

We also feel that the theory takes insufficient note of the distribution of property rights in new technology. As we emphasise, technical change may benefit either the incumbent or the potential entrant. While the regulator cannot know in advance which way developments will go, he can take steps to ensure that the incumbent does not foreclose potential entry by acquisition of rights in competing technologies.

NOTES AND REFERENCES

1. *The Financial and Economic Obligations of the Nationalised Industries*, Cmnd 1337 (London: HMSO, 1961).
2. *Nationalised Industries; A Review of Economic and Financial Objectives*, Cmnd 3437 (London: HMSO, 1967).
3. *The Nationalised Industries*, Cmnd 7131 (London: HMSO, 1978).
4. A good recent example of this has been the arguments about performance indicators. These are widely accepted to be a way of defining social aims, and are advocated as, in principle, useful for 'control' of nationalised industries – that is for every case, to a lesser or greater degree. To us, a leading characteristic of performance indicators is that they represent ways to express external concerns about nationalised industries' performance. Around them, means to bring pressure to bear on nationalised industry Boards can be organised. This is fundamentally anti-Morrisonian. Yet the paradox is that it is in nationalised industries in which the Morrisonian model is still strong that performance indicators could feasibly be applied – and only in those. The industries under continual financial pressure certainly cannot be expected to pay more than lip service to performance indicators; and where they are fighting a tough financial battle, no one seriously expects them to do so. Financially secure industries will, predictably, add performance indicators to the Board's several means of justifying its social aims.
5. M. Beesley and S. Littlechild, 'Privatisation: Principles, Problems and Priorities', *Lloyds Bank Review*, no. 149 (July 1983) 1–20.
6. See, in particular: J. C. Panzar and R. D. Willig, 'Free Entry and the Sustainability of Natural Monopoly', *The Bell Journal of Economics*, vol. 8, no. 1 (Spring 1977) 1–22; W. J. Baumol, E. E. Bailey and R. D. Willig, 'Weak Invisible Hand Theorems on the Sustainability of Multiproduct Natural Monopoly', *The American Economic Review*, vol. 67, no. 3 (June 1977) 350–65; W. J. Baumol, 'Contestable Markets: An Uprising in the Theory of Industry Structure', *The American Economic Review*, vol. 72, no. 1 (March 1982) 1–15; W. J. Baumol and R. D. Willig, 'Fixed Costs, Sunk Costs, Entry Barriers, and Sustainability of Monopoly', *Quarterly Journal of Economics*, vol. 96 (1981) 405–31; E. E. Bailey, 'Contestability and the Design of Regulatory and Antitrust Policy', *American Economic Review Papers and Proceedings*, vol. 71, no. 2 (May 1981) 178–83.
7. Beesley and Littlechild, 'Privatisation', pp. 16–17, p. 11.
8. We have in mind here comparisons among peer groups, challenge from

different professions contributing to similar problems, exposure to media comparisons and criticisms, etc.

9. *A Review of Restrictive Trade Practices Policy*, Cmnd 7512 (London: HMSO, 1979); *Full-Line Forcing and Tie-in Sales*, HC 212 (London: HMSO, 1981).

10. See the chapter by Richardson and Dudley. They discuss the disadvantage in which sponsor Departments of nationalised industries are placed by lack of information and expertise *vis-à-vis* their industry. The same situation will affect the regulator's ability to adjudicate cases of predatory conduct unless the rules devised support him in this.

11. M. E. Beesley, *Liberalisation of the Use of British Telecommunications Network* (London: HMSO, 1981).

12. *The Future of Telecommunications in Britain*, Cmnd 8610 (London: HMSO, 1982).

13. See Beesley, *Liberalisation*, pp. 8–12, and pp. 40–2 for comparison of countries' liberality.

14. *Report of the Inquiry into Cable Expansion and Broadcasting Policy*, Cmnd 8679 (London: HMSO, 1982).

15. *The Development of Cable Systems and Services*, Cmnd 8866 (London: HMSO, 1983).

16. In response to a Parliamentary Question from Mr John Gorst, the Secretary of State announced the following criteria for 'VANS' on 16 Nov. 1981:

    > the criteria agreed with British Telecom are that in order to be licensed telecommunications services should add genuine additional value to the basic telecommunications network services by providing one or both of the following elements:
    >
    > (a) a significant storage of information, apparent to the user of the service;
    >
    > (b) processing of the information by the Value Added Network Services (VANS) operator such that the output information clearly and significantly differs from the input information in format, protocol and content.

17. British Telecommunications Act 1981. General Licence under Section 15(1) for Telecommunication Systems used in Providing Value Added Network Services (21 October 1982).

18. House of Commons Official Report, Standing Committee A, Telecommunications Bill, 17 November 1983 (morning).

19. Commons statement by Mr Baker, Minister for Information Technology, 7 February 1983.

20. Draft licence granted by the Secretary of State for Trade and Industry to British Telecommunications. Department of Trade and Industry, 25 October 1983.

21. The draft Bill to which we refer is: Telecommunications Bill, Ordered by the House of Commons to be printed 27 June 1983.

22. Telecommunications Bill, Clause 47.
23. Telecommunications Bill, Clauses 12 and 13.
24. Telecommunications Bill, Clause 3, subsection (1).
25. Telecommunications Bill, Clause 3, subsection (2).
26. Telecommunications Bill, Clause 82.
27. Commons Statement by Mr Cecil Parkinson, Secretary of State for Trade and Industry, 29 June 1983.

Part III
Methods and Techniques

8 Prices and Planning

RAY REES*

The purpose of this chapter is to examine, in the context of three major nationalised industries, the problems which arise in incorporating prices into the long-run planning process. I begin by setting out a simple theoretical model of the process, based on the standard economic analysis of pricing and investment decisions, and examine the role that prices play in this model. The model provides a framework within which to consider the actual planning processes of the three industries – electricity, coal and gas – in the next three sections. The final section then summarises the main conclusions on the ways in which prices have been treated in the planning processes of these industries.

A THEORETICAL MODEL

The model in this section sets out the economic approach to price and investment decision-taking in the form of a planning process. It will be presented in terms of a sequence of problems. Since the solution to the first step in the sequence – choice of demand forecasts – is not independent of that of the last-choice of prices, we are really looking at one phase of what ought to be an iterative procedure, through which, by trial and error, the solutions at each end of the sequence become mutually consistent.

(i) Demand Forecasts

The starting-point of the process is the derivation of a set of demand

* I am grateful to a number of economists in the nationalised industries who have helped me in preparation of this paper, and in particular to Terry Boley, Ted Denham, Rufus Godson, Colin Gronow, and Michael Parker. None of them of course, necessarily shares the views expressed here.

forecasts for the volume of each type of output the enterprise produces, in each time-period up to some specified time-horizon. Underlying these forecasts will be relationships between demand and its main determining variables. The latter are conventionally thought of as being of two kinds: exogenous variables, whose values are determined outside the enterprise; and endogenous variables, whose values will at some point have to be chosen by the enterprise. Examples of the former are consumers' disposable income, weather conditions, and the prices of close substitutes and complements to the output in question. Examples of the latter are the prices of the enterprise's own outputs, advertising and product quality. This conventional dichotomy is, however, inadequate because it conceals the problem of *strategic interdependence*, the fact that the values of some 'exogenous variables', in particular the prices of close substitutes, may be affected by choice of values of endogenous variables, primarily own output prices.

If strategic interdependence did *not* exist, demand forecasting could proceed by:

(a) making forecasts of the exogenous variables and inserting these into the demand relationships;
(b) making assumptions about the chosen values of the endogenous variables and inserting these into the demand relationships.

If there *is* significant strategic interdependence and competitors' reactions have to be taken into account, some estimate has to be made of the way in which the relevant 'exogenous' variables depend on choice of an endogenous variable: for example, the way in which a competitor will change his price and advertising choices in response to the enterprise's own choices.[1] The extent of strategic interdependence in the nationalised industry sector should not be underestimated. It exists between public and private enterprises selling in the same market, as for example in steel, and in air transport; and between different public enterprises, for example gas and electricity, rail and air transport.

Other major uncertainties can be classified into:

(a) *Uncertainties in the demand relationships* No demand relationship, however fully specified, can predict the value of demand with complete accuracy. There will always be 'random errors' which cause the actual demand value to deviate from that predicted. More seriously, there can be no guarantee that a specific relationship which has held on average in the past will continue to do so in the future, and this adds a further element of uncertainty.

(b) *Uncertain values of the exogenous variables* The future values of even the 'passively exogenous' variables – weather conditions, consumers' income, for example – cannot be predicted with certainty.

At best, then, any single set of demand forecasts must represent 'best-guesses' or 'most-probable' estimates. The question then arises of how this fact should be taken into account in decision-taking based on the demand forecasts.

The theoretical solution is in principle straightforward. A 'state of the world' is defined as a possible realisation of values of all the exogeneous variables and random factors which determine demand, in each future time-period. All possible states of the world are determined and the time-stream of demands corresponding to each state is set out. Any one decision – say a chosen set of prices and an investment plan – will have an outcome which will vary across states of the world. Attaching a probability to each state of the world allows the consequence of any one decision to be represented as a probability distribution of outcomes. Choice among alternative decisions is then made on the basis of an evaluation of these alternative probability distributions of outcomes.

The computational and informational requirements of this theoretical solution are likely to be so large in any practical context as to make its exact application infeasible. Nevertheless it has relevance as an 'ideal solution', and it is of interest to note that each of the industries we shall be examining has made some steps in this direction, in the form of 'scenario-planning'.

(ii) Input Prices

Assuming for the moment a single set of demand forecasts is adopted, these then become 'target outputs' in the remainder of the planning process, or at least in one iteration of it. The next stage is the determination of the input levels required to produce these outputs. The technological input–output relationships are forecast for each future period, and that combination of inputs is chosen that minimises the present value of the total cost of producing the target output stream. A cost of capital is required to discount the time-stream of production costs to a present value, and it is also necessary to forecast input prices in each period. The former may be taken, in the nationalised industry sector, as the Required Rate of Return (RRR) of 5 per cent though the RRR regime does allow industries some discretion in their choice of discount rate. 'Input prices' include wage rates, energy and raw material costs, and the cost of constructing new capacity.

Once again, there is necessarily uncertainty concerning the future values of input prices, and the optimal combination of inputs (including types of capital equipment) is likely to be quite sensitive to the input price forecasts – for example, nuclear v. conventional power. Input prices may be exogeneous to the enterprise – for example, the price of coal on the world market – or, again, there may be a problem of strategic interdependence which severely complicates forecasting. Many input prices are set by negotiation. This is the case, for example, in most labour markets in which the nationalised industries operate, and also in the supply of coal to the electricity industry and the gas industry's purchases of gas from the North Sea. Thus these prices will be the outcomes of a complex bargaining process. Moreover, there is the further difficulty that the values adopted in planning may themselves affect the parameters of the bargaining process, with implications for the outcome which cannot be predicted with certainty. For example, the coal price assumptions the electricity industry makes will determine the amount of coal-fired generating capacity it will have and, therefore, the extent of its future dependence on coal supplies and hence its bargaining power.

In addition, there is necessarily uncertainty concerning future technology: the input–output relationships which will hold in future periods cannot be predicted with certainty.[2] This, in conjunction with uncertainty in input costs, implies that it is in general not possible to speak of 'a cost-minimising input-combination'. Applying the state-of-the-world approach described earlier would show that a given choice of input levels, including scale and type of capital equipment, implies a probability distribution of costs. Choice again requires an evaluation of these alternative probability distributions.

In practice, it is often the case that input-planning proceeds as if the future were certain, with some *ad hoc* adjustments, or crude sensitivity analyses, added on at the end. Again, however, we can regard scenario-planning as an attempt to move away from this unrealistic approach.

(iii) Pricing Policy

Setting uncertainty to one side for the moment, the choice of future input combinations, in conjunction with forecasts of future input prices, will provide estimates of future total costs. Thus we have:

(a) the assumed future output prices underlying the demand forecasts;
(b) the forecast future output levels;
(c) the estimated future costs,

which together imply a future time-stream of profits or losses. The implicit assumption in the discussion so far is that the initial set of prices in (a) is more or less arbitrary, but this now has to be reconsidered. Any enterprise, and nationalised industries are no exception, will have objectives, and will be faced with constraints, which will imply a set of principles or criteria on the basis of which prices will be chosen. These principles or criteria then constitute a 'pricing policy'.

The main constraints which nationalised industries face are, first, in the short run, the external financing limit (EFL) and, in the medium term, the financial target. Since the EFL in general is set for just one year ahead, it is not of primary importance in relation to long-term planning,[3] and so the main constraint will be the financial target. An additional complication is that the period over which a specific target applies – in general, three to five years – is shorter than the time-horizon over which the implications of plans are assessed, which for the electricity industry, for example, may be thirty years.

There are well-known complexities concerning the objectives of nationalised industries and their relation to pricing policy. Let us suppose first that the objective is 'economic' efficiency (in the sense of an efficient allocation of the nation's resources between different uses), and that it is appropriate to regard this as implying a marginal cost pricing policy.[4] Though apparently highly 'theoretical', this supposition is in fact directly relevant for two of the three industries we shall shortly be considering. We then have to consider whether the plan as so far formulated is consistent with marginal cost pricing. For this we have to estimate marginal costs, and so we proceed as follows. In each future time-period, for each output, the plan specifies a price and an output, and we have also determined, in stage (ii) above, the cost-minimising input combination. We then calculate, for any one output in any one period, the change in the present value of total costs which would result from a small increase in that output. In a very simple system that change in cost may arise *only* in the period in which the output will be produced, but in more realistic systems there will be cost repercussions in other periods also, hence the formulation in terms of 'present value of total costs'. It is then a matter of arithmetic to translate this *present value* marginal cost into a *current value* marginal cost, by applying the appropriate compound interest factor. This gives the marginal cost of the relevant ouput in the relevant period. If then the initially assumed price for that output in that period is not equal to this marginal cost, we do not have marginal cost pricing. To achieve a marginal cost pricing structure, we would have to iterate through the process, beginning with prices, deriving output forecasts and associated minimised costs, then comparing prices to the estimated increments in these costs following small changes in the outputs, then readjusting prices, until we converge on a set of prices which equals marginal costs at the output levels implied by those prices.

In reality we know that allocative efficiency is not the only aspect of nationalised industry plans which is of interest to government and the industries themselves. The 'marginal cost pricing solution' just described will itself imply a time-stream of profits or losses, and a pattern of growth or decline in outputs, capacity and employment in the industry. The other implication of economic efficiency – cost-minimisation – will also determine the mix of inputs, not only as between broad categories such as capital and labour, but also within categories – for example the composition of electricity generating capacity as between nuclear, coal and gas turbine plant. We can therefore interpret the departures which may be made in nationalised industry planning, away from the plan which would be implied by economic efficiency alone, as providing evidence of the nature of and emphasis upon other objectives.

To conclude this discussion of pricing policy we reintroduce the question of uncertainty. Since future technology and input prices are uncertain, so are future total and marginal costs. How can we define 'marginal cost pricing' in that case? To pursue that question in general terms would lead us far afield.[5] The practicable, though theoretically imperfect, solution would be to work in terms of expected values, or most probable values,[6] of all the relevant variables, and to treat these *as if* they were certain. This embodies a particular attitude to risk which, though rather special, may be not too inappropriate as a first approximation.[7]

ELECTRICITY

Demand Forecasting

Procedurally, demand forecasting in the electricity industry reflects its organisational structure. On the basis of an agreed set of assumptions, the three sectors of the industry, the Electricity Council, CEGB and Area Board, produce forecasts of demand in the seventh year ahead. These forecasts will not usually be identical. A committee then chooses a single estimate which becomes the 'adopted forecast', for planning purposes. Forecasts are initially derived for sub-groups of consumers – domestic, industrial and commercial. For the first sub-group, consumer durable ownership, consumers' expenditure, energy prices and housing stock composition are regarded as the main determining variables of demand (under average weather conditions). For industrial demand the main determining variable is industrial production, disaggregated by industry group, and price is seen as relatively insignificant. The procedure for the third group is unclear: the Monopolies and Mergers Commission 1981 Report (para. 4.13, p. 43) states, 'the CEGB uses various methodologies, and takes for its forecast the result which it thinks most likely'.[8]

The overall demand for electricity is not seen as being very responsive to price. The CEGB believes the elasticity of total demand with respect to the price of electricity relative to other fuel prices to be 0.1. The systematic tendency to over-forecasting demand described by the Monopolies and Mergers Commission Report (p. 48) is essentially due to overestimates of GDP growth, which led to overestimation of total energy growth. Relatively little was due to incorrect estimation of electricity's share of the energy market, and therefore to incorrect price forecasts. It would therefore appear that in the overall planning process output prices need not play a major role.[9]

The adoption of a single forecast or 'point estimate' of future demand would appear to rule out any consideration of uncertainty. The impossibility in fact of treating the future as perfectly known, however, reasserts itself in two ways. In its investment planning, the CEGB adopts for the long term a 'scenario approach', more fully discussed below. In addition, when deciding on its total required capacity in the year for which the 'adopted forecast' is made, a 'planning margin' is added. This is the margin of capacity added to that required to meet the adopted forecast, as an insurance premium against demand being greater or plant availability lower than is probable. Though the calculations underlying this margin are, from the engineering and statistical viewpoints, quite sophisticated, from an economic standpoint they are extremely crude. An 'engineering judgement' is made on the probability with which power cuts and voltage reductions should be made, without any attempt to weigh up the costs and benefits to consumers of particular degrees of supply reliability. In addition no account is taken of the possibility of using pricing policy to economise on the planning margin.[10] The outside observer is left with a strong impression that the planning margin is currently as high as it is – at 28 per cent of total capacity – largely because past overestimation of demand and consequent overinvestment has resulted in this order of magnitude of spare capacity of quite modern and low-cost generating plant. Reduction of the planning margin would of course further postpone the date when capacity expansion would be required.

Marginal Cost Pricing

The system simulation which underlies the calculation of net effective costs (NECs) for different plant types also provides estimates of marginal costs, consisting of the operating costs of the plant supplying the marginal output at a particular point in the demand cycle, plus the NEC of the type of capacity which would be increased to meet an increment of demand at that time. The Bulk Supply Tariff (BST) at which the CEGB sells electricity to the Area Boards is explicitly designed to be a marginal-cost-based tariff. It can be questioned whether it is in fact one, when short-run price-setting is considered,[11] but in long-run planning, consistency between assumed prices in the BST and marginal costs appears to be achieved. Moreover, the profit stream *implied* by the marginal-cost-based BST seems to be accepted – no attempt is made to extrapolate a different profit requirement for the long term.

The main qualification concerning the economic efficiency of the pricing policy for electricity, even in the long run, is that the fairly sophisticated marginal cost 'message' transmitted by the BST is not actually brought home to consumers at their point of consumption, and therefore it is not at all clear that it can really be claimed that electricity prices do reflect marginal costs. Domestic consumers pay a price which does not vary with time of day or year, unless they choose to go onto a 'White Meter' tariff, which gives a lower rate for night-time consumption. But this is still a very crude reflection of the way in which marginal costs vary through the daily and yearly demand cycles. The response of the industry to this criticism has been (a) to point out the high costs of metering that a more sophisticated retail tariff structure would require, and (b) to express scepticism that consumers would be able or willing to react to more complex tariff structures. However, recent technological developments in metering technology are providing a challenge to the first of these responses, and tariff experiments currently being undertaken with domestic consumers may suggest that the scepticism is unfounded.[12]

COAL

Demand Forecasts

Demand forecasts for five years ahead are prepared annually for the Medium Term Development Plans (MTDPs), which are submitted to government as the basis for the NCB investment programme. In addition there have been a number of major planning exercises, the most recent of which was in connection with the Development Plan to 1990, produced in 1981. The latter was quite a sophisticated exercise, involving predictions of total energy consumption disaggregated into domestic, transport, iron and steel, and nine other industrial sectors. The share of each energy source – coal, gas, electricity and oil – in each of these sub-markets was then estimated, and the demand for electricity further translated into primary fuel demand, much of which is for coal. The result is a set of demand forecasts for coal broken down into its major sub-markets: electricity, iron and steel (coking coal), other industrial and domestic. The main independent variables used in deriving these forecasts were GDP, energy prices, and the contribution of nuclear energy. The NCB bases its oil price forecasts on estimates from outside sources, such as the Department of Energy and oil companies, and regards gas prices as broadly linked to oil prices. The main point of interest is that forecast prices of coal in the UK are based upon the delivered price of imported coal, i.e. the 'world price' plus transport costs, with the world price being taken as the dollar price of coal delivered at Antwerp, Rotterdam and Amsterdam ('ARA', the normal basis for the price of coal imports into Europe). Thus, in its demand forecasts, the NCB appears to adopt the 'theoretically correct' procedure[13] of taking the price of coal in the UK as equal to the world price. This then requires the NCB to forecast future spot prices on the ARA market and the sterling/dollar exchange rate.

Uncertainty is taken into account through a simple form of scenario-planning. Given that the basic demand forecasts are derived for a 'most probable' or 'central' case – i.e. a conjunction of the subjectively most probable values of the independent variables – alternative scenarios are generated mainly by varying the assumptions on GDP growth and oil prices. The four possibilities stemming from combining 'high' and 'low' GDP growth with 'high' and 'low' oil prices have been examined.[14] As a result, demand forecasts are presented not as single point estimates but rather in terms of a range of possibilities. For example, the demand for coal in 1985 was estimated in 1982 as likely to lie in the range 114–121 m.t., and in 2000, to lie within the range 113–142 m.t. No information is given about the respective probabilities of the values within these ranges – for example, whether they are all equiprobable or whether they are, say, 95 per cent confidence intervals about a most likely central estimate. Clearly, however, the extent of the uncertainty is taken to increase, the further in the future the year of the forecast.

The MMC concluded that the NCB's forecasting record was reasonably good under the circumstances. Its over-forecasting of the demand for coking coal was due essentially to over-optimistic expansion plans of its major consumer, the British Steel Corporation. The remainder of its output forecasts had been reasonably accurate, if only because of offsetting errors (which is probably the best any forecaster can hope for). Moreover, the NCB's current forecasts of future demand accord quite well with those of outside forecasters, though this is in large part because the range of demand estimates is so wide as to encompass any reasonable forecast. The important question concerns the *output* level to which the NCB's capacity planning is geared. This is best regarded as part of the general topic of 'input choice', to which we now turn.

Pricing Policy for Coal

In terms of the standard static criteria of economic efficiency, the appropriate pricing and investment policy for coal has the following elements:

(1) the price of coal for domestic consumption should be set at the world price;
(2) coal production capacity should be set at the level at which unit costs at the marginal colliery in operation are just about equal to the world price, where these units costs should be economic or opportunity costs and not simply accounting costs;
(3) any excess of consumption over production should be met by imports; any excess of production over consumption should be exported.

The NCB uses the world price to forecast future demand, but does not appear to do so to determine capacity. It appears to be planning to meet the entire demand out of domestic production, even though this would seem to imply a substantial margin of capacity at which unit costs exceed the world price. Moreover, it is not at all clear that the NCB will actually *charge* the world price on its total production. Where it faces competition from imports it is likely to do so, but in parts of its market where import competition is unlikely, or where it is shielded by import restrictions, the need to meet its financial obligations leads it to charge more than the world price. But this then is inconsistent with its demand forecasting. Perception of this led the MMC to recommend that 'in its planning the NCB should investigate the consequences for its sales of varying the price of its product relative to world market prices'.

The central problem for the NCB is, of course, the rate at which it can eliminate the 'long tail' of excess capacity. However, the appropriate definition of excess capacity is *not* as that set of collieries currently making accounting losses, but rather that set of collieries whose marginal opportunity costs exceed the world price of coal. This latter definition may or may not be more stringent than the former, but it is the one implied by criteria of efficient resource allocation. The NCB explicitly rejects the suggestion that it is pursuing an objective of maintaining output regardless of the implications for profitability,[15] and emphasises its concern to 'achieve break-even on revenue account'. However, there are constraints on the rate of pit closure which, it must be recognised, create a 'second-best' situation, with implications for pricing policy. The elements of such a policy are as follows:

(1) a realistic projection should be made of capacity output, *given* the maximum feasible rate at which excess capacity can be eliminated;
(2) the setting of the domestic price of coal at the world price, and the exporting of any excess of production over demand at this price.

These principles of course imply that NCB revenue is unlikely to cover its accounting costs. However, since the bulk of its output is sold to other nationalised industries, it is both pointless and inefficient for the NCB to distort the cost messages it gives in its prices, to achieve a transfer of revenues from one set of public sector accounts to another.

GAS

Planning and forecasting in the gas industry is, in the first place, a 'bottom-up' process. Each of the twelve regions prepares a 1-year budget and 5–7 year medium-term plan, incorporating not only forecasts of gas sales but also appliance sales and customer service. The centre supplies general macro-economic assumptions, and a forecast of gas prices relative to other fuels. Each region then adapts these to itself. Forecasts are decomposed by markets, again into domestic, industrial and commercial. In forecasting, the regions use their local knowledge of demand patterns and likely developments in housing, industrial location, etc.

Uncertainty is handled at the regional level by requiring not only a central estimate but also upper and lower limits to forecast. These are provided on two bases: (i) that the assumptions given by the centre are correct; (ii) for stated variations in the given assumptions. The centre has then to reconcile these forecasts, and in particular to eliminate 'double-counting' – given industrial development being 'claimed' by two or more areas – and to see that a reasonable aggregate picture emerges. There appear to be no systematic biases in sales forecasting overall, which has been quite accurate, with perhaps some over-forecasting of industrial sales. There is, however, a tendency for 'multi-stage appraisal optimism', i.e. for optimistic margins to be added at each stage of the planning process. A region's past forecasting performance is taken into account when appraising its forecasts centrally. The process following submission of the regional forecasts is essentially a dialogue between the regions and the centre. The outcome of this is again a single 'adopted forecast' for the industry as a whole.

The industrial market for gas is highly price-sensitive, since the main concern is with the cost per thermal unit of heat supplied, and gas is in competition with oil and coal. The so-called 'premium' markets, largely domestic and commercial consumers together with some industrial buyers from whom the controllability, cleanliness and low handling costs of gas are particularly important, are, however, regarded as much less price-sensitive, particularly at existing levels of fuel prices. For example, the recent price increases to domestic consumers of roughly 30 per cent over three years are thought to have had virtually no impact on their demand for gas. Again, therefore, the main determining variables in the premium market are consumer durable ownership, consumers' expenditure, and industrial production in the relevant industry groups.

The relevant price in the bulk industrial fuel market is the future oil price, since this determines the competitive level the gas industry has to meet. An important part of the forecasting effort is therefore devoted to future dollar oil prices and the sterling/dollar exchange rate. Here a 'scenario-planning' approach is adopted, with scenarios ranging from total collapse of OPEC and consequently low world oil prices, to resumed high growth of oil demand at pre-1973 rates. The aim is to derive a series of point estimates of the future prices which can be achieved in the industrial sector, together with a judgement of the risk of variations around these levels.

The BGC is in a very different position to that of the electricity and coal industries in respect of its basic product, in that it is essentially a trader or middleman; it buys gas from the North Sea suppliers and transports it through its distribution network to final consumers. Its distribution costs are relatively well defined and predictable, and so its main planning problem is to relate the prices and quantities of the gas it undertakes to buy on long-term contracts, to the prices and quantities of gas it will be able to sell in future. Thus its demand forecasts are not concerned so much with capacity planning (though of course there will be investment in distribution systems and service facilities for which they are important), as with determining the scale and terms of contractual commitments for future supplies of gas. For this reason decision-taking is very much the exercise of commercial judgement. The BGC uses its demand and price forecasts to decide on the set of supply commitments into which it can enter, such that it has a very high probability (90 per cent was the figure cited to me) of being able to sell the resulting quantities of gas at prices which allow it to meet its financial objectives.

Pricing Policy for Gas

Economic efficiency in gas pricing requires that the price of gas sold on the industrial market be equal to the world price of industrial fuel oil, in terms of thermal content, and that the price to consumers in other markets, net of distribution costs, also be set at this level. Capacity of gas production should be at the level at which the long-run marginal cost of gas (including an allowance for the cost of ultimate exhaustion of reserves) is about equal to the world fuel oil price.[16] As a result of recent sharp increases in prices to domestic consumers, these conditions seem broadly to be satisfied. Again, therefore, the theoretical model seems to find a counterpart in reality, given that the marginal cost of gas is determined by the cost of new supplies from the North Sea, at least over the current planning period.

CONCLUSIONS

In the nationalised industries in general, and the three energy industries considered here in particular, the long-run planning process is complex and confronted with considerable uncertainty. The three industries have developed planning procedures which I would regard as basically adequate for the problem, with one important qualification, the treatment of uncertainty. The crude kind of sensitivity analysis used throughout the 1970s by all three industries has been quite rightly criticised by the MMC, among others, and it is encouraging to see the development of 'scenario-planning', implying the consideration of a fuller set of states-of-the-world, than has hitherto been the case. There are still limitations, of course. The fact that only relatively few states-of-the-world are selected for explicit consideration implies that they may still be drawn from the optimistic end of the spectrum. There is also the more fundamental issue: scenario-planning simply *describes* the nature of the uncertainty which confronts a decision, by giving a small number of points on the overall distribution of outcomes. This still leaves the problem of *evaluation*: exactly how are the risks involved in public sector decisions to be assessed?

It is not, I think, unfair to describe what actually happens in terms of risk evaluation in the following way. The planners in the industry form a view on the decision which they think is the correct one.[17] This will be based in part on objective analysis, but will also be strongly influenced by subjective judgement and, quite probably, the 'internal objectives' of the industry. The analysis of sensitivities, or the more sophisticated consideration of scenarios, tends to be viewed as a means of testing or demonstrating the 'robustness' of the preferred decision to changes in the assumptions. It plays a role in the process of advocacy and debate, at the end of which the decision will be validated and resources committed, or not, as the case may be. It is probably the case that wide scope for the subjective judgement of industry management must always exist: the idea of an objective set of 'decision rules' or techniques for choices under risk, which could be imposed upon managers, is a chimera. The problem is that history has shown the structure of incentives and control in the nationalised industries to be such that very wasteful investment expenditures can be made. The central problem, is, then, to reconcile the necessary degree of managerial judgement which must exist in the face of uncertainty, with the avoidance of decisions which, from the point of view of the public interest, turn out to be costly mistakes. Scenario-planning is a small but useful step toward the solution of this problem.

NOTES AND REFERENCES

1. In the literature of oligopoly theory, these would be known as 'conjectural variations'.
2. In fact, there may well be strategic interdependence creating uncertainty in these estimates. For example, labour productivity in future will depend on the outcome of negotiations on manning levels.
3. Except in so far as it may inhibit investment expenditure in the year in question. But this expenditure will have been largely determined by *past* plans, and is hardly affected by the plan being formulated. Some view, of course, must be taken of how a future EFL will affect the latter. The assumption in practice seems to be that this effect will be negligible provided the plan is consistent with the medium-term financial target, though here we have yet another source of uncertainty.
4. In other words, there are no problems of the 'second-best' and we ignore for the moment the existence of financial targets.
5. The interested reader could consult Chapter 10, and the references cited there, of R. Rees, *Public Enterprise Economics*, 2nd edn (London: Weidenfeld & Nicolson, 1984).
6. The 'expected value' of a probability distribution is its mean. The most probable value is its mode. For distributions such as the normal (Gaussian) distribution these will coincide, but quite plausible distributions could exist for which they are different. My impression is that, in practice, decision-makers tend to focus upon the most probable values, i.e. the modes, of the distributions with which they are confronted.
7. There is a growing literature on the circumstances under which this attitude to risk, which could be described as 'risk-neutrality', is

appropriate for public sector decision-takers. See, for example, K. J. Arrow and R. C. Lind, 'Uncertainty and the Evaluation of Investment Decisions', *American Economic Review*, vol. 60 (1970); L. P. Foldes and R. Rees, 'A Note on the Arrow–Lind Theorem', *American Economic Review* (1977); R. Wilson, 'Risk Measurement of Public Projects', in R. C. Lind (ed.), *Discounting for Time and Risk in Energy Supply* (Washington DC: Resources for the Future Inc., 1982).

8. Monopolies and Mergers Commission, *Report on the Central Electricity Generating Board*, HC 315 (London: HMSO, 1981).

9. This very low price elasticity of demand seems to make economists' perennial concern with electricity pricing policy largely academic. Significant variations in price have negligible influence on output and resource allocation, and electricity prices would make excellent tax instruments. There are several arguments against a too-ready acceptance of this view. One rests on the well-known difficulties of obtaining reliable estimates of long-run price elasticities from time-series analysis. Another is that even if aggregate demand is relatively inelastic, there are still important issues concerning the structure of prices, across times of day and different groups of consumers, which are important for resource allocation. Finally, the low elasticity may reflect the crudeness of the current tariff structure as it confronts final consumers, which gives consumers little incentive or opportunity to reveal their responsiveness to price.

10. These points are discussed at much greater length in Rees, *Public Enterprise Economics*, ch. 10.

11. For further discussion of this, see R. Rees, 'Energy Pricing', *Public Money*, March 1983.

12. For a discussion of the technology involved and its possibilities, see R. A. Peddie, G. Frewer and A. Goulcher, 'The Application of Economic Theory Utilising New Technology for the Benefit of the Consumer', South Eastern Electricity Board, May 1983.

13. For a fuller discussion of this, see R. Rees, 'On Investment in Coal Production' (unpublished, 1983); and Rees, *Public Enterprise Economics*, ch. 60.

14. For fuller discussion, see Monopolies and Mergers Commission, *Report on the National Coal Board*, Cmnd 8920 (London: HMSO, 1983) on which much of this discussion has been based.

15. See National Coal Board, 'Response to the Monopolies and Mergers Report' (unpublished, 1983) para. 1.

16. For the arguments underlying these propositions, see R. Rees, 'Energy Pricing', *Public Money*, March 1983; and Rees, *Public Enterprise Economics*.

17. For example, there is no doubt that the weight of opinion within the CEGB is in favour of a nuclear reactor at Sizewell, because they sincerely believe this to be the 'right' decision.

9 The Role of Forecasting

K. J. WIGLEY*

This chapter discusses relationships between forecasting, strategic planning and decision-taking. No attempt has been made to provide a detailed catalogue of alternative forecasting techniques as this is a subject which already has a substantial literature. However, a number of different approaches to forecasting are discussed and reference is made to experience gained in preparing Energy Projections 1982, included as an Annex to the Department's Proof of Evidence to the Sizewell 'B' Inquiry.[1] Forecasting methods used in the nationalised gas and electricity industries have been described recently by F. K. Lyness,[2] and J. M. W. Rhys.[3]

It is clear that any attempt to forecast the future is a hazardous business. Few forecasts turn out to be correct. In the light of this uncertainty it is tempting to argue that forecasting is a waste of time. In this chapter it is argued that the preparation of alternative forecasts, or projections, which span the range of possible future outcomes, is an essential ingredient of strategic decision-making and planning.

STATISTICAL AND ECONOMETRIC FORECASTS

A forecasting method frequently employed expresses, say, the demand for a product, in terms of economic variables such as the level of economic activity and product price. Such relationships can be estimated statistically and give rise to residual (or unexplained) errors in comparing actual with estimated values for past data, but these are usually small.

This approach is illustrative of a whole class of statistical or

* The views expressed in this paper are those of the author and do not necessarily represent the official view of the Department of Energy.

econometric relationships used in forecasting exercises. The number of explanatory variables may be modified or increased to accommodate the major factors believed to be relevant. The structure may be extended to provide for lagged responses to, or anticipations of, explanatory variables. They may be explicitly derived as a reduced form from more-complex models of interacting supply and demand relationships, or from more basic models of decision behaviour such as the maximisation of a consumer utility function subject to a budget constraint. Such relationships may need to be estimated as one of a set, as in the last example quoted, or because the situation involves a number of like, but distinct, products in competition for a given end-use – for example, individual fuels for heating.

The error term in this type of analysis may be assumed to be independently and normally distributed with zero mean, as for least squares regression, or to have a more complex structure arising from the derivation of the model or from problems arising at the estimation stage. In any event the form of the error term is at least as important as the specification of the structure of the relationship and will determine the method employed for estimating the coefficients.

Forecasting methods using time as the sole explanatory variable, although of use in short-term forecasting, are likely to have only limited application in strategic planning. While this may well apply to key variables such as product demand, these models may be applicable in the longer term to technological coefficients, market shares or relationships employing sigmoid curves for variables tending towards expected upper or lower limits – for example, where saturation levels are anticipated.

In any event, all these forecasting methods are likely to yield alternative forecasts for the following reasons:

(1) For given future values of the explanatory variables a forecast will be subject to an error whose variance may in general be estimated and will increase the further ahead the forecast is made.

(2) Alternative assumptions for the explanatory variables yield different forecasts for a given relationship.

(3) There may be several forecasting relationships with acceptable properties and goodness of fit to the available data which

provide different forecasts for the same values of explanatory variables.

Forecasters, planners and decision-makers need to be aware of the existence of these alternative forecasts and to recognise and take account of the range of forecasts implied.

STRUCTURAL FORECASTS

In many circumstances – for example, where major new investments in an industry are envisaged – it is possible to combine forecasting methods as described in the previous section with simulation calculations for the industry concerned. This process has been used in preparing Energy Projections 1982.

In this exercise, econometric relationships for energy demand for each fuel in a number of consuming sectors have been combined in a single computational framework with a time-phased linear programme of the public electricity supply system in England and Wales which minimises the present discounted value of the capital and operating costs of the system over the planning horizon. This process has been used to prepare eight projections of UK energy demand and electricity supply for alternative assumptions of UK GDP, world fossil-fuel prices and UK industrial structure. In this way statistical and simulation methods have been combined in providing alternative views of the future. This approach is similar in form to the theoretical model described in Professor Rees's chapter in this volume.

TECHNOLOGICAL FORECASTS

As an alternative to statistical or econometric methods, forecasts of product demand are sometimes attempted by building up from highly detailed descriptions of end-use patterns, taking account of possible or likely future technological developments (or possible government measures) and their rates of take-up. Examples are to be found in Bush and Matthews,[4] and Leach *et al*.[5]

It is clear that these studies provide invaluable insights into past and current processes of change. However, experience with these methods indicates that it is extremely difficult to assess the economic attractiveness of new developments for those who must take the decisions to implement them, the effects on that attractiveness of variations in underlying assumptions, the rate of take-up of attractive options or the likelihood of future new developments.

While these technological methods raise considerable difficulties in producing forecasts they can, nevertheless, prove extremely useful in supporting or complementing forecasting exercises using statistical methods.

FORECASTS, PROJECTIONS AND SCENARIOS

A set of projections can be prepared by combining statistical forecasting methods with a simulation model and alternative underlying economic assumptions. The numerical links in such an exercise are well defined and transparent in producing a number of consistent views of the future.

As alternative approach using scenarios has been described in a series of papers by Beck. In a recent example, Beck defines a scenario – as used in Shell – as 'a description of one of a number of possible futures in which the assumptions about social, political, economic and technological developments are all consistent with each other. It is not just one of a number of forecasts.'[6] A similar description of scenarios is provided by Professor Taylor in his chapter in this volume, along with further references.

It appears that a set of projections as described above may lack the degree of social, political and technological supporting explanation included in a set of scenarios. On the other hand it is not clear how consistency between the many elements in a scenario is achieved. What role has statistical inference from available data and explicit simulation modelling to play in the construction of consistent scenarios?

It is likely that orthodox forecasters and scenario builders have something to learn from each other. Thus forecasters may need to provide more justification for the ranges and combinations of exogenous assumptions they adopt and to discuss the wider implications of their results. On the other hand the consistency of scenarios may need to be justified in quantitative terms and the paths explained between the current situation and the alternative scenarios presented. Both groups, if they are indeed distinct, need to provide some justification that they have covered *all* the main dimensions of uncertainty affecting the issue in question.

FORECASTS, SCENARIOS AND DECISIONS

Beck[6] contrasts two different approaches to decision-taking:

(1) The application of decision theory as a cornerstone of management science in which a rational decision-maker decides on the objective function he wishes to optimise; he collects all the data relevant to the decision, determines which option optimises the chosen function and the decision makes itself. He adds that developments of the theory allow for uncertainty by optimising the 'expected value' of the objective function. (He might have added that allowance can be made for decision-makers' attitudes to risk-taking by considering the degree of risk preference held by the decision-maker.)

(2) The view that decisions are essentially based on the judgement of the decision-taker and that the scientific method of decision-taking has little to contribute. Senior managers can inform their understanding of their environment, find it easier to accept uncertainty as a normal way of life and perhaps begin to think the 'unthinkable' by taking part in debates based on a selected number of scenarios (as defined above).

The description of scientific decision-making at (1) above (also see Brown, Katir and Peterson,[7] and Stanford Research Institute[8]) is an idealised one constructed for didactic or analytical purposes. Even in this idealised description the decision-maker must supply judgements on the criterion of choice, the subjective probabilities to be attached to alternative possible futures, attitudes to risk-taking and possibly the range of alternative futures to be considered. In real life these issues are seldom formalised although the elements are usually present in implicit form in the decision-making process. Where the results of forecasting or simulation exercises are provided as supporting material to decision-makers the results of similar exercises carried out by independent bodies are also frequently considered.

An essential question is whether analytical work such as forecasting or simulation exercises can usefully augment the judgements which must be made by decision-takers, especially if these are informed by the debates described by Beck. If the results of forecasts or simulation studies are utilised in achieving consistency within individual scenarios, then the issue reduces to the manner in which these results are presented to decision-makers.

To be specific, consider a simple decision problem which has the alternative options and outcomes as set out in Table 9.1.

TABLE 9.1   *A simple decision problem*

	Alternative possible outcomes		*Expected value of outcome*
	X	*Y*	
Alternative (A)	−2000	+5000	2900
Choice	± 30%	± 30%	
Options			
(B)	+1000	−200	160
	± 20%	± 20%	

Probability of outcome	0.3	0.7

In this problem two options are available, (A) and (B). Two possible future states-of-the-world are identified, *X* and *Y*, which may be thought of as defined by two sections of the ranges of main assumptions which underlie the forecasting model employed. If the future turns out to be *X*, then option (A) will involve a loss of 2,000 units and (B) a gain of 1,000; if *Y* results, then option (A) yields a gain of 5,000 units and (B) a loss of 200. As indicated, these losses and gains appear to be estimated with a larger error for option (A) than for option (B). The probabilities of states-of-the-world occurring are thought to be 0.3 for *X* and 0.7 for *Y*.

The 'expected value' of option (A) is 2,900 units, and for option (B) is calculated as 160. Thus, on this criterion, option (A) gives the best choice. However, there remains a definite risk for either decision turning out to be 'wrong', in the sense that losses could be incurred with either option if an adverse future occurs. The potential loss for option (A) is ten times greater than that for option (B) and is more uncertain. A risk-averse decision-taker may well choose option (B) in the knowledge that it has a lower expected value because it minimises the potential loss. When considering the problem, the decision-taker has to be satisfied that no other options or possible outcomes need to be considered, that the forecasting and other analytical work used in calculating the outcomes is satisfactory, and that the probabilities of the outcomes are acceptable to him.

Although a good deal of sophisticated forecasting and analytical work may have been involved in preparing the material in Table 9.1, a substantial element of judgement is necessary on the part of the decision-maker in reaching his decision. In practice the problem will usually be more complex than that illustrated in this example, involving sequences of decisions and alternative outcomes. Methods are available, using decision trees, for analysing such problems. Inevitably the associated analytical work becomes increasingly complex.

In the view of the author, analytical work is unlikely to reduce significantly the essential uncertainty attaching to the future and may even widen current perception of it. Analytical work can, however, provide a quantitative framework within which attitudes to uncertain future factors may be more easily expressed and combined. This represents a positive and important contribution to decision-making. Whether the results of such work are presented as a 'set of projections' or as a number of 'scenarios' becomes a matter of doubtful distinction.

The role of analytical work in forecasting was considered recently by Sir John Mason in his Presidential Address to the 1983 meeting of the British Association for the Advancement of Science.[9] In his introduction, Sir John stated, 'As scientists we would probably agree that major policy decisions should be based as far as possible on rational analyses of the facts and objective predictions rather than on intuitive and subjective judgements.' It is argued in this chapter that subjective judgements and analytical work do need to be brought together in making decisions. Sir John went on, later in his paper, to say that, 'No extrapolation of past trends, nor any theory or model based on past experience, could have given warning of the dramatic rise in oil prices in 1973 or, for that matter, of the hot summer of 1976 – the hottest in 250 years.' Clearly the timing or extent of either of these events would have been impossible to predict with any degree of accuracy. However, at the risk of an element of hindsight, the effects of such events as these, favourable or unfavourable, can and should be considered in current decision-taking, together with some attempt to assess the probability of their occurrence.

Unless decisions are to be based on the toss of a coin they will require forecasts of the possible future outcomes of alternative options. These forecasts may be supported by analytical work of a greater or lesser degree of sophistication. Judgements are still required to the extent that lessons from the past may be applied to the future. In any event, a thorough analysis of the past provides an important input into those judgements.

SOURCES OF ERROR IN FORECASTING

There are many pitfalls in preparing forecasts. In some cases these arise because in practice the structure of forecasting relationships has to be tailored to the data available which is seldom of adequate quality or coverage. In other cases the factors affecting the variables to be forecast are not properly understood and the structure of the relationships mis-specified.

A major factor affecting forecasting error is the accuracy with which future values of the explanatory variables are known. Many forecasts require a future estimate to be made of economic activity such as gross domestic product. In analysing the past over-prediction of demand in the electricity industry through the 1970s, Boley[10] stresses the importance of the over-estimate of future economic growth – resulting from taking the view commonly accepted by most people at the time – as the most important determining factor.

The reaction to such experience should not be to adopt a correspondingly pessimistic view of economic growth in the future, but to seek a balanced range of assumptions for what are believed to be the determining factors of the forecast variables and for the mechanisms linking them.

FORECASTING AND STRATEGIC PLANNING

Ideally a strategic plan should identify objectives for the organisation concerned, set out alternative assumptions about the future,
analyse the effects on the organisation (and where appropriate on
the assumptions themselves) of alternative strategies under the
various assumptions, and thereby arrive at the key considerations in
deciding a 'preferred' strategy.

For a commercial organisation this means identifying alternative
paths for exogenous key factors such as the general level of
economic activity, prices of inputs, actions of competitors, attitudes
of the labour force, government legislation, etc., and preparing
forecasts of product prices, sales, revenues, costs, production,
investment, plant retirements, new ventures, sources of finance, R
& D, and so on. For each combination of assumptions the plan
would ideally need to prepare the revenue, capital and flow of funds
accounts for each of a number of years ahead over the planning
horizon and consider the effects on these accounts, of alternative
assumptions, and ways of accommodating the consequences.

The results of such an analysis should lead to indicative lines of
decision. For example, the investment in productive capacity might
consider the trade-off between the flexibility of a mix of smaller and
varied types of plant and the returns to scale of larger plant of
similar types with series ordering. It might also consider such major
issues as the future scale of the organisation relative to its
competitors, possible diversification, etc.

The world is not ideal, and strategic planning documents seldom
reach such an advanced stage of development. Even a less-
comprehensive document, if made public, would place either a
private company or a nationalised industry in an adverse commercial position with respect to its competitors or suppliers. It is
understandable therefore that published versions of corporate or
strategic plans fall well short of the ideal.

Nevertheless, the information listed above is likely to be required
by the bankers or large investors financing a major private sector
company or by a government department for a nationalised
industry, on a commercial-in-confidence basis. Nationalised industries draw on forecasts prepared in their regional organisations, at
their headquarters and by outside bodies. They use a variety of
techniques for preparing their forecasts. In addition, banks, major

investors and government departments will generally have their own forecasts and use their own judgements in considering the strategic plans of the organisations they are financing or for which they have a responsibility.

The process of corporate planning in the nationalised industries was outlined in the 1978 White Paper, *The Nationalised Industries*.[11] This process involves a continuing dialogue between the industries and the relevant government departments, which covers long-term strategy, medium-term development plans and annual operating plans and budgets; other topics include economic prospects, industrial policies and, where appropriate, sectoral policies including the social objectives underlying the payment of grants from public funds.

A government department needs to prepare its own perceptions of the future in order to assess the strategic plans of the industries for which it is responsible. These needs become greater if a number of industries is involved, and the department has, in addition, responsibilities for policies for the sector as a whole, as in the case of a number of departments. Departments also maintain wide-ranging contacts with individuals, universities and other bodies to inform their own thinking and to prepare their own views against which to assess the industries' strategic plans. These views of the future provide only one input into the decision-making process, in the form of a quantified framework of alternative possible futures. Energy Projections 1982[1] provides an example of such a framework.

As will be clear from reading the evidence provided by the Department of Energy, CEGB and NCB, to the Sizewell 'B' Inquiry, differences can and do arise in their respective ranges of projections or sets of scenarios. Although there are major areas of overlap in these alternative forecasts there are many differences in points of detail. These differences are inevitable in independent forecasting exercises. It is likely, however, that sound investments will be generally robust to such differences.

Decisions are normally required on individual issues within the life of a particular plan. Decisions on, for example, a particular major investment, are normally supported by an appraisal involving forecasts prepared by the nationalised industries. It is necessary to ensure that the assumptions and forecasts supporting each individual decision application are consistent with the strategic plan.

CONCLUSIONS

It seems inevitable that some perception of the future expressed as ranges of forecasts, projections or scenarios should be required as a necessary part of the process of strategic planning and decision-making. The preparation of these forecasts involves judgements in the form of assumptions, which in turn are bound to rest in the main on a thorough analysis of past behaviour and experience.

In an uncertain world, all single-point forecasts are likely to be wrong – a correct forecast would be a fortunate accident. The aim of preparing a range of forecasts should be to minimise the range of uncertainty while still maintaining an acceptable probability (albeit a subjective probability) that the out-turn will fall within the range.

NOTES AND REFERENCES

1. Department of Energy, *Proof of Evidence for the Sizewell 'B' Inquiry* (London: Department of Energy, 1982).
2. F. K. Lyness, 'Gas Demand Forecasting'. Paper presented to the Institute of Statisticians Conference on Energy Statistics, Cambridge, July 1983 (British Gas Corporation, London).
3. J. M. W. Rhys, 'Techniques for Forecasting Electricity Demand'. Paper presented to the Institute of Statisticians Conference on Energy Statistics, Cambridge, July 1983 (Electricity Council, London).
4. R. P. Bush and B. T. Matthews, *The Pattern of Energy Use in the UK – 1976*, Energy Technology Support Unit (ETSU), Report R7 (London: Department of Energy, 1979).
5. G. Leach, C. Lewis, F. Romig, A. Van Buren and G. Foley, 'A Low Energy Strategy for the UK', Science Reviews (London, 1979).
6. P. W. Beck, 'Forecasts: Opiates for Decision Makers'. Paper to the Third International Symposium on Forecasting, Philadelphia, June 1983 (Shell UK Ltd.).
7. R. V. Brown, A. S. Katir and C. Peterson, *Decision Analysis: An Overview* (New York: Holt, Rinehart & Winston, 1974).
8. Stanford Research Institute, *Readings in Decision Analysis* (Calif.: Stanford Research Institute, 1977).
9. Sir J. Mason, 'Predictability in Science and Society'. Presidential Address to British Association for the Advancement of Science, Brighton, August 1983.
10. T. A. Boley, 'Errors in Electricty Forecasts'. Paper presented to the 4th International Conference on Futures Analyses, Forecasting and Planning for Telecommunications, Energy and Public Utilities, Paris, June 1982 (Electricity Council, London).
11. *The Nationalised Industries*, Cmnd 7131 (London: HMSO, 1978).

10 Planning Models

ANN P. BROWN*

This chapter reports the results of an investigation into the development and use of mathematical models for capacity planning during the last decade, in six nationalised industries – The National Coal Board, The Central Electricity Generating Board, British Gas, British Telecom, British Airways and British Rail.

THE NATIONALISED INDUSTRIES AND STRATEGIC PLANNING

Corporate planning involving the use of computer models is practised in many large private companies. Both these and national-ised concerns share many common characteristics and, of course, have access to the same modelling tools. However, there are some circumstances which apply uniquely to nationalised organisations and which affect the type of planning work carried out by them and hence their use of planning models.

Characteristics Unique to Nationalised Industries

The main difference for planning purposes is that opportunities for change in the nationalised industries are fairly restricted. They exist primarily to supply national needs of particular products and

* I am greatly indebted to the members of the Operational Research and Planning groups of the six nationalised industries which I visited, while this paper was in preparation, who so generously gave their time to explain the working of their own industry and also to comment helpfully on an initial draft. They are not of course responsible for any of the opinions which I have expressed.

services in an efficient manner. Where secondary products exist, the trend recently has been towards privatisation of these peripheral activities. This concentration on a core product or service means that strategic planning in nationalised industries is very much concerned with the provision of capacity to meet projected demand economically, through choice of technology and supply structure.

Moreover, strategic planning is not exclusively the concern of the industries themselves. It will inevitably be a joint activity of both the industry and the government, which as sole or majority owner can and does intervene in the setting of corporate objectives. The government ultimately acts as arbitrator (at least implicitly) between the industries, where conflicts of interest arise as they alternately compete and trade with each other, and between an industry and its customers where there is a monopoly. Finally it provides the necessary external funding, which any major investment may need.

Development of Planning Models

Corporate planning can be divided into three timescales and various functional divisions as shown in Table 10.1.

TABLE 10.1   *Corporate planning*

| Timescale | Functional area | | | |
	Financial	Capacity	Demand	Manpower
Strategic				
Tactical				
Operational				

The functional split corresponds to the areas in which corporate planning is carried out in many private organisations, where the development of products, markets, supply, new technology and size are all seen as important. Very few organisations attempt to deal with all these issues simultaneously. Models tend to develop within functional divisions, and their results can then be used iteratively from area to area. For the nationalised industries, however, where the central problem is that of supplying a core product or service, capacity and demand issues dominate. Demand forecasting is dealt with by Wigley in Chapter 9, so the rest of this chapter concentrates on capacity planning.

TABLE 10.2 *Capacity planning*

Planning level	Typical timescale	Characteristics
Strategic	5 years +	Sizes; main technologies; type of supply structure; scale of investment
Tactical	3–10 years	Facility pattern, developments and closures; modernisation; funding
Operational	1–2 years	Resource procurement, demand allocation

The three timescales in Table 10.2 correspond to the possibilities of change. Over the short term, no great change to the existing system can be made and the issues are clearly the operational ones of making the best use of existing capacity. For some nationalised industries this could be up to five years ahead. Over the medium term, investment or plans inaugurated now could change the pattern of supply, so that the issues are about the change in the system that best meets forecast demand. This could affect the business from between three to ten years ahead. Over the long term, decisions on the scale, nature and objectives of the business come into effect, so that the issues could be many and varying. This could affect the business from any time between five to fifty years ahead.

In the analysis of any strategic issues, such as the rate of implementation of a new technology, discussions of the options (both within the organisation and outside) will be more effective if the tactical path required for each option has been defined. This analysis therefore frequently becomes primarily that of identifying and evaluating the economic consequences of the best tactical plan to meet specific strategic choices. Many of the nationalised industries have complex supply systems (with many options for development, modernisation, and closure) subject to potential changes of technology and market uncertainties, and this type of analysis becomes an obvious application area for models.

It is not unusual for these models to have at their core a simplified representation of the economics of the business at operational level. Their realism will to some extent depend on the information available. Their usefulness, however, will depend more on the appropriateness of the detail included. Indeed, one of the major difficulties of such model design is the achievement of balance between the amount of operational detail necessary for reasonable confidence in the results, and the need to ensure sufficient simplicity for the strategic issues to remain recognisable.

MODELS

The general growth in the use of mathematical models over the last two decades has been more than matched in the nationalised industries, many of whom have been building up extensive knowledge on their use and value since 1970 or before. The range of relevant mathematical techniques has expanded steadily throughout the last half century. This combined with the recent explosive growth in the calculating capacity of computers has made it possible to construct models with the power to deal successfully with large and complex situations. The particular strength of such models includes their ability to take account of many quantities simultaneously, and to handle large amounts of numerical data, yielding results in almost any desired level of details. However, the accumulating body of experience in their use has shown that the degree of their success is variable depending on a number of diverse factors, and has thus generated an extensive debate on their relevance in the analysis of business problems.

Types of Models

The types of models available can be grouped into four sections: optimising, simulation, statistical and stochastic. Optimising models include such techniques as dynamic programming, critical path analysis and linear programming. With these techniques it is possible to maximise or minimise a chosen quantity but only one measure can be set up for an objective. Linear programming, for example, can be used to generate that unique solution which maximises or minimises some required quantity, such as profit or costs, within a situation where constraints limit the range of choices on many of the relevant parameters. This can be done provided that the constraints can be represented in algebraic terms.[1] Allocation models consisting of a set of rules expressing existing best practice can be considered as semi-optimising. They also produce one answer which represents the closest approach currently possible to a minimum or maximum for the chosen quantity. Simulation models do not attempt optimisation; they reproduce physical or other processes in as great a detail as required. Their function is to provide information on the movement of all relevant measures as circumstances are made to change, for example by altering input values. They include the original Monte Carlo simulation method, systems dynamics, most financial cash modelling, input/output analysis, etc. Stochastic models use probability theory in situations of measurable variation. In resolving any one problem, combinations of all these types of models may be used – for example, simulation models often include the use of probability distributions.

Characteristics of a Model

Building a model involves many choices on such factors as: the type to be used, its size, the location of the boundaries, the level and type of detail to be included, etc. The final product is influenced by judgements on an unexpectedly diverse set of issues, which include the resources available, the nature of the problem to be modelled, the circumstances within which it is built and the use to which it is to be put. A successful application will need to take account of all the relevant aspects of such issues.

A model is relatively inflexible. Changes in the nature of the problem or a significant shift in the surrounding circumstances are difficult to accommodate. The common response to this is first to adjust existing models and then to develop new ones.

Appropriately applied, they are extremely powerful tools. As the property of both builders and users the model's existence can expose their basic assumptions to debate and revision. The effort to understand why it produces the results that it does, gives both parties an enhanced insight into the core of simplicity underlying many situations. This contribution to the understanding of complex situations is potentially its most useful characteristic. Even work that is not of immediate application can yield a great deal of benefit of this kind, especially for those departments in which projects of this nature constitute part of a continuing programme of work.

The discipline of formalising a series of mathematical relationships and working rigorously through the consequences in all aspects, frequently turns up unexpected results: for example, a steel plant known to be profitable to the local management, when assessed within the national situation of the whole Steel Corporation, was in fact a clear candidate for closure.

However, it is the key characteristic of 'number crunching' which creates its greatest strength, its greatest limitation, and its greatest potential weakness. It can put together a large number of interlocking relationships and work out consequences which would be tedious and difficult to do otherwise. At its most powerful, it can produce optimum solutions beyond the reach of any alternative approach. All this, however, needs 'hard data' so that only quantities which can be reduced to numerical measures will be included. Finally the relative ease with which further more-detailed relationships can be added exacerbates its two weak points: the time-consuming job of maintaining an up-to-date database, and the difficulty in interpretation of the results. As the size increases, data requirements increase and the complexity makes interpretation more and more difficult. None the less its 'number crunching' capacity does make it peculiarly well suited to assessing the effect of marginal changes quickly. Sensitivity analysis over a realistic range of values becomes possible for the first time, and questions of the 'what if?' variety can be dealt with expeditiously, provided that such questions are only directed towards those factors included explicitly in the model.

THE INDUSTRIES

The following two sections describe the recent experience of the six nationalised industries: the National Coal Board, the Central Electricity Generating Board, the British Gas Corporation, British Telecom, British Airways and British Rail. It is based on a series of discussions which took place in 1983 with planners and model-builders in these six organisations, as well as on some relevant published material. These organisations were chosen both because they are large-scale investors and because they are nationalised concerns which have played a dominating part in their industry. All have been engaged for some time in a wide variety of modelling work, particularly at the operating level.

Common Factors Encouraging Model Development

There have been some factors affecting planning, broadly common to most of these organisations, which have tended to encourage the development of modelling.

(1) The requirement for an annual Corporate Plan was first placed on the nationalised industries by the UK government in the early 1970s. The application of Corporate Planning was developed in more detail since then in various White Papers.[2,3] From the beginning these plans were expected to cover all three levels of strategic, tactical and operational planning.[4] One of their prime original purposes, however, was to support the industry's forecast investment plan over the following five years (required by the government's budgeting process). The government's increasing demand for information will have encouraged the development of models which are prime providers of this commodity.

(2) All these industries had the experience of being nationalised or part of a government department (i.e. British Telecom) since at least the late 1940s, which has significant implications for their organisational structure and hence data availability.

(3) These industries are large investors of capital, both as a proportion of gross domestic fixed capital formation and per employee.[5] Almost all work to long lead times in investments. In planning new capacity, the energy industries will need between five and ten years to see the physical results of an approved project. For British Telecom and British Rail, capacity decisions will involve changing their networks either in shape or quality – a more diffuse process. However, a programme affecting the whole network, such as digitalasation for British Telecom or electrification for British Rail will take a similar period of time to complete. British Airways is perhaps the only industry which can expect to see faster results,

since its major capacity decision is the procurement of aircraft. Even so, the time between placing an order and eventually obtaining the aircraft can be of the order of two or more years. Investment projects not only take a long time to mature, but once operational are also expected to have long lifetimes, generally of a minimum of fifteen years but more frequently twenty to thirty years and longer. These factors coupled with the general variability of demand experienced in the last decade have put an increasing pressure on the planning process, demanding longer timescales, and creating the need not only to examine options in a more systematic way but also to produce accurate demand forecasts.

(4) All are accountable to government for the running of the business. As such they are the subject of scrutiny, to a degree not matched elsewhere, by such bodies as, for example, The Monopolies and Mergers Commission, and their own sponsoring departments.

Description of the Industries

The six industries have been divided into two groups, according to the nature of their investment decisions: 'energy' (NBC, British Gas, and CEGB), dealing with the same market; and 'network-based services' (British Airways, British Rail, and British Telecom), dealing with different markets but with presumably similar problems in analysing, and providing capacity on, a network. The factors considered to have had influence on the choices made are:

(1) the availability of information on current and proposed future operations of the business;
(2) the pattern of supply and demand which dictates the nature of the problem; for many of the organisations there is a potential benefit to be gained in the choice of location and size of plant capacity;
(3) the main economic background, since an organisation's market position affects its range of choices in capacity provision;
(4) the organisational relationship between builder and user (planner), and the ease of access to the relative inherited experience in model building;
(5) the quality and availability of estimates of such factors as future demand and new technology.

'ENERGY'

The industries under this heading compete for the United Kingdom market in energy, which has exhibited little growth since 1974.[6] During the 1970s the relative attractiveness of the different products altered several times, with changes in the relative prices of oil, gas and coal[7] clearly affecting market share, and there seems no reason to assume any greater stability in the future.

National Coal Board

The NCB has recently experienced rapid contraction involving many colliery closures up until the early 1970s.[8] The changes in energy prices at that time indicated a more favourable market for coal in the future, generating demand forecasts which have so far proved optimistic.[9] Plans for expansion were developed and accepted by government in 1975.[10] These proposed not only improvements to existing pits but also at least one major new colliery (Selby). This programme has been followed with some modifications since then. Closures have also continued but at a slower rate.

The NCB is organised into twelve Regional Areas responsible for operating their own collieries, and Head Office responsible for those functions dealt with nationally, such as marketing, planning, finance, etc. Planning is carried out both at an Area level and in the Central Planning Unit at Head Office. Information on existing and proposed new collieries is in general supplied by the Areas. A long-established Operational Research (OR) group provides modelling support for planning at Area-level and for Headquarters Departments. Its activities contribute to a consistency of modelling approaches and assumptions among these groups.

The renewed interest in new collieries development, generated by the 1974 Plan, has led, for example, to a need for improved methods to evaluate their forecast performance. Various models have been developed[11] to meet this need which are now widely used by the Areas. Data on new proposals, making use of such approaches, is submitted to Head Office as part of the industry plans.

Modelling work for national investment planning has been

undertaken both by the Central Planning Unit and its OR section for at least a decade. The capacity decisions centre on the choice of mines to close, upgrade or develop. The original intention was to develop a suite of programmes dealing with such issues as costs of supply, UK demand for energy, energy prices, other supplies of energy and hence the demand for coal. The suite could then be run separately or together. The final link in the chain was the matching of supply to demand.[12]

The supply models appear to have remained unchanged in approach since their original conception. They aggregate data on existing and proposed mining schemes for a preliminary match to any relevant factor such as markets, and then use this data base to create a pit-ranking in order of cost/tonne. Pits can and frequently do change ranking as geological conditions alter. This system picks up such changes and transforms them to a national coal supply curve showing cumulative cost versus tonnage for any chosen future year.

It is in the matching of supply to demand where the major changes have occurred. Up until two years ago the NCB considered that prices were primarily determined by movements in their own costs. The matching model at that time embodied a series of allocation rules to meet a particular demand. In fact, since price was perceived as a variable, the model strictly needed to be run and re-run as adjustments to prices were made. In the last two years this situation has changed. The UK price of coal is now expected to be broadly linked to the coal price on the world markets (as for steel) and so a quantity to be forecast. To meet this changed situation a new linking model has been developed.[13] This is a linear programme which maximises net present value to the NCB for a given projected demand and price profile, by finding the optimal choice of coal production options, imports, exports and stock through time. It has been used during the last year for the current Plan. In essence, the reduction in the range of choice simplified the modelling problem and made optimisation easier.

These models are used frequently, although the amount of work and data required to run even one is considerable. It is more usual to run each model separately. This is because its main purpose is seen as providing results to the planner which can be used both to yield insights into the problem structure and to combine with other aspects of reality not well covered in the model. Running the whole suite together would make the interactive, interpretive mode of use very difficult.

Central Electricity Generating Board

The growth of UK electricity demand (and supply) was high throughout the 1950s and early 1960s, slowing down substantially by the early 1970s. By the late 1970s, growth appeared to have halted,[14] but the CEGB's demand forecasts were slow to accommodate to this change.[15] Investment in new power stations was heavy throughout the 1960s. Since the capacity of individual stations increased substantially over this period, the reduction in the number of stations in operation was also marked (274 in 1952, down to 108 in 1982).[14] Power stations were planned and ordered during the 1970s but at a reduced rate. Since demand is now forecast to be fairly stagnant, new investment is likely to remain at this level or lower. The Board's latest proposal is a new nuclear plant at Sizewell which is the subject of a Public Enquiry at present.

The Board is organised into a Head Office, five Regions, each with responsibility for the maintenance and operation of the power stations and transmission system within its boundary, and three Service Divisions responsible for planning, development and construction of generating plant and the transmission system.[15] It has two main planning functions – investment planning in power stations to provide the appropriate total capacity of electrical generating power, and operational planning to meet varying demand on the existing system at least cost. The existence of the National Grid system and consequent possibility of treating the national resources on the generation and transmission of electricity as a single system, has led to the involvement of the Head Office. From 1974 there has been a suite of models to calculate the system marginal cost and establish a national ranking of power stations according to fuel cost.

Planning new power station investment is carried out at Head Office. Currently there are two types of model used in assessing new projects. One is a linear programme which will minimise net present cost of operation by choice of power stations, from any given available combination. The other is a simulation programme which is used to analyse the future operation of the system over individual years in detail. Data on projected new power station performance is obtained from the Service Divisions, and that on the existing system is clearly available from the routine running of the National Grid. The Planning Department also does much work on forecasting demand which is an input to the model. Although the linear programme takes account of future years, it does not do so on a yearly basis. Development work is currently in progress on a more detailed linear programming model which will include such factors as the seasons, and transport. This is already a large model, in that, for example, it can take account of each power station individually (of which there are still over 100). The development of this (and related models) appears to have been a fairly continuous process.

Prior to 1970 there was a manual non-linear programme which was used for the investment evaluation. The advent of sufficient available computing power prompted a conversion to a larger computerised LP model in the early 1970s, leading eventually to the current one. This is used to contribute to most Annual Plans, and of course intensively at such times as now when a new power station (Sizewell 'B') is under consideration.

British Gas Corporation

For British Gas, recent years have brought rapid growth and a sharp change in the source of supplies. It has changed from being a producer of gas (from oil) and importer of liquified natural gas (LNG) in the mid-1960s, to buying natural gas – in the late 1960s – from an increasing number of fields in the North Sea. Throughout the 1970s, every year has seen an increase in sales of gas, which doubled between 1971 and 1982. This growth is forecast to continue for some time.[16] Its earlier manufacturing capability has been dismantled and substantial investment gone into the creation of the national transmission system[17] and the provision of storage facilities to smooth out seasonal fluctuations in demand. But sometime in the future, as natural gas runs out, possibly after the year 2000, it expects to revert again to manufacturing Synthetic Natural Gas (SNG) (possibly from coal).[18] All these changes have created an unusually wide range of new investment issues for British Gas in recent years.

On nationalisation in 1949, gas was organised into twelve largely autonomous Areas, each responsible for its own investment plan. National investment planning could not therefore develop until there was more central control of the gas supply. The conditions for more central control were initiated with the experiment of importing LNG by the Gas Council on behalf of eight of the Area Boards in the mid-1960s. However, it was the discovery of natural gas which radically altered the situation. The Gas Council was first given powers in 1965 to develop gas supplies in its own right, putting it on a more equal footing with the Area Boards. And by 1972, as the British Gas Corporation, it was finally given total control of gas supply, for the United Kingdom. The Corporation is currently organised into the twelve Regions responsible for the distribution of gas within their own boundaries and other matters such as servicing and sales of domestic equipment, etc., and a Headquarters structured on functional lines and responsible among other matters for the Annual Corporate Plan which includes investment planning.

Operational research has existed in British Gas since the mid-1960s at least, distributed between the Area Boards and the Council (subsequently Regions and Headquarters). A large increase in modelling work generally started with the advent of natural gas,[19] and this has continued since. Operational research and modelling has been closely integrated with the planning function both at Regional and Head Office level. The Economic Planning Division established by the Gas Council and continued by the Corporation includes the operational research staff; it is this division which has the responsibility of producing the Annual Plan which includes provision for long-range investments.

The issue of gas depletion policy, which is central to the capacity investment decision in gas, was first formulated as a linear programme in 1970. This model, which has been developed in sophistication and size since then,[20] aims to match supply and demand so as to maximise present value of net revenues over the long term. The sources of supply are subject to some uncertainty, depending on the outcome of negotiations for the products of various current and newly developed fields. Part of the costs of this supply will be the required investment in storage and transmission. Demand is analysed by market sector, and is seen as partially under the control of British Gas because of its advantage in price and because it can influence the rate at which supply comes forward by changes in depletion rates. Revenue estimates are needed, among other factors. The model can be and is used to investigate effects of differing combinations of assumptions, or of frequent changes in circumstances such as new supply possibilities. Much of the information needed to run this model is derived from current operations and from estimates of future unique schemes for supply, as well as from demand estimates. Like the CEGB, British Gas has a suite of programmes to balance demand and supply within the current system[21] from which information can be taken. It has also developed a series of simulation approaches to deal with such issues as assessing the cost of altering the transmission system to meet new supplies, providing gas gathering systems and determining appropriate storage levels.

Models are seen to be crucial to the running of the industry, and under continuous development to meet the changing nature of the questions asked. They represent a hierarchy of complexity and detail, from extremely specific models dealing with such operational questions as the flow of gas through particular detailed pipe configurations, to the most broad ones used for planning.

NETWORK-BASED SERVICES

The three industries under this heading all serve different markets (with the exception of the very marginal overlap between British Rail and British Airways on long-distance UK travel). They are alike in that a major part of their business is a direct service to the consumer, which could make demand comparatively volatile, reflecting prevailing economic conditions. Their products share an important characteristic in that the service sold is from a specific source to a specific destination. British Telecom sells a telephone/communications link between unique points; British Rail and British Airways sell transport between specific geographic locations. Forecasting of demand must, therefore, deal not only with total levels but also with the demand on each link in the network. Capacity provision cannot be considered simply as a total availability within the whole system, but must also be broken down into at least the major routes of each network. The previous industries also have networks, but these are operated by the supplier for the efficient distribution of his product and not as part of the product sold.

The capacity investment decisions, then, affecting any particular part of the network, will inevitably have repercussions on the rest. The issues are the location and extent of contraction or expansion of the network, choice and speed of development of new technological developments, and the nature of the continued maintenance of the existing network. Both British Telecom and British Rail have a higher investment in their existing routes than British Airways, in that both have physical equipment sunk into each line, which British Airways does not. This must make network change more costly and slow for them. British Airways can reduce its network quickly, but expansion into new routes takes longer (typically up to a year), due to the need for negotiations with all interested parties. It also has to deal with the technology change of each new generation of aircraft, some of which it must buy to keep in business. British Telecom is apparently facing a near-permanent state of technology development. How best to accommodate these changes while maintaining the existing system is clearly a major preoccupation.

British Telecom

The core of British Telecom's business traditionally has been the provision of the public switched telephone network. This network has been growing ever since its inception, doubling the number of exchange connections, for example, in the last decade.[22] Expansion, modernisation of exchanges (to electronic), and the development of an integrated digital network eventually to replace the current analogue network, are all being pursued simultaneously. Technological developments in transmission media, intelligent network functions, and terminals, are leading to new services such as radiopaging, interactive services such as Prestel, and promise future developments such as cable television. As a result, British Telecom has been the largest single investor[23] of all the nationalised industries for many years. It was part of the Post Office until 1981 when it became an independent coporation organised into the four divisions of: Inland, within which lies the Network Strategy department responsible for the investment strategy associated with the telephone network; Enterprises, responsible for the new services such as Prestel; International; and Major Systems, responsible for research and procurement. It will be interesting to see what effect privatisation will have on Telecom's planning procedures.

When investing in a programme of change, such as digitalisation, it would be preferable to know the effect, in terms of cost and performance, of each incremental development on the network, and in particular the optimum path in terms of speed of development and the order in which the changes are made. With a network of over 6,000 exchanges and tens of thousands of links, the resultant complexity defies a detailed modelling approach. The problem is illustrated by work on the comparatively simple area of the trunk transmission network, which connects only 400 trunk exchanges. A model for this network has been attempted (called Cybernet) which aims to minimise the cost of installing new transmission equipment only (i.e. excluding exchanges).[24] It has so far proved feasible, but takes a long period of time to produce any one solution. Telecom continues to contribute to COST 201, a European project on network modelling in telecommunication. For the assessment of the modernisation (including digitalisation aspects) of the network as a whole a different approach has therefore been adopted. A strategic appraisal model has been in use since the early 1970s. It includes all the major elements of the network – i.e. exchanges and transmissions links – but by broad groupings only, and produces the cost of various strategies. It can include any relevant constraints such as equipment shortages,[25] but deals in average traffic intensities between groups of exchange, average route length, etc. It was adapted to allow for the digitalasation options in 1978–80, so that various strategies reflecting differing rates of progress could be costed and compared. This model is currently undergoing further work to allow for the inclusion of a greater amount of detail. The issue of the order of progress to be adopted in, for example, installing new digital exchanges, is dealt with separately. A programme is available which ranks proposals put up by the ten regions according to a constructed measure that reflects both net present revenue and resources used.[26]

British Airways

British Airways' experience of traffic growth in the 1970s has been erratic. Demand grew up to 1974, when there was a short pause. However, within a year or two, growth resumed, until the 1980s during which so far there has been a decline.[27] The prime investment decision is the procurement of aircraft to meet a diverse range of needs, since the range of services offered is so large. At present some reduction of services is being planned, which is in effect a decision to reduce capacity. On the other hand, there are continuing technical improvements in aircraft design – wide-bodied aircraft, less-noisy and more-fuel-efficient engines, and aircraft more closely designed for efficient operation on particular types of routes.

British Airways was created in 1972 when it took over the two state airlines of BEA and BOAC. Planning at that time was carried out in various parts of both organisations, although a central group attempted to ensure consistency on results. Large operational research groups had been in existence in both organisations, which after the merger were immediately organised into one group. This group provides, among other services, modelling support throughout the organisation and in particular to the Planning Directorate (created in 1977).

Both British Airways and British Rail (unlike British Telecom) need to organise schedules and time-tables for their services. Much of British Airways' modelling work is clearly directed at aspects of these problems: forecasting traffic flows, constructing time-tables and obtaining their associated costs;[28] aircrew rostering; matching capacity to demand within the current system with a view to maximising revenue;[29] etc.

The procurement decision, however, needs a model which will assess the cost of varying fleet opportunities on the network of services currently provided (or possibly projected). Since British Airways' business divides sharply between short-haul work in the UK and Europe (mainly involving only one link), and long-haul work throughout the rest of the world (involving potentially many connections in any one trip), provision of two distinct models might have been indicated. In fact a linear programme (ALCOM) was first formulated for the short-haul business within BEA with the objective of minimising the costs of one year's operation. It has been in continuous use since 1972–3, undergoing various changes and modifications to meet airline changes and to increase its scope.[30] Separate models are used to translate its results into yearly cash flows and to produce such measures as NPV. The long-haul business was approached in a similar way, and some optimising models have been tried. However, because of the much greater complexity of the network (involving many different choices of route for any one trip), none has proved to be useful in more than one or two isolated studies. Instead, a number of alternative pragmatic solutions to this problem have been evolved over a series of projects.[31]

Planning is seen as an iterative exercise, generating a large number of 'what if?' questions. The aim in design therefore has been for interactive models which the planner can use directly. Virtually all departments play a part in any major decision of procurement or service change. So this has also affected the design process, and the value of the evolutionary approach in design was emphasised. However, such models imposed a heavy load in data requirements both for the start-up and thereafter in keeping up to date. What level of complexity to build into them was also seen as a serious decision, as the more detail incorporated in it the more complex the results become and the greater the difficulty in interpretation.

British Rail

After the large reduction in its network of permanent track in the 1960s, British Rail has operated with a network of substantially the same size throughout the last decade; there has been only some slight reduction each year, accumulating to an overall reduction of 5 per cent in mileage between 1975 and 1982.[32] The major part of British Rail's revenue comes from two types of traffic: passenger and freight. Freight traffic has been declining fairly steadily since the early 1970s, but passenger traffic appears to be fluctuating around a stable mean value. Investment, therefore, has been aimed predominantly at renewal, improvement of service (which in the passenger business increases the possibility of generating more traffic),[33] and cost reduction. Any 'slimming' of routes contemplated by reducing the numbers of tracks can require further investment to modify track and signalling. Demand (i.e. freight and passenger traffic) depends on plans for investment in traction and rolling stock, in the sense that this establishes rail's competitive position with respect to alternative forms of transport as well as the overall UK transport demand profile. Various rail plans in the early 1970s have proved to have been optimistic in at least the freight demand forecasts. In 1973, British Rail presented to government and had accepted an investment programme which represented a substantial increase over the previous few years. Not all has been implemented, although much has happened since then necessitating alternative approaches.

Planning for the railways is carried out both at head Office, which has had responsibility for the Annual Corporate Plan since 1969, and within the five regions into which the railway network is divided.[34] In its planning, British Rail has to deal with at least two major types of traffic, using some common resources (locomotives and track), and some unique resources (waggons or coaches). Other complications include: traffic generating differing frequencies – high for passenger and low for freight; the need to organise a timetable on a large network with many interlinks (in British Rail's 1982 Annual report this consisted of 10,700 miles and 2,711 stations); differing types of service – for example, intercity, fast trains, stopping-trains, etc.; the interaction between service provided and demand generated; the effect on the existing system and service of any new services created or new investment.

British Rail has been engaged in a continuous attempt to improve the way in which it represents its network since at least the early 1970s. Each new Plan, proposed strategy or investment opportunity has tended to generate further developments. Several approaches have been adopted, including sectioning the network by routes into some 4,000 to 5,000 parts, and grouping services by some 600–700 profit centres. These profit centres represent a specific train service or group of services but individual centres may use track in common with others. They are now a basis on which the Board's budget is analysed. On the operational level, such schemes as TOPS have been and continue to be developed in order to obtain more information on current operations. This is a real-time computer application which started with the freight business but is now being applied elsewhere. Its aim was to have a computer record of all relevant movements on the system immediately available at any time of the day (or night). Since it is from the operational groups that data on the achievement of the existing system is ultimately obtained, this is of key importance for future planning.

Route network investment is just one of the planning issues investigated by the Headquarters planning group in recent years. There has been increasing emphasis on investigations into a series of particular strategies. The network models simulate the operation of the system as changes are proposed. Each question or issue tends to generate its own model, with varying levels of detail but all producing the cost implications. Issues that have been examined in recent years include: the operation of the freight business, the operation of the parcels business, and main-line electrification. The proposed electrification of the main line is an interesting example of an investigation into the application of new investment. In this case the traffic of all businesses was simulated to identify the financial consequences of variation in three factors: traffic levels, the size of the electrified network, and the rate of electrification.

There were four sizes of network, ranging from Option I, which had little additional electrification, to Option V, which had over 3,000 additional electrified route miles. For each combination of the main assumptions, a series of models simulated train operations, traction and rolling-stock requirements, building programmes and infrastructure work. Subsequent models produced cash flows for cost and revenue charges due to electrification. These cash flows were then discounted and the NPVs for the Longer Options were compared with Option I.[35]

THE FUTURE

The Effects of Change

For models there are several types of change that can be significant enough to warrant new developments. An improvement in resources, such as happened in the early 1970s when computing power became progressively cheaper, larger and easier of access, is one. Changes in either the nature of the problem or the circumstances surrounding it is another: this happened to British Gas when the final centralisation of gas procurement established for the first time a need for an industry-wide analysis. Over the last decade such changes have not been a major factor for the six nationalised industries. The immediate future, however, looks different, due to two significant developments: one is the increasing accessibility of computers, hence increasing the power of models; and the other is the changing economic circumstances of the nationalised industries.

The Models

The principal value of models was seen in most organisations to be the increased understanding of the existing supply system that they brought and the chance to evaluate future options. To use them as an investigative tool, however, meant a lot of work on the collection and input of data, not to mention the interpretation of results. So the major limitation on their use was simply the amount of time and labour required to run them.

This limitation should be eased by developments happening now or projected in the near future. Computer power is increasing steadily, and this will not only make the more intractable problems amenable to analysis but also expedite the existing trends of automatic data capture on the operations of any business. The possibility of electronic data handling replacing some of the current manual operations might in the end speed up some of the more labour-absorbing tasks.

Many other developments in computers will contribute to the increasing accessibility and ease of use of models. A whole range of software applications, from off-the-shelf packages to more user-friendly high-level languages, are becoming available and more can be expected. These will not only help data input but also reduce programme development time, thus encouraging the possibility of building a greater variety of models to meet varying purposes. Apart from the now well-established, interactive, on-line facilities available with most main-frame and mini-computers, the increasing development of micro-computers will allow more local power and control in model running.

But perhaps most exciting of all are the opportunities for visual display, most commonly available on micro-computers but clearly an option on any installation. This improvement in display opens up a new dimension in the representation of results, as well as expediting the data input for sensitivity analysis. A visual picture of the results of a simulation model responding to alternate runs will present the effects of investigating 'what if?' questions with far greater impact and clarity than is possible with more static methods. This in turn will widen the range of options which can be seriously investigated. Future developments, then, suggest an optimistic view on the power and use of models.

The Circumstances

There are, however, certain trends which might reduce the need for complex planning models. Privatisation would change the relationship with government, and more significantly any breakup into smaller units which this might entail will reduce the need for the central planning of capacity. The recession has brought the threat of contraction to many industries, and under these circumstances other factors tend to dominate outside the immediate area of analysis of existing models. Emphasis has shifted to the attempt to change existing practice, to negotiate redundancies, etc. Investment in new plant can no longer be seen as the principal source of improvement open to the industry, and this may reduce the use and development of models designed primarily as an aid to investment decision-taking.

CONCLUSIONS

In the last decade models have contributed a great deal to the understanding of the cost implications of various supply possibilities and capacity investment opportunities in the six nationalised industries considered in this chapter. The power of these tools is likely to increase, and hence make possible further fruitful analysis of the current more intractable problems. However, the scope for new investment may in some industries be less than in the past and hence reduce the demand for model-building geared primarily to investment decision-making.

NOTES AND REFERENCES

1. Various textbooks will explain these techniques in greater detail. See, for example H. A. Taha, *Operations Research, An Introduction*, 3rd edn (London: Macmillan, 1982); and G. Hadley, *Linear Programming* (Reading, Mass.: Addison-Wesley, 1962).
2. *Capital Investment Procedures*, the government's reply to the Select Committee 1973/1974, Cmnd 6106 (London: HMSO, 1975).
3. *The Nationalised Industries*, Cmnd 7131 (London: HMSO, 1978).
4. D. J. Harris and B. C. L. Davis, 'Corporate Planning as a Control System in United Kingdom Nationalised Industries', *Long Range Planning*, vol. 14 (Feb 1981) pp. 15–22.

5. National Economic Development Office, *A Study of UK Nationalised Industries* (London: HMSO, 1976) app. vol.
6. Department of Energy, *Energy Trends*; Monthly Statistics on UK energy requirements (1970–82).
7. C. Robinson and E. Marshall, 'What Future for British Coal? Optimism or Realism on the Prospects to the Year 2000', Hobart paper 89, Institute of Economic Affairs (1981), p. 26.
8. National Coal Board, *Report and Accounts 1981/82*.
9. National Coal Board, *Plan for Coal* (1974), and *Coal for the Future* (1977).
10. *The Government's Expenditure Plans 1974–75 to 1978–79*, Cmnd 5879 (London: HMSO, 1975) p. 50.
11. The National Coal Board, *ORE in the Seventies. Review of the Work of the National Coal Board's Operational Research Executive 1970–1978*, p. 19.
12. M. W. Plackett, R. J. Ormerod and F. J. Toft, 'The National Coal Board Strategic Model', *European Journal of Operational Research*, 10 (1982) pp. 351–60.
13. R. J. Ormerod and J. Mcleod, 'The Development and Use of the NCB Strategic model', Energy Statistics Conference, Kings College, Cambridge, July 1983.
14. Central Electricity Generating Board, *Annual Report and Accounts 1981/82*.
15. The Monopolies and Mergers Commission, *The Central Electricity Generating Board* (London: HMSO, 1981) pp. 44–7.
16. British Gas Corporation, *Annual Report and Accounts 1981/82*.
17. S. D. Anderson and A. L. Mongar, 'The Equitable Distribution of Security Expenditure in Local Gas Supply Systems', *Journal of the Operational Society*, vol. 30, no. 9 (Sept. 1979) pp. 785–95.
18. J. A. D. Lister, 'The Next Decade, Supply and Demand Prospects for British Gas in the 1980's', Annual General Meeting of the Eastern Division of the Institute of Gas Engineers, June 1980.
19. I. J. Whitting, 'The Role and Application of Model Building in the British Gas Industry', Symposium of Mathematical and Econometric Models in the Energy Sectors, USSR, 1973.
20. F. K. Lyness, 'OR and UK Natural Gas Depletion Strategy', *European Journal of Operational Research*, 2 (1978) pp. 160–7.
21. O. R. Department Report, *Summary Guide to the Demand and Supply Computer Programmes* (Jan. 1983).
22. British Telecommunications, *Statistics 1982*, p. 24.
23. See, for example, *The Government's Expenditure Plans 1975–76 to 1979–80*, Cmnd 6393 (1976); *1978–79 to 1981–82*, Cmnd 7049 (1978); *1983–84 to 1985–86*, Cmnd 878911 (1983) (London: HMSO).
24. A. C. Piggott, 'An Optimisation System for Inter-City Transmission Network Planning', *Networks 80* (Paris, 1980).
25. C. R. J. Shurrock, 'The Modernisation of the U.K. Telecommunications Network', *Networks 80* (Paris, 1980).

26. K. R. Crooks, 'Programming the Digital Modernisation of a National Local Exchange Network', *Networks 83* (Brighton, 1983).
27. British Airways, *Report and Accounts 1981/82*.
28. K. Rapley, 'Experience with a Macro Economic Model of an Airline', British Airways Management Services, Operational Research (Sep 1973) (unpublished).
29. N. R. Tobin, 'Timesharing, Interactive Models and Operational Research', *Operational Research Quarterly*, vol. 27 (1976) pp. 531–45.
30. K. Rapley, 'Short Haul Fleet Planning Model', AGIFORS Symposium, 1975.
31. K. Rapley, 'Problems, Processes and Purposes: The Systems Approach to O.R.', *Journal of the Operational Research Society*, vol. 34 (1983) pp. 787–95.
32. British Railways Board, *Annual Report and Accounts 1979* and *Annual Report and Accounts 1982*.
33. R. Pryke and J. Dodgson, *The Rail Problem* (London: Martin Robertson, 1975) ch. 7.
34. J. Harris and G. Williams, *Corporate Management and Financial Planning: The BR Experience* (London: Granada, 1980).
35. Department of Transport and British Railways Board, *Review of Main Line Electrification, Final Report* (HMSO 1981) app. 1.

Part IV
Transport and Energy

11 Planning in Transport

JOHN HEATH

THE ROLE OF GOVERNMENT IN TRANSPORT

This chapter is concerned broadly with the role of government in transport and more narrowly with the processes of strategic planning in British Rail and in the British Airports Authority.

Government interest in transport in the UK shows great variety of purpose, method and depth of involvement in every mode, and over almost the whole field of activity. There is no consistent pattern, as Table 11.1 reveals.

Many of the organisations in Table 11.1 are public corporations accountable to Parliament through the Secretary of State for Transport: in *Rail* there is the British Railways Board (BRB) and its wholly owned subsidiary British Rail Engineering Ltd (BREL), with London Transport (LT) at present accountable to the Greater London Council (GLC) but to be transferred to the Secretary of State for Transport; in *Road* there is the National Bus Company, about to be privatised, and LT; in *Air* there is the British Airports Authority (BAA), British Airways (BA), both about to be privatised, and the Civil Aviation Authority (CAA) – a regulatory authority but which also runs some small airports, the national Air Traffic Services and through it controls aircraft movements in British air space – part of the provision of the infrastructure for civil aviation; and in *Sea* there is British Shipbuilders (BS) and Sealink, a wholly owned subsidiary of the BRB and about to be privatised.

Until very recently there would have been Associated British Ports shown as a public corporation, also British Aerospace and the National Freight Corporation; these enterprises also illustrate the range of privatisation structures within which other former state-owned enterprises can be found. The 'least privatised' is Associated British Ports, now a statutory company in which the government

TABLE 11.1   *Public involvement in transport*

	Equipment manufacturing	Provision of infrastructure	Transport operations	Regulation
1. Rail	BREL	BRB PTEs LT	BRB PTEs LT	Dept of Transport
2. Road Passenger	BL	Dept of Transport	LT Nat. Bus. Co. Local authorities	Dept of Transport Treasury (Taxation)
Freight	BL	Dept of Transport		Dept of Transport Treasury (Taxation)
3. Air	BR Aerospace (48.5%)	CAA BAA Local authorities	BA	CAA Dept of Transport
4. Sea	BS	Ass. Br. Ports plc. (48.5%) Local authorities Other public authorities	Sealink	Dept of Transport

retains 48.5 per cent of the shares, appoints two Directors to the Board, retains the power to authorise (and hence not to authorise) all investment over £3 million, and guarantees their bank overdrafts. The 'most privatised' is the former National Freight Corporation in which the government has retained no interest or special powers of any kind. British Aerospace is in an intermediate position. The purpose of such a wide range of residual government interest is not clear.

As Table 11.1 also illustrates, the involvement of government in transport is much wider than its concern for public enterprises. It includes, for example, the provision of roads, the taxation of road vehicles and the negotiation of air traffic rights for UK and foreign airlines. Because of this wide involvement, and because of the strongly competitive nature of transport in which to a greater or lesser degree all modes interact, the government's own strategies towards the industry assume great importance. These strategies provide the framework for the whole transport industry, and in particular have great influence over the public enterprises which are present in every transport mode and in almost every kind of transport activity.

Ownership and accountability of the transport public corporations are centred in the Department of Transport. The role of that Ministry is clearly much wider than would be necessary to control these public corporations, as Table 11.2 illustrates.

TABLE 11.2 *Some roles of the Department of Transport*

1. *Owner* (of the nationalised industries)
2. *Minority shareholder* (in Associated British Ports, for instance)
3. *Banker's agent* (the Treasury is the banker for nationalised industries)
4. *Provider*
   – Directly (trunk roads)
   – Indirectly (BR rail services)
5. *Promoter*
   – Road safety
6. *Enabler*
   – Authorising the provision of airport capacity
7. *Regulator*
   – Road haulage licensing
   – Aviation route licensing
8. *Sponsoring Department*
   – for the whole transport industry

This is a formidable list. In the formulation of its own strategies the Department has to be sensitive to all of these different roles it is performing, to the different shares of the market over which it can have direct or indirect influence, and to the interactions between the different parts of the transport industry. Some implications of this are discussed later.

This brief survey of the ways in which the government – and the Department of Transport in particular – is involved in the transport sector of the UK economy provides a framework within which to consider strategic planning in just two public enterprises – the BRB and the BAA. These were chosen partly because of personal involvement by the author in both of them, but mainly because they offer contrasts in scale, growth, profitability and in their past history.

STRATEGIC PLANNING IN THE RAILWAYS

Strategic Framework

Over many years the government failed to provide the British Railways Board with a workable strategic framework for its operations. Attempts to do so were always frustrated by the pressure of events – the growth of competition, the rise of private car ownership, changing population and habits of the travelling public – so that their currency was short-lived. The clearest and most simple statement was, however, in 1974 when the government required the BRB from 1 January 1975 to 'operate its railway passenger system so as to provide a public service which is comparable generally with that provided by the Board at present'.

This was, however, too negative a statement and too brief to be a useful guidance in a rapidly changing transport competitive environment. *Rail Policy*, published by the BRB in 1980, was an attempt to draw the government's attention to what was required by stating clearly its own policies in what was believed to be a rapidly deteriorating situation, and in the absence of an adequate response the now notorious Serpell Committee was promoted by BRB as an attempt to force the pace. The outcome has been a long letter dated 24 October 1983 from the Secretary of State to the new Chairman of the BRB which described the priorities of the government for British Rail, set a tougher overall financial target than had existed previously and gave some limits for independent action.

Role of Corporate Plans

In any organisation which has such a close and continuing relationship with government, which depends upon the government for such a substantial part of its total income and which has not had a satisfactory strategic framework provided by the government, it is perhaps inevitable that Corporate Plans should come to be seen as part of that continuing negotiation with government – in the past, British Rail was no exception.

In these circumstances the role of a Corporate Plan was to provide reassurance to the government, to give support to policies which BR wished to pursue, to provide briefing material for Department of Transport Ministers in argument and negotiation with ministerial colleagues, and to provide an atmosphere of professionalism and control over the business which governments – and the public – expect. It would be going too far to describe earlier Corporate Plans as aspects of public relations, but the truth is that line management was little involved in their formulation and did not feel a high level of commitment to the achievement of the Plans put forward.

Since the 1983–1988 Corporate Plan that has now changed. Nothing goes into the Plan without the full commitment of management for its achievement, and where new policies are put forward they would only be incorporated if Action Plans existed and if management had accepted specific commitments to them. This will not, of course, guarantee that the outcome will be as predicted – economic and market forecasts (including assumptions about the effect of the M25 and of the development of regional air services on rail traffic, for example) may prove to have been wrong; unforeseen strikes or other events may occur. Moreover, the succeeding Corporate Plan will always incorporate new Action Plans to which management is committed, and there will be new forecasts and perhaps a different perception of the success of competitors, and so on. Nevertheless, to put it crudely and unfairly in relation to past endeavours, the Corporate Plan is now firmly a tool of management and not of public relations.

Thus the new Corporate Plans in British Rail have become rather more than a compass by which to guide management action, but less than a blueprint for what will happen over the five-year Plan period. The change is considerable and is perceived to be such by managers themselves.

This change in the role of corporate planning has been associated with the setting-up of five profit accountable business units within the Railways, which took place early in 1982, and with the decentralisation of the corporate planning function largely – but not wholly – to these individual business units (these were: InterCity, London and the South East; Provincial Passenger Services; Freight; Parcels).

Of course a corporate function at the centre had to remain, to pull together the separate business unit plans, to provide a challenge to the appropriateness of these plans, and to consider and resolve conflicts or interactions between these separate propositions within the corporate rail system. Thus the highly centralised corporate planning process which used to exist has been replaced with essentially a decentralised system based upon these five individual business units.

And having net revenue responsibilities, these individual business units have a significantly better appreciation of the likely impact of cost proposals on future revenue, and vice versa, than had hitherto been possible.

Associated with this decentralisation of the planning process was the establishment of a new committee of the Board called the Strategy Committee, under the Chairmanship of the Board Member for Finance and Planning. This advises the Board and acts on its behalf in connection with the formulation of strategy at the business unit and the corporate levels. Thus the basic assumptions would be agreed by the Strategy Committee, as would the framework of policies and the ground rules under which business unit plans would be developed. This provides a coherence to the planning process without undermining the responsibilities and initiatives of the five separate business units. Since the Chief Executive (Railways) is a member of this Committee, and since he is also Chairman of Rail Executive (effectively the Executive Board of the railways), the links between strategy formation, railway corporate planning and management aciton are very close.

The Strategy Committee has also conducted its own studies into key issues of relevance to the formulation of the Board's policies, including, for example, the problem of joint costs between individual business units. And the Committee itself has exercised discipline in relation to the plans put forward by railway, subsidiary and associated businesses where they are not thought to be good enough. In all of these functions the Strategy Committee is supported by the Central Policy Unit as well as an expert and experienced team of management accountants.

With the appointment in September 1983 of the former Chief Executive (Railways) as the new Chairman of BRB some changes of the processes described in the two previous paragraphs are bound to occur, but the Strategy Committee itself is well established and has been seen to be very successful.

Content

Each business unit needs to have a clear statement of its objectives and targets, and where these have not been provided by the government British Rail itself has invented its own, recognising that for management control purposes these are essential.

Basically the rail business is divided into two segments: the 'commercial' business units (InterCity, Freight and Parcels) and the 'social' railway (the Provincial Services, and London and the South East commuter services). In the 'social' railway, effectively the government is purchasing rail services on behalf of the community and making them generally available. The method of purchase is through the Public Service Obligation (PSO), which is formally authorised by the EEC Commission.

The government has, for example, set an objective for the InterCity business, that it shall break even by 1986 and achieve a 5 per cent real rate of return on its assets (on a current cost accounting basis) as soon as possible thereafter; and the government has set the freight sector the objective of achieving a 5 per cent rate of return on assets employed after charging depreciation at current cost.

The Corporate Plan incorporates detailed plans and forecasts over the period 1983–8 for the rail business as well as for the other subsidiary and associated companies within the British Rail group (these include BREL, Travellers Fare, Freightliner, Property Board, BTA, Transmark and the R & D Plan). The financial consequences are also aggregated to the corporate level.

In the formulation of individual business unit plans the introduction of the five sectors of the rail business has also provided the framework for, and given a clear impetus to, the development of higher-level strategic planning. The Inter-City management are in the process of completing a 3-volume strategic review of their entire business, volume 1 being a detailed business analysis of InterCity, volume 2 being a thorough examination of options, and volume 3 being their proposed strategy. This Report will be presented to the Strategy Committee and to the Board for their consideration and approval, and the agreed policies will be included in future Corporate Plans when Action Plans exist, with the agreement and commitment of all those concerned. This way of developing pro-active policies is a new departure for British Rail and contrasts sharply with the style and approach of earlier studies, such as the

Passenger Business Sector Strategy, completed after immense effort by the then Planning Department only four years ago. It is a consequence of delegating authority to individual businesses, giving them clearly defined net revenue responsibilities and setting them unambiguous targets. It is also a consequence of appointing the right people to these important new posts.

Problems

The first problem is that certain key authorisations are decided by the government only on an annual basis – the External Financing Limits and the limits to the PSO payments – whereas railway planning has to be long-term. Assumptions have to be made therefore about these limits over the next five years, and they could turn out to be wrong (but since the expected future requirement is for a steadily and steeply declining PSO there is some chance of their proving to be acceptable to the government). The Investment Ceiling has not in the past been an operative limit because the EFLs have imposed lower levels of investment than had previously been authorised as a result of the Investment and Financing Reviews.

The railways constitute a total network, and train services provided by each of the separate business units will incur joint costs when they use the same infrastructure. These pose particular problems in management and in planning. There is no unique solution to this problem – indeed one would argue that there have to be compelling reasons in the first place for wanting to allocate joint costs (in the British Rail situation there are two such reasons: as a firm basis for sector management responsibilities, and because part of the railway system is supported by the PSO and part is 'commercial'). Different allocation systems must be used for different purposes.

Moreover the railway business is organised on a three-dimensional basis: first are the five business units which have high levels of net revenue responsibility and where plans and policies emerge; second there has to be strong geographical management because the railway system is geographically dispersed, with local depots, train services which originate in many parts of the country, and which terminate after short or long journeys; third there is functional management, with a strong engineering focus, with the need for a central railway operations activity (to ensure the effective use of locomotives between the various business unit uses, for example), with personnel, finance and accounting, etc. being important functional activities also.

In such an organisation, one dimension has to be dominant and the leading edge of policy and change. This is the role of the Directors of the five individual business units. But of course they cannot act in isolation because of the unity of the network and the importance of joint costs. So while the broad framework is very clear, as are the responsibilities of the five Sector Directors, there has to be a great deal of working together for the common good, through discussion, negotiation and agreement.

The most acute difficulties arise where actions that Directors of the 'commercial' sectors see as being in their commercial interest have an impact on the 'social' sectors, with implications for the required support by government. Thus it may seem inconsistent for the government to be supporting little-used cross-country rural services where perhaps revenues from passenger fares do not even pay the direct costs of providing the service, while the InterCity business, because it has a break-even target, may want to close down much more heavily used routes which do not achieve that target (or the higher 5 per cent return) but which fully cover their direct costs.

Inevitably these strategic issues bear heavily upon government strategy for the railways: they are not capable of resolution by British Rail alone.

These are, however, problems to be overcome within the existing framework which has now been introduced. There are many examples already of sound business decision-making which almost certainly in the past would have been dominated by engineering considerations or unduly influenced by other specialist interests. The changes described took nearly three years to work out and to bring to the point of introduction; and the full impact at lower levels in British Rail have yet to be experienced. There is much still to be done.

STRATEGIC PLANNING IN THE BRITISH AIRPORTS AUTHORITY

Probably the key strategic issue covering all sectors of civil aviation is the question of privatisation. The purposes of privatisation appear to be as follows: in the short term to make a financial contribution to government revenue and to reduce the PSBR; in the longer term to lead to greater efficiency through private sector market discipline and greater competition, and to reduce the need for government involvement, thus saving Ministerial and civil-service time.

Privatisation raises several kinds of strategic issues for the enterprises concerned. In the case of British Aerospace and Associated British Ports, there is an issue concerning the longer-term implications of these continuing relationships with the government, mentioned earlier. If there is public money in the enterprise there must be a public purpose; and if there is a public purpose there must be accountability. Furthermore, government representatives on the Board must presumably account for their performance in some way, at least at the time when they come up for reappointment. To have these substantial interests in an enterprise without specific purpose or accountability would appear to indicate a failure in public responsibility. This is an issue which should be clarified in future privatisation proposals.

The major issue for the British Airports Authority and for British Airways is, of course, the form in which privatisation will take place (will the British Airports Authority be sold as a single concern, as it strongly desires, or will individual airports be sold separately?); and there are questions of timing, residual government involvement, capital structure, etc. These would all have an impact on the strategic policies of these two enterprises (British Airways is also the largest single customer of BAA).

The deepest involvement by government in the strategic policies of the BAA arises from the need to undertake planning enquiries for major airport developments (by far the largest of these is the enquiry recently completed into the further development of Stansted, and its major alternative – Terminal 5 at Heathrow). The outcome of such enquiries are fundamental to the strategic policies of the BAA, and in the past there have been occasions when ministers made different decisions from those recommended by the planning inspectors. Planning enquiries introduce delay as well as uncertainty (periods in excess of one year between the receipt of an Inspector's Report and a government decision have been experienced).

The BAA also illustrates an issue concerning the specification of objectives. As a result of the report by the Central Policy Review Staff in 1981, special efforts were made by the government to reach agreement with nationalised industries on their objectives. An attempt to persuade the BAA to adopt a set of objectives proposed by the government was thwarted by the fact that BAA has statutory duties laid down by parliament, and it could not fetter itself against the fulfilment of those duties. (A compromise was reached, but the BAA were clearly right in giving priority to their statutory duties over a set of objectives which would have had no statutory basis or authority.)

In 1982, following the reappointment of the Chairman, a study was undertaken of the top-level organisation of the management of the BAA, following which the responsibilities for corporate planning of the Director Planning were widened. A more pro-active approach was adopted as a result of this change and certain gaps in coverage which had been identified in the previous system were effectively closed. The 1984 Plan will reflect these changes and will adopt a more decentralised approach, with individual airport business plans taking a leading role. Major assumptions and strategic options are considered by the Board to provide the framework for the development of these plans.

The Corporate Plans themselves, however, cannot be like those in British Rail because of the fundamental importance of the outcome of planning enquiries to the future development of the BAA. For example, a completely different approach to the forward planning of the London area airport system would be required if the government were to decide (against its present policy) in favour of the BAA developing a fifth terminal at Heathrow instead of developing the existing airport at Stansted. British Rail excludes Electrification of its InterCity routes from 1983–8 Corporate Plan because this has not been approved by government: the BAA has to include developments at Stansted in its 1983 Corporate Plan even though there is no government approval for it, because without it the whole future of the BAA would be different.

The BAA has also changed its planning system in response to events, although not as radically as has British Rail. It is, however, a financially successful public enterprise which reduces the concerns of government, although the government has to take a public stance on its major strategic policies towards the BAA because of the need for public enquiries before airport terminals can be built or developed. The fact that, over the years, governments have changed their minds several times over the 'Third London Airport' issue makes forward planning by the BAA more difficult – but at least at any given time there is a strategy.

TRANSPORT CO-ORDINATION

Transport activities are almost all subject to considerable competition. The private sector is substantial, in some modes wholly dominant, and always a potential threat to the public sector. Entry barriers vary widely and are low in some key sectors (road haulage and inter-city buses, for example). In these circumstances, even though the government and its agencies and enterprises are extremely important, co-ordination of the industry from the centre is an impossibility.

The market is – and undoubtedly will remain – the means of co-ordination. What people are prepared to pay for must be the principal guide to resource allocation. But the market signals must be appropriate to efficient resource allocation objectives. In certain situations – where congestion costs are significant, or where there are thought to be other strong social reasons for maintaining services where customers would not be prepared to pay enough to cover costs – free market pricing is unlikely to result in efficient or appropriate resource allocation. So a public authority must step in.

Furthermore, the government must co-ordinate its own involvement in the various transport activities, where it decides that intervention would be appropriate, and that such intervention should be reasonably consistent. As has already been outlined, the government has assumed many roles more interventionist than simply being 'an enabler'.

To provide an appropriate framework within which competition can operate is, however, a key task for government – no one else can do it. That framework, to enable competition to work both within and between modes, is perhaps the most important aspect of government policy.

Co-ordination of the government's own involvement in transport should be made easier now because of the concentration of government responsibility in the Department of Transport. While this makes for a large department with many different concerns and pressure groups, co-ordination of the government's own policies and programmes to provide consistency should improve.

In practice, however, there will remain many problems which are simply too difficult for the government to solve. Probably the main reason is political, with many pressure groups which, in terms of support for the government, cannot be completely ignored, even if all parties know that there is no logic in the case put forward.

The proposed new London Regional Transport looks as though it was the victim of such pressure groups. An original proposal, which seemed sensible at the time, was that there would be a strong transport executive, with four operating divisions: London Transport underground; London Transport Buses; Country Buses; and British Rail London and the South East Services. But now the LRT is to be for London Transport only, with (according to Cmnd 9004) 'new liaison arrangements' with British Rail, and the possibility of transferring the 'support of British Rail's London commuter services' to the LRT later.

However these – and other matters – are resolved, it is most important that managers in transport enterprises should be motivated to stretch themselves to achieve good performance, that the right market signals should be given, and that transport undertakings should have sufficient discretion in the way they work, and in the directions of possible change, to allow for flexibility and innovation. The government also has wide responsibilities in the industry and it is reasonable to expect it to discharge these responsibilities with efficiency and effectiveness. Where political considerations are dominant and where there are many technical problems involved in arriving at appropriate solutions, these simple desiderata are far from easy to achieve.

CONCLUSIONS

Four conclusions emerge from this chapter. First, corporate planning in transport public enterprises is greatly influenced by government policies and the consequences of the government's own strategic planning. In particular this places a heavy burden of responsibility on the Department of Transport which itself has a wide range of other concerns in transport. It has many distinct roles, which require to be well co-ordinated.

Second, governments find that control of public enterprises through the specification of strategic objectives is extremely difficult to achieve successfully. Given that governments are politically dominated with inevitably short-time horizons, perhaps the problems of strategy formation are just too great.

Third, the role and practice of planning in some transport public enterprises has been subject to fundamental change in recent years, with generally a more pro-active market-orientated approach being adopted, usually as a consequence of important organisational change in the management of the business concerned.

Finally, there is a clear need for the co-ordination of strategic policies within the Department of Transport. The implementation of these policies will determine the framework within which market forces in transport will operate, and so the Department must be aware of the likely impact of their chosen policies on the operation of the market. Ultimately it is the market for transport activities, through consumer choice and the rates of return of businesses, public and private, that allocates those resources not provided by the government itself: but the government is such an important actor, particularly in the provision of roads, the support of some rail and bus services and through its taxation policies, that it cannot itself escape having a responsibility for the outcome of these market forces. In formulating its policies, therefore, the government must be sensitive to market pressures and act *as if* it were subject to them. In doing so, however, it should respond on the basis of social costs and benefits if national resources in transport are to be allocated efficiently.

12 Strategies for Coal and Electricity

RICHARD PRYKE

The most interesting and difficult policy problems in the energy industries are to be found in coal and electricity. Before discussing what should happen in the future I want to examine the developments that have taken place since the energy crisis of 1973. I shall throughout be primarily concerned with investment policy because it is here that the decisions may properly be described as strategic.

COAL: DEMAND FORECASTS

During the early 1970s the coal industry's capital expenditure was at a very low ebb, but in 1974 the NCB published *Plan for Coal* and embarked on a massive programme of modernisation and reconstruction. The Board argued that, due to the huge increase in the cost of oil, the industry's prospects had greatly improved and stated that demand might range up to 150 million tons.[*][1] In fact its central estimate was that it would be able to sell 135 million tons, including 5 million tons of exports.[2] In 1977, *Coal for the Future* 'reaffirmed' the figure of 135 million tons.[3]

However, demand was only likely to reach this level if the economy expanded at an improbably high rate. In 1977 the Department of Energy forecast that domestic consumption would amount to 130 million tonnes* in 1985, but this assumed that the growth rate would rise to about 3 per cent per annum.[4] At that time large private firms were assuming for planning purposes that the GDP would increase by 2.5 per cent per annum.[5] Some idea of the

* Throughout this chapter figures are given in tons (i.e. imperial tons) or tonnes (i.e. metric tons) according to the way the original forecasts, etc., were expressed.

extent to which the NCB's target was excessive can be obtained by looking at the prospective power station market. The NCB forecast that the electricity industry would consume 90 million tons in 1985. By averaging the CEGB's estimates of coal consumption for high and low economic growth it is possible to see what it would have forecast if, like private industry, it had been assuming that the GDP would rise by about 2.5 per cent per annum. On this basis the CEGB's Corporate Plans for 1976 and 1977 show a consumption of 65–70 million tonnes, after allowing for Scotland.[6] Only if there were to be rapid economic growth and a large rise in oil prices – an improbable combination – would power stations' demand reach the NCB's figure at 89 million tonnes.

In *Coal for the Future* the NCB forecast that by the year 2000 there would be a market for about 170 million tons of British coal. It was estimated that power stations would consume around 85 million tons, but this assumed that a considerable amount of new coal-fired capacity would be installed.[7] A sensible planning assumption would have been that nuclear power would take over the base load. In this case only around 70 million tons of coal would be needed, granted the NCB's reasonable assumptions about the growth in power stations' total fuel consumption. The Board allowed for the use of around 10 million tons of coal in the production of substitute natural gas and expected that by 2000 industrial consumption of natural gas would be in decline.[8] However, British Gas was not expecting the supply of natural gas to tail off until after 2000.[9] It would not have been unreasonable for the NCB to assume that there would be a market for 135 million tons of coal: the figure at the bottom end of the Board's range.

The NCB not only made forecasts that were unrealistic but it was very slow to revise them downwards. Early in 1979 the Board was still predicting a demand for around 175 million tonnes in 2000, and as late as 1981 it was hoping that the home market would absorb around 145 million tonnes, although by then independent experts were forecasting that the figure would be no more than about 120 million tonnes.[10] Moreover, it was not until 1980 that the Board abandoned its forecast of 130 million tons of inland sales by 1985.[11] During 1979 inland consumption had, it is true, climbed sharply to 129 million tonnes because of the huge rise in oil prices when the Shah fell. However, economic prospects had deteriorated. By 1979 large private firms were expecting the economy to grow by only 1.7

per cent per annum.[12] Furthermore, although cheap foreign coal had become available, the NCB went on assuming that almost no coal would be imported. The Board was relying on being able to prevent the CEGB from importing, as it had in the autumn of 1977 when cheap Australian coal was on offer, and during 1979 when the Board was forced to dump previously contracted supplies at a loss on the Continent.[13]

MEETING ESTIMATED DEMAND

I now want to look at the supply side. It was stated in *Plan for Coal* that deep-mined capacity, which then stood at around 120 million tons, would by 1985 be reduced by 33 million tons through the exhaustion and closure of collieries. It was proposed to create a corresponding amount of new capacity; and with 8–9 million tons through the better use of existing capacity, and 15 million tons of opencast coal, 'the industry would be within close reach of satisfying a possible demand of 150 million tons'.[14]

By the time of *Coal for the Future*, the Board had dropped the idea of providing capacity to meet a demand that, even on its own estimates, was unlikely to occur: a proposal that had originally been justified with the ironic argument that it would 'provide the industry with a stable future'.[15] The Board's target was now limited to 135 million tons, but on the other hand it was no longer thought that production could be increased by improving the use of existing capacity, and it was now forecast that new mines would provide 10 million tons less than had originally been planned.[16] The problem of how to make good this shortfall was overcome by deciding to close pits more slowly. It was now decided to limit colliery closures to a total of 23 million tons.

This was considerably less than the Board's loss-making output. During 1976–7, those mines that made an operating loss, after depreciation at historic cost, had an output of 49 million tonnes, and of this, 32 million tonnes was produced at collieries which did not make a profit at any time during the following five years. Moreover, pits that only made a profit in one year out of six and were still losing money at the end of the period accounted for 9 million tonnes.[17] These figures must include the output of some pits which the Board had planned to close. Between 1973–4 and mid-1982, mines that produced about 14 million tonnes were shut, although it had been intended that 23 million tonnes of capacity would be eliminated.[18] Hence up to 9 million tonnes of the output from grossly unprofitable pits was accounted for by collieries that the NCB was planning to close. It follows, however, that those mines which were persistently or almost persistently unprofitable over the period from 1976–7 to 1981–2 were responsible for more than 30 million tonnes of output. This strongly suggests that the Board's plans implied that a large part of its output would be produced at a loss for many years to come.

The only escape from such a conclusion would be to argue that the Board underestimated its costs, which is a poor defence, or that it overestimated its revenue. At first sight the latter seems likely, and excusable, because the NCB can scarcely be blamed for failing to foresee the present world recession and the reduction in coal prices that has resulted. However, it turns out that the Board's revenue per tonne of deep-mined output was 3 per cent higher (in real terms) in 1981–2 than it had been in 1976–7.[19] The Board could have been expecting a larger increase but it would not have been prudent in 1977 to have expected any great rise before the mid-1980s.

By 1976 the NCB had already exhausted the scope for raising its prices which the escalation in the cost of oil had provided. In the autumn of 1975, the Chairman of the Coal Board warned that:

> the average effective price advantage of coal over oil delivered to power stations . . . has now been eroded to little more than 10% by a virtual doubling in the price of coal. Substantial tonnages are already very close to the crossover point where coal could again become uncompetitive against oil. Our coking coal prices have increased by about 140% over the past year and, as a result, imported supplies of many qualities of coking coal are now cheaper than ours at coastal steel works.[20]

During 1976–7 industry paid about as much per therm for coal as for oil, after allowing for coal's non-price disadvantages.[21]

No great rise in the real price of oil seems to have been expected before about 1985 either by the Board or the Department of Energy. The latter concluded that in 1985 the demand for OPEC oil would probably lie between 1,500 and 2,050 million tonnes, whereas OPEC's capacity would amount to 2,250–2,350 million tonnes. 'OPEC' it concluded, 'is likely to hold significant quantities of spare oil production capacity, but will nevertheless be able to maintain the real oil price and perhaps to increase it'.[22] A rise in the price of oil was therefore scarcely something which, over the medium term, the Board could bank on, and no great increase was to be expected. The NCB appears to have taken the same view as the Department of Energy. At the beginning of 1977 one of the Board's full-time members stated that the next decade or so would be a 'difficult and confused period, with a possible surplus of energy'.[23]

This does not necessarily mean that the NCB was not expecting some rise in the price of coal, but in order that all its prospective output might become profitable it would have had to have been hoping for a very large increase. During 1981–2 a substantial tonnage was produced at a huge loss. This included the output of many pits that, back in 1976–7, the Board had been hoping to close. I have assumed, although it is unrealistic, that the 9 million tonnes of additional capacity which the Board had been planning to shut (by 1985) would have coincided with the most unprofitable output in 1981–2. If it had, the revenue per tonne at the most unprofitable collieries that would still have been open would have had to be as much as 50 per cent higher than it was during 1981–2 in order for them to have covered their operating costs in that year.[17]

It is therefore difficult to avoid the conclusion that the Board's plans implied that a large part of its output would continue to be produced at a loss. The NCB would no doubt reply that it was unable to shut its unprofitable pits because the NUM would only permit the closure of those that were completely exhausted. However, the Board did not, until 1981, even try to overcome union opposition, because it was aiming to produce all the coal that its over-ambitious plans suggested it would be able to sell. As this could only be achieved by continuing to produce at many loss-making collieries they had to be kept open. If the Board had wanted to accelerate the closure of unprofitable pits it could, for instance, have publicised how much they were losing. However, this was a closely guarded secret which even the Department of Energy was not supposed to know. Another obvious step was for the Board to refuse to embark on its investment programme without a firm commitment by the NUM to allow the closure of unprofitable pits.

None was sought. Instead the NCB proceeded to invest heavily in pits that were hopelessly unprofitable. Let us now examine the industry's massive programme of capital expenditure.

THE ESTIMATED RATE OF RETURN

Some projects appeared to show a high rate of return. This was true in particular of investment in new drift mines and of projects that would raise the output of existing collieries. It was estimated that for schemes of the latter type the average internal rate of return was 30 per cent.[24] Some of the life-extension and modernisation projects also appeared to show good rates of return, but many were not very profitable – although they should have shown internal rates of return of at least 10 per cent, since this was the Board's normal cut-off point.[25] The life-extension schemes were almost all at collieries which had previously been candidates for closure. Consequently they had been starved of capital, and in many cases relatively large amounts of replacement investment were necessary if production was to continue. Moreover, the prolongation of collieries' lives often meant that inferior reserves would have to be opened up. Thus in some cases productivity would fall, and in others a low grade of coal would be produced.

Unfortunately, the Coal Board's profitability estimates had, and still have, serious weaknesses. The rate of return on new investment was calculated by forecasting what the net cash flows would be if the project were carried out, and then subtracting the likely net cash flows in its absence and/or with a feasible alternative. The internal rate of return was then found by discovering what rate of discount would reduce the difference between the two sets of net cash streams to zero.[26] This meant that where, but for the project, a pit would incur cash losses, the Coal Board treated them as part of the benefit. In other words, the NCB regarded a loss avoided as being equivalent to a profit earned. However, the correct way of handling losses is to count them as a cost while the contemplated investment project will be in progress, and to ignore them thereafter. The rationale for this is that losses can always be avoided by closing down.

The Coal Board would argue that unless the pit in question was completely exhausted, closure was impossible, because the mineworkers' union was so powerful and recalcitrant. Something has already been said about this and I shall merely remark that, if the Board refused to invest, closure would become inevitable, and that the NUM would have had to be unbelievably powerful to have forced management to engage in capital expenditure. The Board could always, as a last resort, close unprofitable pits but continue to pay their workers: an option which has in some cases become financially advantageous. Because so many collieries were making losses, or would soon do so but for investment, the Board's method must often have given an exaggerated impression of the likely return on capital expenditure, especially in the case of life-extension and modernisation projects.

The Board tried to guard against investment in pits that would remain unprofitable by discounting the cash flow of the colliery (including the costs and revenues of the project but ignoring all previous investment) over the period of the project by a rate that reduced its value to zero. The general rule was that this rate of return must be 5 per cent or more, after allowing in some cases for the risk that the planned results might not have been achieved.[27] However, the 5 per cent rule was sometimes waived. When the Monopolies Commission examined major projects that were already in operation it found that six of the fifty-nine collieries were not expected to be viable on completion.[28]

Moreover, investment in mining machinery was not fully taken into account. Collieries obtain such machinery from Area plant pools and pay charges that are based on the value of the equipment at historic costs.[29] These charges were regarded as an operating cost but, because interest was ignored and depreciation was only partly covered, the prospective rate of return was exaggerated. If the Board disregarded a large part of the cost of using mining machinery, the question arises of whether it also ignored the substantial amount of ongoing investment that is required in order to keep a pit in operation.

A further weakness of the Board's system for avoiding invest-ment at pits where prospective costs exceeded prospective receipts, was that it generally assumed that there would be no increase in the real level of miners' earnings.[30] This was wholly unrealistic: not only were they likely to rise in line with the general increase in incomes but miners had not managed, by 1976, to re-establish the lead over other workers which they enjoyed when the demand for coal had previously been strong.[31] It is true that the Board did not, on the other hand, allow for any increase in the real price of coal. However, as we have seen, no rise was expected until the mid-1980s. Because the NCB ignored the prospective increase in miners' wages, the Boards estimates must have conveyed a very exaggerated impression of pits' future profitability. It was to guard against such errors that the government had told the nationalised industries in the second White Paper 'to make allowance for the likelihood that the real price of labour will rise continuously through time'.[32]

PROJECTS IN PRACTICE

As might have been expected, the Coal Board turns out to have devoted a large part of its capital expenditure to unprofitable pits. Between 1977–8 and 1981–2 it appears to have invested £180 million, at current prices, at collieries which are not classified as having a life of more than five years or a satisfactory history and prospects. This represented 7 per cent of total capital expenditure. A further £435 million, or 17 per cent was invested at mines which, though they are regarded as having satisfactory prospects, failed to make an operating profit at any time over the period; and pits that made losses for three or four years out of the five were responsible for another £675 million of investment.[33] This meant that pits which were unprofitable in most years, or throughout the period, accounted for almost half of the Board's capital expenditure.

A substantial part of the investment devoted to large projects has not yet fructified. However, the performance of those mines at which major schemes have been completed is extremely disappointing. Out of the sixty-four projects, thirty-seven, or 58 per cent, were at collieries where there was an operating loss in 1981–2. The NCB says that thirty-seven out of the fifty-nine pits involved were profitable, or were expected to become profitable. This left twenty-two 'where prospects were more problematical'.[34] These mines accounted for 35 per cent of the total investment that had been made. According to the Board, half of the dud pits had been adversely affected by the collapse of the market for coking coal, and it has been argued that until late 1977 the NCB was encouraged to plan coking-coal production to match the BSC's expansion plans.[35] But it was obvious long before 1977 that BSC's plans were over-ambitious, and in the autumn of 1975 the Chairman of the Coal Board recognised that imported coking coal was often cheaper. The NCB's investment plans were based on the hope that the Steel Corporation would not wake up to the fact that British coking coal was of poor quality and relatively expensive. During 1979 it did.

The main reason why investment projects have provided such poor returns is that their cost and duration were under-estimated, and that production and productivity were over-estimated. The cost of those projects that have been completed was 4 per cent greater than anticipated, and they were, on average, fourteen months behind schedule. The shortfall in production averaged 7 per cent, and ouput per manshift was 10 per cent lower than had been estimated.[36] As the gain in productivity was estimated at around 30 per cent, it appears that only about 55 per cent of the projected rise was being achieved.[37] That the benefits of capital expenditure were exaggerated is scarcely surprising in view of the Board's over-optimism about the industry's prospects.

Moreover, in some areas it was probably necessary to exaggerate, if they were to share in the investment bonanza. It is noteworthy that in North Nottinghamshire – the most profitable area – output and productivity have been above the forecast level, but in South Wales – the most unprofitable – production was around 20 per cent below the projected figure and productivity was about 30 per cent lower.[38] South Wales and Scotland were obviously risky places in which to invest, but their proportion of the Board's total capital expenditure on major projects at existing mines, over the period between 1974–5 and 1981–2, was only a little lower (12.4 per cent) than their initial share of deep-mined output (16.2 per cent).[39]

ELECTRICITY INVESTMENT SINCE 1973

While capital expenditure in the coal industry has boomed since 1973, electricity investment has been in the doldrums. This contrast is at first sight puzzling, because the rise in the price of fossil fuels should have made nuclear power more attractive, and it is, of course, highly capital intensive. However, in contrast to coal, the electricity industry was already at an advanced stage of a huge investment programme. This was intended to provide for a large increase in demand, but the rate at which this was growing had fallen and was to fall further. Hence there was ample capacity, and although the CEGB tried to launch an ambitious programme for the construction of Pressurised Water Reactors (PWRs), the Board's case lost its force when it became evident how slowly demand was now increasing.[40]

The PWR was a proven reactor system for which (along with the BWR) almost every country in the world had opted, and our disastrous experience with the Advanced Gas Cooled Reactor (AGR) had shown the danger of being outside the technological mainstream. Nevertheless, in mid-1974 the government opted for the Steam Generating Heavy Water Reactor, although even the South of Scotland Electricity Board, which appeared to be its one strong partisan, conceded that a PWR or BWR would be more economic.[41] The Steam Generator turned out to be far more difficult to develop than the government had anticipated. In the end it was decided to stop working on it and to build two more AGRs. The construction of one AGR was necessary in order to keep this reactor system alive – though it would have been better dead – and the other was sanctioned for the compelling reason that if England was to have a new AGR, Scotland must have one too.

The total outcome of the period since the energy crisis has been the commencement of these two AGRs, the building of a coal-fired station that was not required, and the ordering of oil-burning capacity equivalent to two-and-a-half nuclear stations.[42] This capacity will be wildly uneconomic, and the CEGB calculates that, even if the price of coal remains at its March 1982 level, it is preferable to construct a PWR rather than a coal-fired station (because the PWR has a lower net effective cost).[43] Furthermore, according to the CEGB's latest estimates, which merely confirm earlier figures, an AGR costs 25 per cent more to construct than a PWR, without any compensating advantages.[44] Not a single PWR was started, although, as we shall see, the construction of some capacity would have been justified simply on cost-saving grounds.

AVOIDABLE ERRORS AND WHY?

The investment policies of the coal and electricity industries have been marred during the past decade by a series of major errors which could and should have been avoided. It may be said that I am simply being wise after the event, and that it was impossible to foresee how gloomy economic prospects would become. But my strictures do not for the most part relate to the industry's demand forecasts. In electricity, power stations were not of the right type, and in the case of coal, the Coal Board greatly overestimated the physical benefits from investment, employed misleading methods to estimate the financial yield, and must have been planning to supply a large tonnage on which a loss would be incurred. These are supply-side criticisms. In the case of coal, I have also found fault with the NCB's demand projections, but this is not because they are now turning out to be too high, but because they were over-optimistic even when they were made and prospects appeared more rosy. Early in 1975 I forecast that inland demand for NCB coal would be about 120 million tons in 1981. This compares with the NCB's then figure of 130 million in 1980.[45]

Most of the criticisms that I have made were voiced years ago by Duncan Burn and Professor Gerald Manners, or appeared in my book *The Nationalised Industries*.[46] My critique of the NCB's planning was written during 1979 but was based on some disturbing interviews which I conducted in the latter part of 1977. Moreover I was sceptical about the Coal Board's investment programme from the time that it was launched in 1974. It is now possible, because of a Monopolies Commission report, to provide a fuller and better-supported account of the NCB's planning and the poor results that are being achieved at pits where major investment schemes have been completed.[47]

If it is accepted that serious and avoidable mistakes have been made, the question arises of why this occurred. In the case of the NCB, the basic explanation for past errors appears to have been the belief by those in charge that because oil was running out there was a *need* for coal. They were convinced that there would sooner or later be a market for more coal, and that if for some reason demand was less than expected the Government should provide the industry with support and protection. The Board did not view itself primarily as a commercial undertaking but as the guardian of the public interest, and it believed, and believed passionately, that this would best be served by the maintenance and then the expansion of its own capacity.

In this situation, which was not difficult to discern, it was more than usually necessary for the sponsoring Department to vet the NCB's plans and ensure that investment was being properly appraised. This did not happen. One important reason was that Labour, which was in power until mid-1979, was emotionally committed to coal and closely tied to the mineworkers' union. Hence when the Coal Board submitted its plans they were readily endorsed after tripartite examinations. Instead of exercising a restraining influence, the Department suggested in its Green Paper of 1978 that there would be a market for 220 million tons of coal in the year 2000, and raised the spectre of a nation unable to buy abroad at any price. How, in a world in which energy was in such short supply, the British economy would manage to grow at a faster rate than ever before (just under 3 per cent per annum), was not explained.[48] It is evident, moreover, that politicians must take the blame for many of the mistakes that have been made since 1973 in power-station ordering.

SIZEWELL B

The CEGB is now trying to obtain permission to construct a PWR at Sizewell, and if its estimates are correct it ought to be the harbinger of a series. In this case the expenditure will be huge and there will be a large reduction in the demand for coal. The decision over Sizewell B is therefore a strategic choice of the first order. I propose to look at the Board's case and to try to throw some light on the economic issues that are involved.

To discover whether it is worth constructing a new station, and of what type it should be, the CEGB estimates the extra capital and operating expenditure that will be incurred year by year over the plant's life; it works out the saving in system fuel costs that will arise each year, because other more-expensive stations can be operated less intensively; and it discounts the net benefit or disbenefit for each year at 5 per cent and finds the net present value, converts this into an annuity to facilitate comparisons between stations that have different lives, and divides the annuity by the station's capacity, because stations differ in size. The outcome of this calculation is known as the net effective cost (NEC), and if it is negative the station is worth constructing because the fuel savings which it will provide exceed the costs that it will involve. Even if the fuel savings are insufficient to justify a new station, its construction may nevertheless be worthwhile because old plant can then be closed. So long as the new station's NEC is smaller than the NEC for obsolescent capacity, the new plant is economic because it will lead to a reduction in costs.

The CEGB made estimates for five future scenarios. Scenarios A and B assume that the economy will expand rapidly, with GDP increasing by 3.4 per cent per annum between 1983–4 and 2000; C assumes moderate growth, with the GDP rising by 1.4 per cent per annum; and D and E presume that the GDP falls by 0.4 per cent per annum.[49] Sizewell B's NEC has been estimated for each of these scenarios assuming a low nuclear background, which means that no further nuclear stations will be built; against a medium nuclear background, under which nuclear plant builds up until it accounts for 40 per cent of all capacity (by the year 2010 in Scenario C); and against a high nuclear background, by which nuclear stations ends up forming 70 per cent of all capacity (by 2020 in C).[50]

Nuclear plants have very low fuel costs, and the smaller the amount of coal- and oil-burning capacity the less scope there is for reducing system fuel costs. Hence the NECs for Sizewell B are lowest for the high nuclear background. They range, according to the CEGB's estimates, from −£108/kW per annum for Scenario B, to −£1/kW per annum for Scenario D.[51] Moreover, it is estimated that the least-efficient plant on the system during the 1990s will have an NEC of +£14/kW per annum.[52] This suggests that both Sizewell B and subsequent PWRs would be economically justified. The Board reports that calculations for Scenario C with a high nuclear background show that PWRs commissioning in 2000 would still have a negative NEC.[53]

SCENARIOS AND IMPORTED COAL

At first sight it seems very impressive that Sizewell B turns out to be economic over growth rates which range from 3.4 per cent per annum, which is unbelievably fast, to −0.4 per cent per annum, which is implausibly slow because it would almost certainly mean a massive and unacceptable growth in unemployment. However, more careful examination of the CEGB's figures shows that this robustness is due to the assumption that if the rate of growth is negative, and demand for electricity falls, it will construct far less capacity. Under Scenario B, where the peak demand more than doubles by the year 2030, the CEGB commissions almost 110 GW of nuclear and coal-burning plant, whereas under Scenario E, where peak demand falls more than a quarter, it commissions less than 38 GW.[54] Hence, the Board's scenarios do not reveal the impact that differing rates of growth *per se* would have on Sizewell B, because other variables, including the amount of future capacity, are not held constant. This provokes the question of why the scenarios have different NECs.

The principal reason is the large variation in the amount by which it is assumed that coal prices will rise. If this increase were to be the same, at 0 per cent, for each of the scenarios, their NECs would not differ very greatly.[55] According to the CEGB, what it pays for coal will largely depend on the price at which it can import. This, in turn, will depend on the UK exchange rate and the price of coal on the world market. The Board distinguished three possible cases: high world growth and a rapid increase in world coal prices, medium growth, and slowly increasing prices. Each of the possibilities for UK economic performance was then associated with one of the cases for world growth and world coal prices. However, as the Board itself remarks, 'except at the extremes the world economic outlook does not restrict UK economic performance. It is quite possible, for example, to assume that the UK economy is relatively successful even if the world economy is somewhat depressed'.[56]

The Board chose in Scenario C to associate moderate growth for the UK economy with moderate growth abroad, but it would be almost equally plausible to assume low world growth.[57] This would not, up to the year 2000, involve the implausible supposition that the UK will grow as fast as other developed countries. If medium domestic growth were to take place in the context of low world growth, our relative performance in productivity would be better than the Board's figures imply and the exchange rate may not deteriorate in the way that it is assuming for Scenario C.[58] Hence it is quite possible to envisage another Scenario which combines moderate domestic growth, an exchange rate of $1.50 to the pound and the Board's low case for world coal prices. Back-of-an-envelope calculations suggest that in these circumstances, and with a high nuclear background, Sizewell's NEC would deteriorate from Scenario C's −£32/kW per annum to around zero.

The question arises of whether the CEGB was right to construct its scenarios (and indeed of whether this approach has any great merit). The possible futures that it considered were based on various rates of UK growth, most of which were implausible – although the pivotal but largely unrelated factor that determines Sizewell's economic desirability is the amount by which the cost of coal increases. The scenarios divert attention from the main issue and must have absorbed time and energy which would have been better devoted to the consideration of coal prices.

The CEGB forecasts that with medium world growth the cost of steam coal on the international market will rise in real terms, from $60 per tonne (at March 1982 prices) in 1980–1 when it appears to have been around its long-run equilibrium level, to $90 in 2000 and $140 in 2030.[59] The Board's estimates for the period up to the turn of the century were based on forecasts of the principal coal exporters' marginal costs. These were obtained by escalating the various components at different rates. For instance, in the case of Australia, which is the marginal producer, it was assumed that, over the period 1978–2000, real wage costs per tonne will rise by 2 per cent per annum and other operating costs by $3\frac{1}{2}$ per cent per annum (although part of this increase arises because of the presumed appreciation of the Australian dollar against the US dollar).[60] The cost escalation factors for Australia, and the other producers, assume that technical progress will not be sufficient to offset the rise in real earnings, or the tendency for costs to rise as the best reserves are exhausted. This may turn out to be the case, but it is somewhat disconcerting to discover that virtually all the CEGB has to say about the subject is that 'There would appear to be little prospect of any changes in technology that would offset these cost increases.'[61] Furthermore, the Board seems to have assumed without further anaysis that world coal prices will go on increasing at a rapid rate after 2000. This is questionable in view of the huge reserves of medium-cost that are known to exist.[62]

The CEGB's view of the development of world coal prices is not the only one that can be taken. The NCB, on the basis of work by its separate coal research branch, is forecasting that the price at the turn of the century will lie between $60 and $90 per tonne. The CEGB's forecast for medium world growth is therefore the NCB's top figure, and the CEGB's estimate for low world growth corresponds to the mid-point of the Coal Board's range. Moreover the NCB is not expecting the price of coal to go beyond $100 per tonne.[63]

Two reasons have now emerged as to why the CEGB should have considered a scenario with moderate UK growth but lower coal prices than those the Board assumed. First, moderate growth at home may be combined with low instead of medium growth abroad and, second, the CEGB's estimates of coal prices may be on the high side, especially for the period beyond 2000. If such a medium-UK-growth/lower-coal-price scenario had been constructed, the case for Sizewell B would have appeared much weaker, because the results of the Board's possible futures would have been far less clear cut. This is scarcely surprising. If a scenario exercise is well conducted, and a wise range of possibilities are considered, it is quite likely that diverse answers will be obtained.

THE MARGINAL COST OF NCB COAL

Hitherto I have assumed, like the Board, that what is relevant is the price at which it can buy coal and that this will reflect the world market price, even though imports will continue to be shut out or tightly restricted. The latter seems a safe assumption, unless the coal industry's monopoly-hold on the electricity market is broken through a nuclear power programme. Hence the coal which Sizewell B will displace will come from the NCB, and, since it is produced at home, what is relevant from the point of view of the national economic welfare is not its price but what it costs to produce. The great weakness of the CEGB's case for constructing Sizewell B, and of the counter-arguments that have been advanced is that they relate to the price of coal. It is true that the projected pithead price is, until 2000, below the forecast average cost of producing British coal, including interest. But this does not help, because the CEGB's cost estimates are anything but convincing. It is, for instance, simply assumed that because expenditure per tonne on such items as power, light, materials and contract work has been rising rapidly, it will escalate by 4 per cent per annum at long-life pits, and by 2 per cent per annum at new mines. As a result, these costs rise by nearly three times between 1981–2 and 2030, and exert a powerful upward influence on the industry's average costs.[64]

Moreover, what are required are estimations of marginal and not average costs.

Two sets of marginal costs (MCs) must be distinguished. First there is the medium-term MC, which is the cost of mining the highest-cost coal that is produced at existing collieries. This includes all avoidable costs, including the capital charges on the ongoing investment which it is necessary to carry out. Second, there is the long-run MC, which is the cost of production at a new mine, including capital charges. The industry's future equilibrium position will be where the medium-term MC is equal to the long-run MC. I shall now try to throw some light on the medium-term MC.

Figures are available for each pit's operating costs per tonne during 1981–2.[65] These should approximate to medium-term avoidable costs because, although they only include a little historic cost depreciation, they embrace social costs, which are a transfer payment and not a resource cost. Coal is not a homogeneous product, but it was possible to estimate roughly what it would have cost to produce coal of the average electricity grade, by reducing (or increasing) each pit's costs per tonne by the amount by which its revenue per tonne exceeded (or fell short of) the average price that the CEGB paid. Those collieries which the Board has already closed, or regards as having a short life, were omitted, because they should have been shut by the early 1990s.[66] They accounted for nearly 20 million tonnes of output in 1981–2. Also, it has been assumed that by the year 2000, pits producing a further 16 million tonnes will have been shut, as the NCB believes that exhaustion will each year necessitate the closure of collieries with a capacity of 2 million tonnes.[67] These further closures would, it was assumed, involve pits with the same distribution of costs as the Board's short-life mines.

Opencast output was put at 15 million tonnes, and in addition the Board should, by the early 1990s, have 12.3 million tonnes of output from Selby and other new collieries that are under construction.[68] The CEGB postulates in Scenarios A and B that, in 2000, new mines will be able to provide 40 million tonnes.[69] However, this includes various developments such as Hose, Saltby, Margam and Park that are unlikely to go ahead. Thirty million tonnes is a more realistic figure.

The CEGB's estimates for Scenario C with a high nuclear background suggest that inland coal consumption will increase from

111 million tonnes in 1982 to 125 million tonnes in 1990, and 129 million tonnes in 1995, but then fall to 114 million tonnes at the turn of the century.[70] The Board's forecast for 1990 now seems on the high side, but even if demand is only 114 million tonnes in the early 1990s, the NCB's marginal cost will be £67.5 per tonne, at March 1982 prices. This compares with the CEGB's Scenario C forecast that the pithead price will be just under 144 per tonne in 1990, and that the equivalent cost of the imported coal and oil to be displaced by Sizewell will be about £67 per tonne. In 2000, the NCB marginal cost will, according to my estimates, be £53 per tonne, which is a little higher than the CEGB's forecast of £51.8 for the pithead price.[71] However, my figures assume that unit costs at the NCB's existing pits will remain at their 1981–2 level.

It is possible to believe that the NCB will, over the period up to 2000, prevent its average costs per tonne from rising, although this may be an optimistic assumption. The mines that are closed have above-average costs, and Selby's operating costs will be below average, implying a rise of 11.8 per cent at the Board's continuing collieries. Such a rise does not seem plausible. The Coal Board's forecasts imply that output per manshift at its long-life collieries will increase by only 1.5 per cent per annum between 1981–2 and 1990–1.[72] Moreover, the rate of productivity growth will probably tail off during the 1990s because it is improbable, and undesirable, that expenditure on the modernisation and reconstruction of collieries will be maintained at its existing high level. If the average cost at existing collieries does rise by 11.8 per cent, and the cost structure remains the same, the Board's MC will be £59.5 per tonne in 2000 (given a demand for 114 million tonnes). This is, of course, substantially above the pithead price estimate (£51.8) which the CEGB employed when it estimated Sizewell B's NEC for Scenario C with a high nuclear background.

After 2000, the medium-term MC of coal should decline, as new mines come into operation and old high-cost pits are closed (unless the world price has already risen above the NCB's MC and thereby forced it up). The reduction in the medium-term MC should continue until it becomes equal to the long-run MC (and the price of imported coal, which must ultimately rise). Without making a major investigation it is impossible to know what the long-run MC is likely to be, but even if it (and the world price of coal) is lower than the CEGB's Scenario C forecasts for the pithead price of British coal for the period beyond 2000, it does not follow that the case for nuclear power collapses. If the cost of coal were to be relatively low, the appropriate response would be to so restrict nuclear construction that Sizewell B and successor stations remain on base load throughout their lives.

Under Scenario C with a high nuclear background, Sizewell B is pushed off base load between the years 2005 and 2010.[73] If it were to remain on base load, it would provide greater savings in system fuel costs during its latter years and its NEC would fall. Despite the mass of figures which the CEGB has provided for the Sizewell B inquiry, it is impossible to discover by how much the station's NEC would be altered by lower prices and/or increased base load operation after 2005. However, it appears that under Scenario C with a medium nuclear background, where Sizewell B never goes off base load, its NEC would be no greater than +£17/kW per annum, even if the price of fossil fuels were to remain at the March 1982 level.[74] As the marginal cost of the coal that Sizewell B will displace is bound to be very much higher than this price up to 2000, and is likely to be considerably higher beyond, the station's NEC will almost certainly be negative.[75] It also seems likely that the earlier PWRs that follow Sizewell when there is a medium nuclear background – and nine are assumed by 2000 – will be economically justified, because if they are not constructed, and the demand for coal is greater, its MC will be astronomic.[76]

It may therefore be concluded that, if the case for a nuclear power programme is based (as it should be) on the cost of producing the British coal that is likely to be displaced, there are strong grounds in its favour. The weakness of the CEGB's argument for Sizewell B is that it rests on estimates of average costs and prices, which may (or may not) be too high. It seems most unlikely that the Board's failure to take account of the MC of producing British coal is due to any want of economic expertise: the CEGB is obviously a highly sophisticated body. It may be partly explained by the absence until recently of comprehensive and reliable information on the costs of production at each pit. However, the main reason is probably that the Board's duty is to manage electricity generation. If, as it assumes, the price of British coal will come to be determined by the price of imports, the fact that part of the NCB's output is and will continue to be produced at a very high cost is of no direct concern to the CEGB. However, it should be of concern to the Department of

Energy as the guardian of the public interest. It is regrettable that the Department, in its evidence to the Sizewell inquiry, saw fit to produce yet another set of scenarios – eight this time – and to confine itself to question-begging platitudes. It declares that 'prices should reflect market pressures where reasonably open markets exist, or the costs of supply in other cases. The Government considers it is then up to the consumer to rank his own investment priorities in the light of prevailing prices.'[77] What this ignores is that investment planning will continue to be defective, even if prices approximate to world levels, unless marginal costs are then adjusted downwards to these prices.

In coal, this would mean closing down all those collieries that are hopelessly unprofitable. Unless the government is able and willing to instruct the NCB to adopt such a policy, the CEGB needs to use shadow-pricing and base its investment strategy on the marginal cost of British coal, in which case the Coal Board will ultimately be compelled to shut loss-making pits because the construction of nuclear capacity will reduce its sales to its major customer: the electricity industry.[78] It is disappointing that the government has failed to face up to the fact that the NCB has always practised cross-subsidisation and that it is likely, even under Ian MacGregor, to continue to do so. The government needs to do more than utter slogans and construct scenarios. It ought to have formulated a coherent and economically defensible energy policy.

CONCLUSIONS

It has been shown in this chapter that the investment strategy that the Coal Board has pursued since 1973 has been marred by serious errors. The Board has been over-optimistic both about the level of demand and the pay-off from its capital expenditure projects. Moreover, it has been prepared to go on producing coal at a loss, and has devoted a substantial proportion of its investment to pits that have been persistently unprofitable. Grave mistakes have also been made in electricity, where, instead of constructing Pressurised Water Reactors, capital expenditure has been used for uneconomic oil- and coal-fired plant and for high-cost Advanced Gas Cooled Reactors.

In view of this, and the poor results that have been achieved in coal, the CEGB's decision to construct a PWR at Sizewell, and its desire to follow this up with further stations of the same type, should be a welcome one. However, the Board's case rests on the assumption that there is likely to be a large and continuing rise in the cost of coal, and it is quite possible that the world price will increase more slowly than is being assumed and/or that the exchange rate will deteriorate less. On the other hand, the Board bases its argument for Sizewell B on the price that it will be charged, although what is relevant in terms of economic welfare is the cost of producing the British coal which the station will displace. This will remain high even if, over the period between 1982 and 2000, the NCB closes down exhausted pits that mostly have high costs and which produce 36 million tonnes. After the turn of the century the marginal cost of British coal may decline, as more new mines come into operation and the remaining high-cost pits are closed, but the appropriate response would then be to limit the construction of nuclear capacity in order that Sizewell B and successor stations remain on base load, and provide large fuel savings, throughout their lives.

The government ought to have recognised that the NCB practises cross-subsidisation and instructed the CEGB to base its estimates on the prospective marginal cost of British coal. It has not done so. One of the most striking features of the last decade has been the government's failure to play a constructive role with respect to coal and electricity. Perhaps the time has come to abandon the hope that it ever will, and to devise an alternative system in which public ownership and monopoly are wherever possible replaced by private ownership and competition.

NOTES AND REFERENCES

1. NCB, *Plan for Coal* (NCB, 1974) pp. 8, 9.
2. Monopolies and Mergers Commission, *National Coal Board* (HMSO, 1983) pp. 70, 89: henceforth referred to as Cmnd 8920.
3. *Coal for the Future* (Department of Energy, 1977) p. 22.
4. Gerald Manners, *Coal in Britain: An Uncertain Future* (London: George Allen & Unwin, 1981) p. 29; *Plan for Coal* assumed growth of around $2\frac{1}{2}$ per cent per annum (Cmnd 8920, p. 64).
5. Monopolies and Mergers Commission, *Central Electricity Generating Board* (HMSO, 1981) p. 48.

6. CEGB, *Corporate Plan 1976* (CEGB, June 1976) fig. 2, p. 31; *Corporate Plan 1977* (CEGB, April 1977) fig. 2, p. 35.
7. *Coal for the Future*, pp. 15–17.
8. Robert P. Greene and J. Michael Gallagher (eds), *World Coal Study: Future Coal Prospects: Country and Regional Assessments* (Boston: Ballinger, 1980) p. 411.
9. Manners, *Coal in Britain*, p. 41.
10. Greene and Gallagher, *World Coal Study*; Cmnd 8920, p. 71.
11. Cmnd 8920, pp. 82, 89.
12. Monopolies and Mergers Commission, *CEGB*, p. 48.
13. Cmnd 8920, pp. 88, 90; CEGB *Annual Report and Accounts 1978–79*, pp. 14, 15.
14. *Coal Industry Examination: Interim Report June 1974* (Department of Energy) pp. 10–12.
15. NCB, *Plan for Coal*, p. 8.
16. *Coal for the Future*, p. 9.
17. Cmnd 8920, vol. 2, pp. 30–41; etc.
18. Cmnd 8920, p. 174.
19. Cmnd 8920, p. 31, vol. 2, p. 25.
20. *Colliery Guardian*, September 1975, p. 389.
21. Department of Energy, *Digest of United Kingdom Energy Statistics*, 1979 (HMSO, 1979) p. 117; *Energy Policy: A Consultation Document* (HMSO, 1978) p. 29: henceforth referred to as Cmnd 7101.
22. Cmnd 7101, pp. 8–10, 14.
23. Leslie Grainger, 'Coal and Nuclear Power', *Coal and Energy Quarterly*, Spring 1977, p. 12.
24. *Coal for the Future*, p. 11.
25. Cmnd 8920, p. 192.
26. Ibid.
27. Cmnd 8920, pp. 192, 193.
28. Cmnd 8920, p. 210.
29. Cmnd 8920, pp. 32, 308.
30. Cmnd 8920, p. 190.
31. Pay Board, *Relative Pay of Mineworkers*, Cmnd 5567 (HMSO, 1974) p. 31; Richard Pryke, *The Nationalised Industries: Policies and Performance since 1968* (London: Martin Robertson, 1981) p. 49.
32. *Nationalised Industries: A Review of Economic and Financial Objectives*, Cmnd 3437 (HMSO, 1967) para 29.
33. Cmnd 8920, pp. 196, 197. If £2,320m represented 89 per cent of total investment this amounted to £2,607m, and if £1,317m is deducted in respect of pits that were consistently or mainly profitable, and £1,110m for those that were consistently or largely unprofitable, then £180m remains and presumably relates to CD2 collieries.
34. Cmnd 8920, pp. 210, 211.
35. Cmnd 8920, p. 78.
36. Cmnd 8920, pp. 203, 204.
37. *Coal for the Future*, p. 11; NCB *Reports and Accounts 1978–79*, p. 16.

38. Cmnd 8920, p. 206.
39. Cmnd 8920, vol. 2, p. 65.
40. Duncan Burn, *Nuclear Power and the Energy Crisis* (London: Macmillan, 1978) p. 225.
41. Ibid, pp. 226–30.
42. Central Electricity Generating Board, *Annual Report and Accounts: 1973–74*, p. 9 and Appendix 4; *1976–77*, Appendix 6.
43. *Sizewell 'B' Power Station Public Inquiry: CEGB Proof of Evidence 4* (November 1982) figures 5–8. Henceforth this and other CEGB Proofs are referred to by P and the number.
44. P4, p. 80; P8, table 21.
45. Richard Pryke and John Dodgson, *The Rail Problem* (London: Martin Robertson, 1975) pp. 64, 69; Cmnd 8920, p. 6.
46. Burn, *Nuclear Power*; Gerald Manners, 'Alternative Strategies for the British Coal Industry', *Geographical Journal*, 1978, pp. 224–34; Richard Pryke, *The Nationalised Industries*, pp. 60–6.
47. Cmnd 8920.
48. Cmnd 7101, pp. 74, 85, 95.
49. P5, pp. 57, 62, 68, 72, 76.
50. P5, pp. 34, 111, 113.
51. P4, additional material (henceforth ADD) 3, p. 8.
52. P4, pp. 121, 122.
53. *Sizewell B Power Station Public Inquiry: CEGB Statement of Case* (April 1982) p. 60.
54. P4, pp. 104, 106; P4 ADD 3, p. 1.
55. P4, figures 5–8; P4 ADD 3, p. 11.
56. P5, p. 27.
57. P5, figure 1.
58. P5, pp. 50, 65, 79.
59. P6, p. 89.
60. P6, p. 30.
61. P6, p. 29.
62. Ray Long, *Constraints on International Trade in Coal* (IEA Coal Research, December 1982) pp. 33, 34.
63. Sizewell B Public Inquiry, NCB/P/1 (ADD 1), see paragraphs 14(i), 16 (iv).
64. P6, pp. 56, 57, 96.
65. Cmnd 8920, vol. 2, pp. 30–41.
66. *Minutes of Evidence taken before the Energy Committee: Pit Closures: Thursday 25 October 1982* (HMSO) pp. 28, 113, 114.
67. Cmnd 8920, p. 92.
68. Cmnd 8920, p. 43.
69. P6, pp. 63, 65.
70. P6, p. 91.
71. P4, p. 143; P6, pp. 96, 98.
72. Cmnd 8920, p. 164; vol 2, pp. 30–41.
73. P4, figure 14.

74. P4, p. 86.
75. Unless, of course, the CEGB is being grossly over-optimistic about the construction time, cost and performance of Sizewell B.
76. P4, p. 105.
77. Department of Energy, *Proof of Evidence for the Sizewell 'B' Public Inquiry* (October 1982) p. 3.
78. The NCB might conceivably dump its unwanted high-cost coal aboard. However, it seems doubtful whether this would continue for long because it would not benefit UK consumers. Another objection to my line of argument is that the marginal resource cost of UK coal is below the financial cost because the miners involved will not be able to obtain alternative work, and so produce other goods and services. But what, among other things, this ignores is that if there is general unemployment the same reasoning can be used to justify the retention of unprofitable activities in other industries. There is, other things equal, no case for according special treatment to coal. Moreover, if the level of unemployment is necessary because of the need to depress wage claims, it is wrong to exempt miners who have been particularly militant.

Postscript: The Future of the Nationalised Industries

JOHN GRIEVE SMITH

The theme of Bernard Taylor's contribution in the first chapter is the increasing emphasis on planning for change. Whether or not change is any more rapid now than in the past, the direction of change in recent years has tended to be adverse, and the business environment has become more hostile. The nationalised industries are for the most part highly susceptible to changes in macro-economic conditions and have suffered accordingly.

Recent emphasis on the importance of designing organisations able to cope with strategic change throws some interesting light on the present structure of these industries. The original nationalisation acts were designed to create a national monopoly in utilities which were 'natural' monopolies like gas or electricity. Coal was treated in the same way partly as an aftermath of centralised wartime control and partly because state ownership was equated to such a monolithic structure. The same form of organisation was then extended to manufacturing industries like steel, shipbuilding, and aerospace two decades later.

The statutory provisions, and the administrative framework which has developed subsequently, place a number of constraints on the industries which make it difficult for them to adapt to change. The basic approach of the nationalisation acts has been to specify closely the products or services which the coporations can provide. Where diversification is permissible under the statutes, governmental pressure has generally been against it. Conservative governments have not only tended to set their faces against further diversification but have recently compelled industries to hive off existing diversified activities. Although Labour administrations have been better disposed to diversification, the corporations have been reluctant to adopt strategies which were likely to have to be reversed with a change in government.

The nationalised industries are therefore for the most part locked into providing specified groups of products. This does not prevent them developing better products, new designs of aircraft or ships, or higher-quality steel; nor does it prevent them developing new methods of production. Indeed the existing organisations are, perhaps most effective in responding to the challenge of new, capital-intensive techniques. The British Steel Corporation's most successful achievement has been the replacement of open-hearth steelmaking by oxygen steelmaking in less than a decade.

The nationalised industries are at their most vulnerable when demand for their products is being depressed by competition from products which are regarded as the province of another industry (for example, coal by gas, or tinplate by aluminium), or by the stagnation of the UK economy. In such situations, the restrictions on the industry's field of activities tend to give it a strong vested interest in the status quo. Not only is the labour force naturally concerned to preserve jobs in existing plants and trade-union pressure in this respect is particularly strong, but management's *raison d'être* is threatened unless they can keep their industry in its present form as large as possible. The nationalised industries are thus much better geared to the need to expand than the need to contract. Indeed the whole tone of successive White Papers is based on the realistic assumption that management in these industries is biased towards over- rather than under-investment.

In one respect the difficulties which nationalised industries have in adapting to rapid change is common to all our industrial organisations, public or private: that is the fact that it is impossible rapidly to adjust the size or nature of the workforce. It is no longer possible suddenly to reduce employment when the market falls. Correspondingly, management hesitates to increase employment when demand increases, for fear that the increase in demand may be short-lived and they will then be left with too large a labour force that cannot easily be reduced. This greater stability in employment conditions is an inevitable, and from most points of view desirable, consequence of economic progress; it is a concomitant of rising educational and living standards and a greater degree of equality in bargaining power between managers and the work force. For the majority of the population it is one of the major benefits of a more advanced economy. To try to reverse it in the interests of economic progress is perverse. The problem is to live with it and indeed harness it to facilitate economic progress: the fact that the Japanese economy is now the most rapidly developing in the world is clear evidence that this can be done. In considering the future of the nationalised industries, their high degree of trade unionisation and their pioneering attempts at industrial participation should be seen as important factors which can be used to facilitate industrial change rather than obstruct it. The fact that both the present political climate and the high level of unemployment have recreated the 'hire and fire' approach to management, seems more likely to be a temporary deviation from a long-term trend towards greater participation than a reversal of it.

ORGANISING FOR CHANGE

To put the problems of adapting to change in the nationalised industries into perspective, it is instructive to compare the approach to change of three different types of organisation: the conglomerate, the diversified company, and the single-industry enterprise. The pure *conglomerate* is essentially a holding company regarding its subsidiaries as investments to be bought or sold in accordance with their performance and prospects. The portfolio approach to strategic planning in conglomerates emphasises the need to construct a portfolio of businesses: (a) whose cash flow characteristics are complementary (i.e. some generate cash surpluses and others provide profitable outlets for investment); and (b) with a spread of products in different stages of their life-cycle, so that as some become obsolescent and unprofitable, other new products take their place. Thus the holding company itself aims to continue to flourish even though constituent businesses may be disposed or shut down.

Hence, in effect, the owners and top management at the centre are assured of continuity. But neither the management in the individual businesses nor the rank-and-file workers are in any better position to cope with the problems of changing markets and the life and death of products than if they were in independent firms: indeed they are in a worse position, because while the individual firm has a strong instinct for survival, the pure conglomerate (at any rate as conceived by the management theorist) would as soon sell a problem firm as resolve its problems. In fact it may not be possible to dispose of businesses in declining industries. Nevertheless, the essential point remains that the conglomerate approach, in the sense of a financially oriented holding company, does not provide any solution to the managerial problems of coping with industrial change within the individual business unit.

The *single-industry company*, whether it is in the private or the public sector, finds it more difficult to deal with a decline in demand in the products in which it has specialised. Capital-intensive industries present a particular problem because all the available funds tend to be needed for the existing business; this hinders diversification when business is good, and when business is bad and profits are low, the shortage of funds may be acute. This is, for example, one of the reasons why few private sector steel companies have diversified, save where they were traditionally part of a steel/heavy-engineering complex as in Germany.

The nationalised industries suffer from the same difficulties as the single-industry firm in the private sector, but in addition they are further handicapped by statutory and political constraints on diversification. Thus the tendency for such industries to take an over-optimistic view of their existing products and to over- rather than under-invest in their statutory fields of activity, is a natural reaction of ambitious management locked into such a situation. Moves to privatise diversified or successful new activities while leaving the older and less profitable ones in the state sector, will intensify the problem of nationalised industries having a vested interest in the status quo. This may be politically satisfying for those whose overriding motive is to furnish proof of their own belief in the superiority of the private sector, but it does little service to the need to facilitate industrial change. The problem is, rather, to consider ways of removing the straitjackets constraining the nationalised industries, so that the large corporations in the state sector are free to use their considerable skills and resources to develop new activities, rather than creating a constant bias towards devoting too many resources to their existing fields of endeavour.

Beesley and Gist make, in a sense, a parallel point when they distinguish between privatisation and stimulating more competition. Privatisation may lead to constraints on competition in order to increase the attraction of the proposition to would-be investors.

Increased competition, to be constructive, should surely have as a concomitant the removal of restrictions on the public sector's ability to respond, rather than additional restraints. The aim should be to ensure that industrial organisations in which for various reasons the state has a major stake, are not only efficient operators in their original fields of activity but also have every opportunity to react to changing markets by exploiting new opportunities as they arise.

THE 'HYBRID' ENTERPRISE

So called 'privatisation' has obscured the overdue need to reconsider the constraints under which partially state-owned firms operate. I say 'obscured' because shares are now being floated in companies in which the state remains the largest shareholder, without any clarification of the relationship between the state and the company or any safeguards for the remaining shareholder. It is a wry comment on the investing public's enthusiasm for privatisation (and the short-term horizon of the market) that critical judgement on these points seems to have been completely suspended. There is urgent need for some basic thinking about the powers of the state and the conventions under which they should be exercised in the case of such 'hybrid' enterprises. The problem of the Company Act format is that the state can have effective control as the largest shareholder while owning less than 50 per cent of the shares, and thus potentially greater power than when it was a statutory organisation. Partly for that reason I advocated some time ago that consideration should be given to devising a new form of statutory corporation for part-public/part-private enterprises with a view to specifically *limiting* the powers of the state and giving them greater freedom to manoeuvre than the traditional nationalised industry.[1] To achieve the same state of affairs without such legislation would require some clear-cut statement of government intention and some confidence that this would not be contravened or amended as and when it suited the government to do so. It would also require parliamentary scrutiny of the terms, if there is to be any sort of parliamentary accountability for the public stake in the company.

One of the points that will no doubt emerge into public discussion in due course is that it will be difficult for the government to absolve itself from all responsibility for the appointment of the Chairman and Managing Director of such organisations and leave the top management to be completely self-perpetuating. Allied to this will be the question of whether there should be an identifiable representative of the government as shareholder on the Board. Whereas the public is used to established large firms such as ICI being run by a self-perpetuating management, the publicity attaching to privatisation may call for more effective accountability for management. Moreover, in the case of the public utilities, it seems unlikely that people will be satisfied for long with such a key service as the telephone network being run by a management with no direct accountability to the public through Ministers or Parliament. It could well be that the longer-term public reaction to any widespread privatisation of essential services and key industries could lead to a call for greater public accountability for all major corporations, which is perhaps not what its most enthusiastic advocates would intend.

There seem to be two basic lines of approach to the 'hybrid' (part-public/part-private) enterprise. One is to use the Company Act company but to clarify and formalise the conventions under which the government will use its powers as the major shareholder. The other is to legislate for a new form of corporation with part-public, part-private capital and with the government's powers specified (and limited) by statute. The former approach is more flexible, but in a sense too much so; because the government can always alter the rules in the middle of the game and the management and private shareholders only know where they are as long as current policy prevails. The experience of the nationalised industries suggests that such a policy can be uncomfortably volatile.

The statutory solution requires more thought and careful definition, which in present circumstances would be a good thing. It does, in addition, require the legislation to be administered in the right spirit. At present, the far-reaching powers of control of departments over the nationalised industries depend as much on the fact that they control the supply of capital as on the terms of the statutes. It is no good carefully limiting the government's statutory powers if the government uses its financial clout as a major source of capital to re-establish detailed control.

The key areas in which greater latitude is needed are, product mix and diversification, and the ability to establish joint ventures with companies at home and abroad. It should be said straight away that these are all sensitive areas in which there is no case for going from one extreme to another. To be successful, diversification has to be into related areas rather than indiscriminate. We do not want a corporation, whose prime purpose is to produce and sell steel, for example, suddenly to diversify into a completely unrelated area with a consequent dilution of management effort. On the other hand the BSC has suffered, compared with other companies, from lack of forward integration into steel processing and related areas; hence, when demand has fallen it has found itself fighting in a fiercely competitive market without the benefits of tied customers. It has also been strongly inhibited from improving its position in Continental and North American markets by joint ventures or investment in finishing facilities. But at a time when cross-frontier industrial ventures are more important than ever before, it is wrong to establish forms of organisation for major international corporations which tend to confine their operations to one country; nor is there any necessity for organisations with some state capital to be inhibited in this way, provided they or their subsidiaries obey the normal legal requirements of other countries. This applies particularly within the European Community, where many of the industries employing state capital could reap economies of scale from multi-national projects: for example, steel, aerospace, nuclear power.

THE KEY ISSUES

There is a genuine need to reconsider the organisation and structure of the state-owned section of British industry which has come to be referred to as 'the nationalised industries', but the question at issue is not simply where to draw the frontier between the public and private sector – if indeed there can be a clear-cut frontier. It may, for example, be more important in practice to consider whether the bulk of our seaports (or airports) should be in one organisation or separate enterprises, than whether they are publicly or privately owned.

There is a need to examine carefully at least four different elements in the discussion about the future of the public corporations apart from the extent to which they should be financed by public or private capital:

(1) the extent to which public or private utilities are given monopoly rights or otherwise protected against competition;
(2) the method and rules by which the government or some public body will regulate 'public' utilities in private ownership: for example, rival telephone networks;
(3) the method and extent to which the government will use its power in relation to hybrid organisations in which it is a substantial shareholder;
(4) the constraints on wholly or partly state-owned enterprises operating in competitive markets, in particular the attitude towards diversification and joint ventures.

Recent obsession with the Public Sector Borrowing Requirement and 'privatisation' has led the government to concentrate almost exclusively on establishing private shareholdings in as many of these organisations as possible, without adequate consideration of the industrial implications. Indeed, the preparation of some organisations for privatisation seems to have become an end in itself, dominating both their financial arrangements and their immediate planning. Since the industries in question (aerospace, off-shore oil and gas, telecoms, airways, airports, steel) all represent crucial elements in the British economy and are ones in which the governments of most of our fellow EEC partners are involved in one way or another, it is important to consider any potential changes in terms of their effects on the long-term strategy and operating policy of these industries. Nor has adequate consideration been given to the future of those public enterprises which are not profitable enough to be candidates for sale.

There is a need for change. But the objectives to be sought are more complex than the advocates of privatisation recognise, and the future organisation of these industries cannot be isolated from the strategic problems they face. The aim must be to seek a political and organisational structure for public enterprise which will: provide the infrastructure needed by industry and the public; maintain or create industrial organisations with sufficient resources and market power to develop new products and technologies, free if necessary to ally themselves with other enterprises, British or foreign; and facilitate industrial change by minimising the creation of vested interests in existing products and technology.

NOTES AND REFERENCES

1. 'Taking the Shackles off State Industry', *The Times*, 22 April 1981.

Index